Improving the Communication
of People with Down Syndrome

Improving the Communication of People with Down Syndrome

edited by

Jon F. Miller, Ph.D.
University of Wisconsin–Madison

Mark Leddy, Ph.D.
University of Wisconsin–Whitewater

and

Lewis A. Leavitt, M.D.
University of Wisconsin–Madison

·P A U L · H·
BROOKES
PUBLISHING C?

Baltimore · London · Toronto · Sydney

Paul H. Brookes Publishing Co.
Post Office Box 10624
Baltimore, Maryland 21285-0624

www.pbrookes.com

Typeset by Barton Matheson Willse & Worthington, Baltimore, Maryland.
Manufactured in the United States of America by
Versa Press, East Peoria, Illinois.

The photographs appearing in Chapter 9 were taken and provided by Jeanne
Ramsey and are reproduced with permission.

The case studies appearing in this book are based on actual people and actual
circumstances, but the individuals' names have been changed to protect their
identities. The case studies appear herein with permission.

Library of Congress Cataloging-in-Publication Data

Improving the communication of people with Down syndrome / edited by
    Jon F. Miller, Mark Leddy, and Lewis A. Leavitt.
        p.   cm.
    Includes bibliographical references and index.
    ISBN 1-55766-350-5
    1. Down syndrome.   2. Mentally handicapped children—Education—
Language arts.   3. Mentally handicapped—Means of communication.
4. Developmentally disabled children—Education—Language arts.
5. Verbal ability in children.   6. Communicative competence in children.
I. Miller, Jon F.   II. Leddy, Mark Gene.   III. Leavitt, Lewis A.
RJ506.D68I47   1999
616.85'8842—dc21   98-18258
                                                                CIP

British Library Cataloguing in Publication data are available from the British
Library.

Contents

About the Editors vii
About the Contributors. ix
Preface xiii

1   Introduction: The Communication Challenges that
    People with Down Syndrome Face
    Jon F. Miller, Mark Leddy, and Lewis A. Leavitt. 1

I   **Communication Characteristics of People with
    Down Syndrome and Their Families** **9**

2   Profiles of Language Development in Children with
    Down Syndrome
    Jon F. Miller 11

3   Language Development in Children and Adolescents
    with Down Syndrome
    Robin S. Chapman 41

4   The Biological Bases of Speech in People with
    Down Syndrome
    Mark Leddy. 61

5   Verbal Fluency, Speech Intelligibility, and
    Communicative Effectiveness
    Jon F. Miller and Mark Leddy. 81

6   Individual Differences in Mothers' Communication
    with Their Young Children with Down Syndrome
    *Mary A. Roach, Marguerite Stevenson Barratt, and
    Lewis A. Leavitt* 93

II **Assessment and Intervention** **117**

7   Evaluating Communication to Improve Speech and
    Language Skills
    Jon F. Miller, Mark Leddy, and Lewis A. Leavitt. 119

8   Communication Interventions: Improving the Speech
    Intelligibility of Children with Down Syndrome
    Peggy Rosin and Edie Swift 133

9   Assistive Technology: Strategies and Tools for
    Enhancing the Communication Skills of
    Children with Down Syndrome
    Jamie E. Murray-Branch and Julie E. Gamradt 161

10 Enhancing the Speech and Language Skills of
    Adults with Down Syndrome
    Mark Leddy and Gary Gill. 205

III   Thinking About the Future **215**

11   Families of Adults with Down Syndrome
     Marsha Mailick Seltzer and Marty Wyngaarden Krauss 217
12   A View Toward the Future: Improving the Communication
     of People with Down Syndrome
     Jon F. Miller, Mark Leddy, and Lewis A. Leavitt 241

Appendixes

 A   Resource List 265
 B   World Wide Web Sites on Down Syndrome and
     Related Topics
     Helen Hartman 271
 C   Medical Care of Children with Down Syndrome 275

Index 277

About the Editors

Jon F. Miller, Ph.D., Professor and Chair, Department of Communicative Disorders, University of Wisconsin–Madison, 1975 Willow Drive, Madison, Wisconsin 53706. Dr. Miller is Director of the Language Analysis Laboratory at The Waisman Center at the University of Wisconsin–Madison. He has published extensively in the areas of child language development and disorders, language assessment, and language intervention. In addition, he has been investigating early language development in children with Down syndrome in a longitudinal research project funded by the National Institutes of Health since 1988.

Mark Leddy, Ph.D., CCC-SLP, Assistant Professor and Clinic Director, Department of Communicative Disorders, University of Wisconsin–Whitewater, 800 West Main Street, Whitewater, Wisconsin 53190; Fellow, Communication Processes Unit, The Waisman Center, University of Wisconsin–Madison. Dr. Leddy has worked extensively with children and adults with Down syndrome, providing clinical assessments, directing intervention programming, and conducting clinical research protocols. He has presented at various international, national, and state meetings, and he has co-authored several book chapters about the communication characteristics of people with Down syndrome and their speech-language assessment and intervention needs.

Lewis A. Leavitt, M.D., Professor, Department of Pediatrics, University of Wisconsin–Madison, 1500 Highland Avenue, Madison, Wisconsin 53705. Dr. Leavitt is also Coordinator of the Social and Affective Processes Research Unit and Medical Director of The Waisman Center at the University of Wisconsin. He has been widely published as an author or co-author of numerous journal articles and book chapters on infant speech perception; communication, stress, and coping in infancy; and developmental issues in children with special needs. His research includes work on the psychological effects of violence on children. He co-edited *Psychological Effects of War and Violence on Children* (Lawrence Erlbaum Associates, 1993).

About the Contributors

Marguerite Stevenson Barratt, Ph.D., Director, Institute for Children, Youth and Families, Michigan State University, 27 Kellogg Center, Lansing, Michigan 48824. Dr. Barratt has published widely since the late 1970s on issues concerning the role of families in supporting social and communication development in young children. Her recent research has addressed issues concerning children at risk for developmental delay, cross-cultural perspectives on family interaction, and longitudinal change in attachment and play patterns in infants and toddlers. She has been particularly interested in adolescent motherhood and the role of fathers in early child development.

Robin S. Chapman, Ph.D., Professor of Communicative Disorders, Department of Communicative Disorders and The Waisman Center, University of Wisconsin–Madison, 1500 Highland Avenue, Madison, Wisconsin 53705. Dr. Chapman is Principal Investigator and Coordinator of the Communication Processes Unit at The Waisman Center at the University of Wisconsin–Madison. Her research has focused on language development and language disorders, particularly in children and adolescents with Down syndrome. She is the Editor of *Processes in Language Acquisition and Disorders* (Mosby–Year Book, 1992) and co-creator of *SALT: Systematic Analysis of Language Transcripts* (University of Wisconsin–Madison, The Waisman Center), a computer program designed to assist in language transcript analysis and coding.

Julie E. Gamradt, M.S., CCC-SLP, Speech-Language Pathologist and Augmentative Communication Specialist, Communication Development Program, The Waisman Center, University of Wisconsin–Madison, 1500 Highland Avenue, Madison, Wisconsin 53705. Ms. Gamradt graduated from the University of Wisconsin–Madison with a master's degree in communicative disorders in 1986. Since that time, she has worked as a therapist and director of the Communication Development Program at the TRACE Research and Development Center. She is a specialist in augmentative communication with expertise in context-based services and providing services for individuals who have developmental disabilities. She has been actively involved in interdisciplinary training efforts focusing on augmentative communication for students at the University of Wisconsin–Madison. Her experience includes presenting at local, state, and national conferences on the topic of augmentative communication. Her research interests include developing better ways of documenting functional outcomes of augmentative communication interventions.

Gary Gill, Ph.D., Speech-Language Pathologist, Swallowing and Speech Research Laboratory, GRECC 11G, Wm. S. Middleton Veterans Administration Hospital, 2500 Overlook Terrace, Madison, Wisconsin 53705. Dr. Gill received his doctoral degree in language pathology from the University of Wisconsin–Madison in 1975. From 1971 to 1997, he was associated with the Department of Communicative Disorders at the University of Wisconsin–Madison in various roles: clinical instructor, lecturer, and clinical director. Most of Dr. Gill's professional work has focused on children's language development and developmental disabilities. In the fall of 1997, he changed his focus to the geriatric population, joining a research team at the Swallowing and Speech Research Laboratory, a joint program of the Wm. S. Middleton Veterans Administration Hospital and the University of Wisconsin–Madison Medical School.

Helen Hartman, Administrative Assistant, Communication Processes Research Group, The Waisman Center, University of Wisconsin–Madison, 1500 Highland Avenue, Madison, Wisconsin 53705. Ms. Hartman received her bachelor of fine arts degree from the University of Iowa and taught art for several years. She is the mother of three children, including Hannah, age 9, who has Down syndrome. Since 1983, Ms. Hartman has worked with professionals and school systems to develop optimal health and education programs for all of her children.

Marty Wyngaarden Krauss, Ph.D., Associate Professor, Heller School, Brandeis University, Post Office Box 9110, MS 035, Waltham, Massachusetts 02254. Dr. Krauss is an associate professor of social welfare and is Director of the Starr Center for Mental Retardation at the Heller School at Brandeis University. She is Co–Principal Investigator of a 12-year study of older families of adults with mental retardation, Senior Investigator of the Early Intervention Collaborative Study, and author of numerous publications on family issues and disability. She is chair of the Governor's Commission on Mental Retardation in Massachusetts.

Jamie E. Murray-Branch, M.A., Clinical Instructor, Department of Communicative Disorders, University of Wisconsin–Madison, Goodnight Hall, 1975 Willow Drive, Madison, Wisconsin 53706. Ms. Branch is a clinical instructor in the Department of Communicative Disorders at the University of Wisconsin–Madison, where she teaches graduate students in the clinical training program. A major emphasis in her clinical work has been in the enhancement of language and communicative skills in children and adults with severe and multiple disabilities who use augmentative communication systems. In 1998, she completed work on a 5-year interdisciplinary training grant focusing on preservice-level training of students in the area of augmentative communication and assistive technology. Ms. Branch earned her master's degree at the University of Texas–Austin. She has worked as a speech-language pathologist in hospital, school, and clinical environments. She served as a diagnostician for 3 years on a National Institutes of Health research project focusing on early lexical acquisition in children with Down syndrome.

Mary A. Roach, Ph.D., Associate Scientist, The Waisman Center, University of Wisconsin–Madison, 1500 Highland Avenue, Room 559, Madison, Wisconsin 53705. In addition to being an associate scientist at The Waisman Center, Dr. Roach is a lecturer in the Department of Child and Family Studies at the University of Wisconsin–Madison. Her research interests include parent–child interaction, with a particular emphasis on the developmental outcomes of children with Down syndrome.

Peggy Rosin, M.S., CCC-SLP, Clinical Instructor, Department of Communicative Disorders, University of Wisconsin–Madison, 1975 Willow Drive, Room 337, Madison, Wisconsin 53706. Since 1991, Ms. Rosin has worked in early intervention, providing training and technical assistance to personnel across the United States on issues related to infants and toddlers with special needs and their families. She co-authored the book *Partnerships in Family-Centered Care: A Guide to Collaborative Early Intervention* (Paul H. Brookes Publishing Co., 1996) and is first author of several training guides and videotapes on early intervention. One focus of Ms. Rosin's career has been communication assessment and intervention with young children with disabilities. She and her colleague Edie Swift have collaborated since 1983 on issues related to the communication of people with Down syndrome. Together they have published articles and have made state- and national-level presentations related to speech intelligibility and Down syndrome.

Marsha Mailick Seltzer, Ph.D., Professor, The Waisman Center and School of Social Work, University of Wisconsin–Madison, Waisman Center, 1500 Highland Avenue, Room S102, Madison, Wisconsin 53705. Dr. Seltzer is a professor at the University of Wisconsin–Madison with appointments in the School of Social Work and The Waisman Center. Her research focuses on the well-being of caregiving families across the life course, particularly families who have a son or a daughter with developmental disabilities. Among her publications are *The Parental Experience in Midlife* (University of Chicago, 1996), which she co-edited with Carol Ryff, and several articles in the October 1997 issue of *Family Relations,* which she guest edited with Tamar Heller. She has served as a member of several editorial boards of journals in the fields of developmental disabilities, family relations, and aging.

Edie Swift, M.A., Clinical Instructor, Department of Surgery/Otolaryngology, University of Wisconsin Medical School, 600 Highland Avenue, Madison, Wisconsin 53792. Ms. Swift received her master's degree from Northwestern University, Evanston, Illinois. She has worked as a speech-language therapist in Denver, London, San Francisco, and Wisconsin. In each of these settings, she was responsible for both therapy and diagnostic work for children and adults. Since coming to the University of Wisconsin, she has helped establish a clinic that is dedicated to the study of motor control problems in children and has been a diagnostician at The Waisman Center and in the Department of Communicative Disorders. She is presently working in the Department of Surgery Voice Clinic at the University of Wisconsin, where she continues to do diagnostic work with children and adults. Her special interest in children with Down syndrome dates from the early 1980s, when she began working with Peggy Rosin to try to define the often-observed speech-motor control problems that appeared to have a substantial impact on the frequently seen reduction in speech intelligibility of these children. Her interests have continued to include a search for therapeutic techniques to improve the speech intelligibility of people with Down syndrome.

Preface

This book is a compilation of past and present research by clinicians and researchers at The Waisman Center at the University of Wisconsin–Madison. The Waisman Center is one of the original mental retardation research centers established during the Kennedy administration to promote research on mental retardation and developmental disabilities. Since 1973, The Waisman Center has brought together scientists from a variety of disciplines to investigate the causes, consequences, remediation, and prevention of developmental disabilities. It is extraordinary to find so many talented people with an interest in people with Down syndrome in one research center. Our research and clinical collaboration since 1983 has given rise to this unusual interdisciplinary book, which details the challenges that children with Down syndrome face as they acquire communication skills and provides a wealth of ideas and suggestions for improving their communication throughout childhood, adolescence, and adulthood. The work presented in this book was supported by research grants from the National March of Dimes Foundation, the National Institutes of Health (Grant No. HD22393), and the National Institute on Aging.

To the children and families who have participated in our research over the years and to an optimistic future for all people with Down syndrome

1

Introduction

The Communication Challenges that People with Down Syndrome Face

Jon F. Miller, Mark Leddy, and Lewis A. Leavitt

This book provides a description of the speech, language, and communication abilities of people with Down syndrome; a review of assessments and interventions that have proved effective in promoting the development of communication skills; and a summary of long-term family outcomes. It focuses on individuals' specific abilities, the relationships among their specific cognitive and language skills, and how these abilities contribute to the communication development process from childhood to adulthood. The goal of this book is to bring together research of the 1990s with advances in intervention strategies that have been successful in optimizing the development of communication skills in children, adolescents, and adults with Down syndrome.

An entire book on language and communication of children with Down syndrome is necessary for several important reasons:

1. Down syndrome is the most frequent identifiable cause of mental retardation currently known.
2. Language and communication are key areas that constrain social and personal development of children with Down syndrome.
3. Research conducted in the 1990s requires revision and restructuring of previous advice on the management of speech and language problems of children with Down syndrome.

Among the important advances in the field of developmental disabilities in the 1990s is the recognition that specific biologically based causes of mental retardation have distinct profiles of cognitive and language functioning as well as development. To serve children with Down syndrome and their families properly, we must be knowledgeable about their similarities to and differences from the performance and development of children who are developing typically.

What can be expected from a child with Down syndrome with regard to the development of communication skills? The answer to this question is complex and requires an appreciation of the cognitive, environmental, and anatomical and physiological contributions to communication development. Adults communicate without effort almost everything or anything that can be imagined or perceived. Children must develop their communication skills over the course of many years, coordinating their abilities to perceive and produce the sounds of the language spoken around them; recognizing words; combining sounds to produce words; and combining words into sentences and sentences into logical descriptions of experiences, stories, or other communication needs. The marvel of this process is that it happens so effortlessly in typical children and presents so many challenges to children with Down syndrome. These challenges become evident when one reviews the research literature and when one engages in conversation with individuals with Down syndrome. The speech intelligibility of individuals with Down syndrome limits the effectiveness of their messages. Their messages are limited in complexity either because of their recognition that their speech is difficult to understand or because their expressive language is limited. Their language comprehension is difficult to judge without further exploration. The language comprehension of individuals with Down syndrome is almost always better than their language production skills. Their language comprehension skills can be predicted by their nonverbal cognitive skills, which supports the notion that cognitive skills are necessary for language to develop but are sufficient in most individuals with Down syndrome because their language production is not as advanced as their language comprehension.

This book germinated with a research project aimed at describing the early language abilities of children with Down syndrome. The literature prior to 1987 had emphasized the impairments in speech and language skills of children with Down syndrome and offered few causal constructs to account for the particular difficulties that these children were having in acquiring effective oral communication skills relative to their other cognitive abilities. The original questions that the research project sought to answer concerned their rate of acquisition of several skills simultaneously rather than focusing on a single aspect of language and communication independently. The review of the previous research undertaken in the project appeared to show a trend toward asynchronous development when individual features of language performance were reviewed. The development of vocabulary skills in children with Down syndrome seemed to be more advanced than that of their syntax or the grammar of their language. At the same time, children with Down syndrome were better able to understand language spoken to them than to produce spoken messages of equal complexity. These differences were evaluated in detail through a series of research projects involving several hundred children between 1987 and 1995. Our goal in this book is to share the improved understanding of how the extra copy of chromosome 21 affects the cognitive, speech, language, and communication skills of children with Down syndrome.

There is still a great deal that is not understood about human communication and the processes that underlie its development. This book is organized to provide a readable account of research on the communication skills of people with Down syndrome, with the goal being to inform readers of the ways in which specific anatomical and physiological differences associated with the syndrome explain or fail to explain the communication abilities of and opportunities available to these individuals. The discussion begins with an overview of human communication to remind readers of the nature of the human communication process and its component parts. The chapters of this book review language and communication development and provide insight into expectations and challenges that parents and their children with Down syndrome face on their road to achieving communicative competence.

Communication involves generating an idea or a thought that needs to be transmitted, initiating and receiving a message with a medium for transferring the message between the sender and the receiver, and understanding the meaning of the message:

Idea ---▶ Message initiation ---▶ Medium ---▶ Message reception ---▶ Understanding

Human beings are usually capable of both message initiation and message reception. The exceptions to this might involve people with perceptual impairments, hearing or vision impairments, or motor problems limiting their speech production or the use of their hands and arms. Communication is usually thought of as involving speaking and listening, and the medium is usually thought of as the air transferring the acoustic energy to the message recipient's eardrum for conversion to neurological energy routed to the brain for interpretation. The communication process can be hindered in many ways, such as by the speaker's failure to produce an intelligible message or by the listener's experiencing limited hearing acuity, language-processing impairments, or limited knowledge of the spoken language. Messages are also transferred by means other than speech, including writing, gestures, and symbols. These modes use alternative media to transmit the message, including print, visual images, and graphics. To receive these message types, the message recipient must have the faculty of vision and specific knowledge of the system (e.g., printed alphabet and written language, American Sign Language [ASL], Signing Exact English [SEE], specific graphic symbol systems). These detailed components result in a more complete communication model that specifies how a message is initiated, transferred, and received:

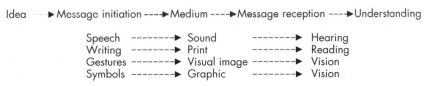

Speech is usually accompanied by gestures, facial expressions, and body postures that elaborate the spoken message and aid the recipient's message reception. Detailed study of speech communication reveals the rich complexity and paradoxes of human communication, including the ability to convey one message via speech and another by facial expression and body posture. Some experts (D. Yoder, personal communication, October 1985) have claimed that only about 30% of the content of face-to-face verbal messages is conveyed by verbal language; the remaining 70% is communicated by gestures, facial expressions, and body postures.

As the communication of people with Down syndrome is evaluated in this book, the conception of human communication must be expanded beyond speech to include reading and writing and the use of gestures and sign systems as well as graphic symbols. People use variations of each of these systems every day in their communication with adults and children. Each of these different modes of communication can complement the others when limitations in the sender, the receiver, or the medium reduce effective message delivery.

In this book, Murray-Branch and Gamradt, in Chapter 9, review the use of symbol systems for communication, specifically discussing the use of augmentative and alternative communication (AAC) systems that have proved beneficial to children with Down syndrome. Clearly, knowledge of how the world works is fundamental to the child's acquisition of a language with which to map that knowledge. Children who are typically developing acquire their language over a number of years from childhood through adolescence seemingly without instruction. Instruction is delivered by parents and others who engage children in the communication process in a variety of subtle ways. A number of specific features of this communication interaction process are particularly important for fostering children's language and communication skills development. Parents who talk more to their children promote their children's rapid vocabulary learning. Parents who respond to their children's communication attempts promote more verbal initiations by their children. Parents who take their children on more outings enhance their children's development of more advanced language skills. All of these factors are products of environment and therefore can be modified. Language intervention programs focus on these features to promote children's more rapid language learning. In Chapter 6, Roach, Barratt, and Leavitt review these aspects of parents' communication with young children who have Down syndrome. They document how parents of children with Down syndrome can cope effectively by modifying their interaction styles to meet the language and communication needs of their children. The specific challenges facing speakers with Down syndrome can be elucidated by examining the human communication process. The listening or comprehension side of the process has been documented as a strength of people with Down syndrome in spite of the fact that such individuals have more frequent middle-ear infections that continue through childhood and, for some, into adolescence and adulthood. Although there is an increase in mild to moderate hearing loss among these individuals, the impact of hearing loss on individuals with Down syndrome appears to be on their phonological speech processing and speech production rather than on their word- and sentence-level linguistic knowledge. These effects may have an impact on their reading skills acquisition as well as on their speech intelligibility throughout their lives.

With regard to speech production, speech intelligibility impairments of people with Down syndrome result in listeners' failing to comprehend these individuals' messages. Many children who are striving to overcome limited speech intelligibility reduce their messages to a minimum, selecting one- or two-syllable words and using single-thought-unit utterances in their efforts to be understood. These adaptations are made by all communicators whose listeners evidence difficulty in processing their messages. Speakers with Down syndrome and their conversational partners have been observed to adapt rapidly to the speakers' abilities. Whereas speakers with limited speech intelligibility shorten their messages by selecting their most intelligible words, partners reduce their demands by asking direct questions that elicit short answers rather than risk having to process a lengthy explanation or description. These adaptations leave many individuals with Down syndrome with the appearance of having limited language production skills. The importance of alternative methods of message production for these individuals is obvious. The use of gestures, graphic symbols, or writing is helpful as an alternative to speech, particularly early in the child's development. The work of Buckley (1985, 1995a, 1995b, 1997) in England has demonstrated that children as young as ages 2 and 3 years can learn to sight-read a large number of words. These abilities suggest that children have visual information–processing strengths that can be used to support and improve their auditory processing systems. The language strengths in comprehension of oral language and reading of people with Down syndrome suggest that more attention should be directed at the phonological level to improve both reading abilities and speaking abilities. This strength may exist at all ages, regardless of language and speech development in people with Down syndrome.

CONCLUSIONS

This book provides an interdisciplinary focus on language and communication skills with contributions from professionals in speech-language pathology, social work, assistive technology, pediatrics, and developmental psychology. In addition to separate chapters by Miller (Chapter 2) and Chapman (Chapter 3) reviewing the language and communication progress of children and adolescents with Down syndrome, several chapters discuss the speech production challenges that these children face. If one were to name the biggest challenge to effective communication for people with Down syndrome, it would have to be speech intelligibility. Improved speech intelligibility improves social interactions, offers exposure to language, and induces more language practice. Leddy, in Chapter 4, reviews the physical ability of people with Down syndrome to produce speech and discusses, with Miller, speech intelligibility and fluency in Chapter 5. In Chapter 7, Miller, Leddy, and Leavitt describe speech, language, and communication assessment procedures. In addition, Rosin and Swift, in Chapter 8, present case studies describing specific methods by which to improve speech intelligibility and communication for those individuals who experience difficulty in producing speech; and Leddy and Gill, in Chapter 10, document improvements in communication in adulthood resulting from speech and language therapy.

The future holds promise for finding solutions to the most troubling challenges that people with Down syndrome face. Viewing the future in context provides people with Down syndrome and their families hope that solutions to their challenges will be found. The long-term family perspective is provided by Seltzer and Krauss's (Chapter 11) description of life-span issues that families of people with Down syndrome face. Their findings provide some optimism, and their chapter provides an uplifting view, for families with young children with Down syndrome. Finally, Miller, Leddy, and Leavitt (Chapter 12) offer suggestions for the future, including recommendations for integrating new approaches to assessment and intervention into school systems, health care services, and communities.

REFERENCES

Buckley, S. (1985). Attaining basic educational skills. In D. Lane & B. Stratford (Eds.), *Current approaches to Down syndrome* (pp. 211–234). Eastbourne, England: Holt Saunders.

Buckley, S. (1995a). Improving the expressive language skills of teenagers with Down syndrome. *Down's Syndrome Research and Practice, 3,* 110–115.

Buckley, S. (1995b). Teaching children with Down syndrome to read and write. In L. Nadel & D. Rosenthal (Eds.), *Down syndrome: Living and learning in the community* (pp. 158–169). New York: Wiley-Liss.

Buckley, S. (1997, April). *Links between literacy, language and memory development in children with Down syndrome.* Paper presented at the 2nd International Conference on Language and Cognitive Development in Down Syndrome, Portsmouth, England.

I

Communication Characteristics of People with Down Syndrome and Their Families

The first section of this book discusses the speech, language, and communication abilities of children with Down syndrome. The chapters in Section I set the foundation for the chapters in Sections II and III, which implement the information in Section I in developing evaluation and intervention methods as well as discuss expectations for the future of research in these areas. The chapters provide both new data and a review of published research to document performance. The intent of this section is to integrate the authors' new research into a model of abilities that can be used to guide parents and professionals toward optimizing the communication skills of their children with Down syndrome. The second section of the book includes chapters on assessment and intervention that highlight the unique speech-language approaches that professionals have used with success. The third section provides a glimpse of the future from the perspectives of families, the increased societal demand for communication and literacy skills, and the need for changes in public policy to meet the future needs of individuals with Down syndrome.

Section I begins with Chapter 2, in which Miller describes the outcomes of a 5-year study of more than 150 children with Down syndrome that was aimed at documenting early developmental progress from single-word comprehension and production to using simple sentences. He documents patterns of language development, which he calls *profiles*, found in children with Down syndrome, which seem to show that there are three predominant profiles that can help professionals plan therapeutic programs to meet the needs of children with different patterns of development.

In Chapter 3, Chapman provides a detailed review of the literature from the onset of simple sentences. Her review of the research data on later language development in children with Down syndrome shows how development continues beyond early childhood. Her work contradicts previous research that suggested that development was arrested at the simple-sentence level in these children. Chapman's work is pivotal for motivating language and communication interventions with older children.

After the chapters documenting the abilities of children with Down syndrome, Leddy, in Chapter 4, revisits communication, examining the biological constructs that underlie speech performance and the biological differences of these children that may affect their speech production. Understanding musculoskeletal variations in children with Down syndrome as well as their nervous system development is vital for constructing effective intervention programs to improve their speech intelligibility. In Chapter 5, Miller and Leddy continue the focus on speech production by providing some scaffolding for the conceptualization of verbal fluency in children with Down syndrome.

In the final chapter in Section I, Roach, Barratt, and Leavitt place the parent into the equation of child development. They show how mothers of children with Down syndrome modify their patterns of communication in step with the developmental levels of their children. The work of these authors demonstrates that styles of interaction such as high directiveness, which may seem counterproductive with children who are typically developing, can be viewed as adaptive when used to foster the language and communication performance of children with Down syndrome.

2

Profiles of Language Development in Children with Down Syndrome

Jon F. Miller

Reviews of research on the language and communication skills of children with Down syndrome have concluded that language skills do not keep pace with the development of other cognitive skills (Chapman, 1995; Miller, 1987, 1988). The research reveals that they have particular difficulty with language production rather than with language comprehension, but research documenting the relationship between these two language modes through the developmental period is sparse at best. The relationship between language comprehension skills and language production skills is important for several reasons. Theoretically, discrepancies between language comprehension and production abilities of children with Down syndrome provide information about their general linguistic abilities. If their comprehension of language is better than their language production, it can be inferred that there is not a general impairment in learning linguistic material. If their language comprehension and production skills were similar but not as advanced as their other cognitive skills, it might be inferred that their problem is more general and perhaps is associated with their understanding of all linguistic or representational material. As a practical matter, monitoring developmental progress is expensive, so knowing in which areas to expect problems provides a needed focus for assessment and intervention. Furthermore, understanding how the relationship between language comprehension and production might change through the developmental period informs interventions to reduce the

11

gap between their comprehension and production as children with Down syndrome grow older. Finally, the language interventions can take advantage of the comprehension strengths of children with Down syndrome to improve their language production.

Research on children who are developing typically suggests that the relationship between their language comprehension and their language production is consistent with advances in their general nonverbal cognitive skills, with their comprehension skills emerging before their production skills. The research on this relationship is not particularly detailed; but the relationship among cognition, language comprehension, and language production may not be constant through the developmental period either, because aspects of language acquired early (e.g., vocabulary) are easier for children with Down syndrome as compared with aspects of language acquired later (e.g., syntax) or because their difficulty with language production may compound, resulting in an increasing gap between their language comprehension and their language production as they age. Documenting changes in the relationship between comprehension and production skills is important for designing intervention programs for prevention as well as for contributing to understanding language development.

This chapter presents the results of several years of research aimed at describing the developmental progress of language comprehension and production in two groups of children with Down syndrome. The goal of the research was to characterize the changes in language comprehension and language production of children with Down syndrome relative to their advances in other cognitive skills. At first glance, this task may seem straightforward; but, in reality, the problem is complicated by the nature of language itself, the body of research devoted to describing acquisition, and the way in which Down syndrome alters the abilities required to learn language efficiently. Consider that, to learn language, it is necessary to recognize the sound system of the language; the rules used in combining sounds into words; that words represent objects, actions, and relationships from everyday experience; the rules used to combine words into sentences to express thoughts; and the rules for using language to serve a variety of purposes such as to get something, to comment, to convince, to ask for information, or to clarify. The rules for sounds, words, sentences, and uses of language are unique for each human language. Note that acquiring a second language is relatively easy for young children but is increasingly difficult for people with advancing age. Acquiring a language takes a great deal of time and effort, though this factor is not usually attended to because young children seem to acquire language so easily.

There are several issues to keep in mind as children progress in acquiring language and communication skills. Languages are composed of several levels (sounds, words, morphemes, syntax, semantics, and pragmatics), each with its own rules governing permutations and combinations to form messages. The rule systems continue to evolve as children acquire more language, with each level becoming more elaborate and more interrelated with the other levels. Rules characterizing children's early language development may be different from those characterizing their later language development. Documenting developmental progress of a single linguistic level (e.g., vocabulary) is not likely to yield useful information about progress with regard to the syntax of the language. How, then, can useful developmental descriptions be constructed that are capable of capturing changes in individual linguistic levels in both comprehension and production?

The problem of describing developmental progress has perplexed researchers for hundreds of years. Early solutions usually focused on a single language level such as vocabulary. Counting words became an accepted method of describing developmental progress from the 1920s through the early 1960s. It is now understood that vocabulary size and composition make up but one of the interrelated levels of language performance and that counting words provides no information about how those words are combined to form messages through the developmental period. Developmental progress on one level (e.g., vocabulary) does not necessarily predict developmental progress at other levels (e.g., syntax). Nor does performance at one language level describe an individual's ability to communicate. That is, having a large vocabulary does not automatically mean that the individual can use those words to make sentences or that the sentences that the individual uses communicate a message effectively.

The solution to this dilemma has been to attempt to characterize developmental progress by using a profile approach, documenting the simultaneous acquisition of language components (Miller, 1978, 1981; Miller & Paul, 1995). This approach has the advantage of describing the multiple levels of language as they develop individually and provides the opportunity to describe the relationships among language levels as they develop in both comprehension and production. In thinking about this complex system, it is easy to imagine that problems at one level (e.g., vocabulary production) will affect other levels (e.g., syntax) because fewer words would be available to form sentences following the grammatical rules of the language. Describing developmental progress requires documenting the absolute gains at each level (e.g., increases in vocabulary size) and syntactic diversity as well as the synchrony of progress across linguistic levels in comprehension and production. The relationships among levels relative to the chronological age or the cognitive skills of the child with Down syndrome reveal a child's strengths as well as his or her impairments. The relationship between language comprehension and production status reveals something about the information-processing skills or utterance formulation abilities available to the child. Children with both language comprehension and language production problems are thought to have more serious language-learning problems than children with only language production problems.

PROFILES OF LANGUAGE DEVELOPMENT

This section reviews the work aimed at describing language comprehension and production development relative to other cognitive skills.

Role of General Cognitive Skills in Language Learning

Progress in language learning can be charted relative to a child's increasing age or to the increasing maturity of the child's general cognitive abilities. Theories of language acquisition suggest two primary factors associated with language growth:

1. General cognitive skills related to acquiring knowledge from experience that underpin learning the language skills to represent that experience
2. Environmental stimulation, ranging from having a language spoken in the child's presence, to the frequency of language directed to the child, to the responsiveness of the other language users to the child's attempts to communicate

Both of the preceding aspects are essential to foster children's language growth. By measuring nonverbal cognitive skills, an expectation for language progress can be established that assumes that children's language growth should be equal to their development of other cognitive skills. Other researchers (Chapman & Miller, 1980; Cromer, 1974, 1991) have referred to this hypothesis as the weak form of the cognition hypothesis, in which cognitive skills are necessary but are not a sufficient condition for language to develop. Although this view has been contested (Cole, Dale, & Mills, 1992), it does provide a rationale for describing the progress of language in comprehension and production relative to nonverbal cognitive skills and chronological age. Without the cognitive measures, one would be left to assume that language skills were solely the result of advancing chronological age. Whereas this assumption may be true by association, if for no other reason, for children who are experiencing typical development, it is not true of children with identified or expected cognitive impairments. It is important to include measures of cognitive skills even if measurement of cognitive skills is controversial relative to its predictive validity for language learning. Measures of nonverbal cognitive performance, even if flawed, provide the best mechanism available for documenting the developmental progress of children with cognitive impairments. As a result of this perspective, the protocol used here for describing language change includes a measure of nonverbal cognitive skills, comprehension of vocabulary and syntax, and the production of vocabulary and syntax. Profiles enable clinicians and researchers to document the consistency of children's growth across linguistic levels of vocabulary and syntax as well as between comprehension and production. The result is a profile of language growth over time both within and among these measures.

What Is a Profile? A profile of language performance has been used in the past to refer to the relationship between language comprehension and language production (Miller, 1978, 1981) as well as the relationships among language levels within language comprehension and language production (Miller, 1988). The language profile is used to provide a visual image of the relative synchrony among language levels within language comprehension and language production as well as between language comprehension and language production in general. The term *profile* assumes that typical development is described by a flat profile and that atypical development shows some deviation from a straight line (see, e.g., Figure 1). From a measurement point of view, the notion of a profile requires either standard scores or age-equivalent scores for all measures in order to show the relationship among the scores. That is, the scores must be on the same scale. The language profile, then, is a model of the theory of language development described here and as such allows one to chart predictions about the relationships among language levels and processes and how they might change over time. This model can predict that children will understand more of the language than they will be able to produce because, for example, our theory recognizes that children comprehend words and sentences before they can produce them to form messages. Because vocabulary is the building block of learning grammar (i.e., syntax), vocabulary scores would be equal to or more advanced than syntax.

A profile provides a tool to describe how the development of language comprehension relates to the development of language production and how progress in vocabulary relates to syntax for comprehension and for language production relative to other cognitive skills. The profile is nothing more than a snapshot of progress in language development. With a series of these snapshots, the changes in these rela-

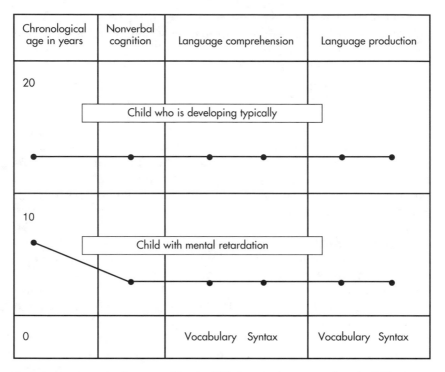

Figure 1. Language development profiles of a child who is developing typically and a child with mental retardation.

tionships over time can be described. The power of profiles to describe the developing language performance of children with Down syndrome is apparent as the data from our research are presented in this chapter. Documenting changes in the language performance of children with Down syndrome relative to their other cognitive skills through the critical stages of the developmental period captures the dynamic changes within processes and among the levels of their language system. These data provide information about the unique character of the language-learning system available to children with Down syndrome. The following sections describe how Language Development Profiles (LDP) can provide a visual map of the complexities of the language development process for children with cognitive impairments.

Why Are Profiles an Important Method of Investigating the Language Performance of Children with Down Syndrome? The language development of children with cognitive impairments has been studied since the 1920s. Summaries of this research appear from time to time, and, for the most part, the results are reported for a single group or by the level of cognitive impairment (mild, moderate, severe, and profound using 1983 American Association on Mental Retardation [AAMR] definitions [Grossman, 1983]; or requiring intermittent, limited, extensive, or pervasive supports using the AAMR's 1992 definition and classification system [Luckasson et al., 1992]). The summaries of this research paint a picture of language emerging as a slow-motion version of typical language development. All children acquire some communication skills, regardless of the severity of their impairments (McLean & Snyder-McLean, 1978). The language system that they learn is the language that they hear spoken around them and follows the rules of that language. Children with cognitive impairments are not learning a different or "degraded" version of English. Regardless of the severity of their cognitive impairments, these children's acquired language resembles the structure of the language that they hear every day. These data demonstrate the contribution of children's communication environment on their language learning as well as the biological capacity of all children to learn a language system. If one were to construct a profile of this view, the language profiles would be represented by a relatively straight line between comprehension and production skills, showing their equal development. The present author's theory would further predict that children's nonverbal cognitive skills would be equivalent to their comprehension and production skills. (See Figure 1 for an example LDP for a child with general mental retardation.)

One might conclude from this discussion that nonverbal cognitive skills are the best predictors of language development in children with cognitive impairments. The disparity between children's chronological age and their cognitive skill attainments defines the severity of their cognitive impairments. This research reflects the theory that cognitive skills are necessary but are not sufficient for language to develop, with the remaining impetus for language development coming from environmental stimulation. The general prediction from this theory for any child with cognitive impairments is synchronous language development consistent with nonverbal cognitive skills. This view predicts that all children with cognitive impairments have similar profiles. The problem with this view is that it ignores the fact that children's cognitive impairments are the result of many different causes, traumas, genetic syndromes, disease processes pre- and postnatally, the prenatal substance abuse of the children's mothers, and environmental deprivation.

Research (Miller, 1997) has documented different neurodevelopmental syndromes for different etiologies. There is no reason to expect children with different patterns of brain development to have similar language-learning abilities. This view is reflected by the practice of researchers of grouping children by etiology rather than by general cognitive impairment. As a result, research conducted since the late 1980s has begun to document different language outcomes with different neurodevelopmental syndromes. To illustrate this point, the communication characteristics of children with fragile X syndrome show strengths in vocabulary and syntax but impairments in pragmatic skills (see Figure 2 for a sample LDP). Children with Down syndrome show strengths in verbal comprehension and pragmatic skills, as well as impairments in syntactic production (see Figure 2 for a sample LDP). Children with Williams syndrome show strengths in all verbal abilities but have impairments in spatial cognition (see Figure 2 for a sample LDP). Girls with Turner syndrome, though they do not necessarily have cognitive impairments, show cognitive patterns similar to girls with Williams syndrome: good verbal skills with significant impairments in spatial skills. The profile approach to describing language performance allows identification of strengths and weaknesses in both comprehension and production and comparison of language abilities to cognitive skills as well as chronological age. The LDP also allows comparison of individual children as well as documentation of change

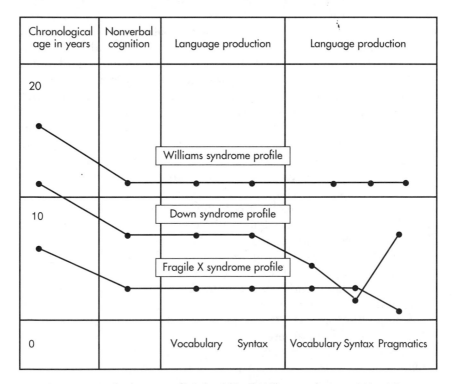

Figure 2.   Language development profiles of a child with Williams syndrome, a child with Down syndrome, and a child with fragile X syndrome.

over time. The next section reviews research using this method to measure the language skills of children with Down syndrome.

Language Development Profile
Studies of Children with Down Syndrome

Research characterizes children with Down syndrome as having particular difficulty in acquiring language production skills compared with their abilities with regard to language comprehension (Miller, 1987, 1988, 1995). In their profile study, Miller and colleagues (Miller, Rosin, Pierce, Miolo, & Sedey, 1989; Miller, Streit, Salmon, & Lafollette, 1987) found that two profiles of language performance accounted for 95% of the children studied. Of the individuals studied, 60%–75% had impairments in language production. As these children got older, more of them exhibited this profile. Of the remaining individuals, 20%–35% exhibited profiles in which language comprehension and language production were consistent with their cognitive status, and only 5% of these children had impairments in both language comprehension and language production.

It appeared from these data that these children's language production skills were developing more slowly than their language comprehension and other cognitive skills. It is important to note that these data are cross-sectional; only one set of data or LDP is available for each child. Figure 3 summarizes these individual profiles. The impression that these data give is that language skills are consistent with other cognitive skills through the early stages of children's development. As children with Down syndrome get older, they experience increasing difficulty in acquiring complex language production skills. The language production of these children indicates impairments at both the lexical and syntactic levels. The problem with these data is that it is not known whether individual children will follow the course of development suggested by the combined group data, whether all children will exhibit the same developmental profiles, or whether individual children will exhibit unique profiles relative to their peers. Each of these questions is critical to understanding the development of language in children with Down syndrome and the possible causes for their apparent difficulties in language development. Several causal constructs may be involved, including speech-motor control problems that cause difficulty with the production of coordinated sequential movements of the articulators; neurophysiological impairments in those areas of the brain associated with language learning; or lack of appropriate environmental experience with language, including opportunities to talk. Would these causal mechanisms result in similar developmental profiles of language performance?

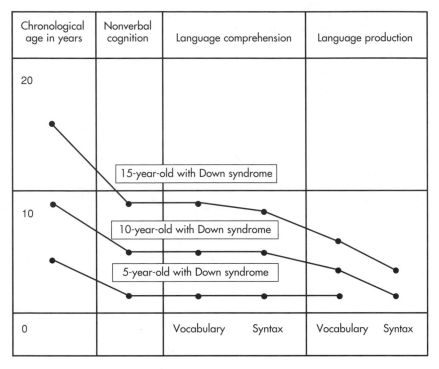

Figure 3. Language development profiles of a 15-year-old with Down syndrome, a 10-year-old with Down syndrome, and a 5-year-old with Down syndrome.

Although no direct measures are available, one can speculate on how each cause might affect language learning. Impairments in speech-motor control would reduce speech intelligibility and overall verbal production. Such impairments might result in children's using shorter sentences and selecting words that listeners can understand. The result would be an appearance of significantly impaired production skills. If practice with language is an important feature of language acquisition, then reduced speech intelligibility can be suggested as a cause of language production problems. Impairments in speech-motor control should affect only language production performance, however, not comprehension. Alternatively, environmental impairments associated with overall stimulation, language input, or social interaction impairments should reduce language learning in both comprehension and production.

Neurophysiological impairments have been documented in the brains of people with Down syndrome. The research data do not suggest that these children's language production would be affected more than their language comprehension. Researchers are far from understanding the direct links between the neurophysiological impairments in specific areas of the brain and their consequences for learning, particularly for behaviors requiring higher cognitive functions such as language and communication. There is some behavioral evidence to suggest that short-term memory (STM) is adversely affected in this population and that STM may be linked to poorer performance in language production, which requires word selection and formulation skills that are memory dependent. Based on this review of the causes of language impairments in children with Down syndrome, a study of longitudinal changes in language comprehension and comprehension skills would provide insight into causal constructs that could account for the language-learning problems of these children.

Longitudinal Change in Language Development Profiles

As part of a research project funded by the National March of Dimes Foundation, this work attempted to document the developmental synchrony of language learning in young children with Down syndrome based on a longitudinal study. It was clear that examining profile types over time would provide insight into the forces that influence the language development of children with Down syndrome. Two features of profiles were important to document as children progressed through the most volatile period of language development: the type of profiles exhibited and the stability of the profiles. Stable profiles may reflect the language-learning abilities of the child, including perceptual, motor, cognitive, and linguistic skills. Alternatively, changing profiles may be attributable to environmental or adaptive forces. The study attempted to address three questions:

1. Do children with Down syndrome exhibit similar profiles of language development?
2. Do these profiles remain constant over time?
3. What can language development profiles tell us about improving the communication skills of children with Down syndrome?

Attention was focused on the first 4–5 years of cognitive development, when the most active period of language development was expected to be captured. The children with Down syndrome studied were between ages 1 and 5 years chronologically at the beginning of the project and were followed for 2 years. Their mental ages were between 8 and 36 months. There were 43 children with Down syndrome participating in the study. They had a mean chronological age of 37.2 months and a mean mental age of 22 months. Chronological age and mental age distributions for each of the four data points can be found in Table 1.

The individuals studied were from the state of Wisconsin. Each family was seen four times during a period of 2 years. The first three visits occurred 6 months apart covering a period of 12 months, and the fourth visit occurred 12 months after the third visit. It was predicted that the 24 months that the study covered would allow documentation of about 12 months of these children's mental age development.

Assessing Developmental Progress

An assessment protocol consisting of developmentally appropriate tests and procedures to measure cognition, language comprehension, and language production was administered to each child at every visit. The period of development that this study covered required some rather unconventional practices in order to derive scores for cognitive skills, language comprehension, and language production for each child. Measurement formats typically used for children's behaviors up to the first 24–30 months of development are different from those documenting their performance thereafter. None of the measures used in the present study, therefore, covered the entire developmental range investigated. The appropriate test for the child's developmental period at each visit was chosen even though it might have resulted in different tests being used to derive the cognition score, for example, for three of the four visits because three different tests were used. Researchers cringe in these situations because different tests are likely to measure different skills and abilities so that changes over time might be attributable to what is measured rather than to real changes in overall performance. Given these decisions, there is no answer for this criticism. If the criticism is valid for these data, one expects to see a great deal of variability in the results. If there is a robustness in the

Table 1. Subject distribution by chronological age and mental age for each visit

Age range (in months)	Time 1		Time 2		Time 3		Time 4	
	CA	MA	CA	MA	CA	MA	CA	MA
Birth–12	2	10	—	1	—	1	—	1
13–24	14	26	8	31	3	26	—	11
25–36	14	7	14	11	15	10	2	18
37–48	9	—	11	—	13	6	14	12
49–60	4	—	10	—	8	—	14	1
61–72	—	—	—	—	4	—	10	—
73–84	—	—	—	—	—	—	3	—

CA, chronological age; MA, mental age.

cognitive, comprehension, and production skills assessed, then one expects to see consistency in the data even though different measures were used. Clinicians face this situation with every child they treat for several years. Suffice it to say that until measures are created to measure children's developmental progress through the first 5 years of life, researchers are forced to use different procedures and cope with the limitations in arguing the results. This strategy was the only alternative available to investigate this critical period of language development. The impact of this measurement problem on the outcome of the study should bias against finding consistent results. The use of different tests to evaluate the same variable for children over time should introduce variation into the data that would result in no clear pattern of developmental change in outcomes.

The cognitive measures used included the Bayley Scales of Infant Development–Mental Scale (Bayley, 1969) for those children whose mental ages were between 6 and 30 months. This procedure was used for the majority of the children through Time 3 and for about 50% of the children at Time 4. The Symbolic Play Test (Lowe & Costello, 1988) was given to all children as a backup procedure. The Stanford-Binet Intelligence Scale, Fourth Edition (Thorndike, Hagen, & Sattler, 1986) nonverbal subtests (bead memory and pattern recognition) were given to children who performed at ceiling on the Bayley mental scales. By Time 4, about half of the sample had been given this procedure. The Symbolic Play Test was very useful in providing data on those children who were at ceiling on the Bayley scale but could not achieve baseline on the Stanford-Binet scale.

Two measures were used to assess language comprehension in children functioning up to mental age 24 months, the Sequenced Inventory of Communication Development (SICD) (Hedrick, Prather, & Tobin, 1984) and the Miller–Chapman procedures (Miller, Chapman, Branston, & Reichle, 1980). These measures allowed parent report data on comprehension to be gathered by using the SICD as well as context-based comprehension assessments of lexical and early two- and three-word combinations using the child's own vocabulary and the Miller–Chapman procedures[1] (see Miller & Paul, 1995). Children whose mental ages were above 24 months received the Test for the Auditory Comprehension of Language–Revised (Carrow-Woolfolk,

---

[1] *Reader's note:* The Miller–Chapman procedures are published in a more accessible form in Miller and Paul, *The Clinical Assessment of Language Comprehension* (Paul H. Brookes Publishing Co., 1995), which provides 26 comprehension-testing procedures covering the developmental period from ages 7 months to 10 years. Procedures provide several response modes, object manipulation, picture pointing, and looking; and they cover all language levels from vocabulary to discourse features.

1985) and the Peabody Picture Vocabulary Test–Revised (Dunn & Dunn, 1981). Age-equivalent scores were derived by using the normative data found in the test manuals. Aggregate scores were calculated when more than one measure was given.

The developmental status of language production was derived from videotaped and audiotaped children's language samples in a play context with a standard set of toys. The sample duration was 30 minutes' total time for each subject (15 minutes with parents and 15 minutes with the examiner) at each visit. Sample length was determined by time (30 minutes) rather than by the children's number of utterances because of the tremendous variation in children's language productivity in this period of development. The time-based samples allowed use of the temporal measure descriptively while controlling for the children's opportunities to talk. The samples were transcribed in two ways. For those children who were producing more than 20 different words, an orthographic transcript using standard *SALT: Systematic Analysis of Language Transcripts* transcription conventions (Miller & Chapman, 1993) was completed. For children whose productive language was limited to fewer than 20 different words, the intentional productions were transcribed using the International Phonetic Alphabet. The videotape was reviewed and scored for the prelinguistic communicative behaviors found in Table 2. The age assignment for each sample was based on the frequency of occurrence of each category, with the final assignment reflecting the most frequent, oldest age-related category. The orthographic transcripts were analyzed by using *SALT: Systematic Analysis of Language Transcripts*, a computer program designed to provide quantitative measures of language sample data.

Two measures were used in this study: mean length of utterance (MLU) in morphemes as a measure of general syntactic advancement and the number of different words (DW) as a measure of vocabulary diversity. Age-equivalent scores were derived for MLU by using the prediction equation found in Miller (1981) using the Miller and Chapman (1981) data. In addition, a database of language samples from 252 children who were developing typically (Miller, 1990, 1991) was used when the ages assigned by the Miller and Chapman (1981) data were exceeded. The age-equivalent scores for the number of different words were derived from a prediction equation calculated according to the Miller (1990) reference database on the number of DW produced in conversational contexts.

Defining a Profile

The major issue at this point was to set up a system to transform the individual age scores for each category—cognition, comprehension,

Table 2. Criteria for establishing language production age

Behavior	Age assignment (in months)
Pre-intentional period	
Reflexive crying	0–2
Cooing and laughter	2–5
Vocal play	4–7
Reduplicated babbling (nonintentional)	6–8
Intentional period, prelinguistic	
Intentional action	8–12
Reduplicated babbling	
Communication games	
Differentiated cries	
Linguistic period	
Performatives	12–18
Gesture and vocalization	
Hi–Bye routines	
Request attention or object	
Number of different words (Miller, 1988, 1990)	12+
Mean length of utterance (Miller, 1990; Miller & Chapman, 1981)	18+

and production—into profile types. The goal was to be able to accomplish two things: first, to have the scores sort themselves into distinct profile types, and second, to have nonoverlapping profile types. This process might be judged more clinical than experimental, but it was the only solution available to monitor children's language development through the early period of language learning in children whose skills were quite variable. Previous attempts to document profiles in children with Down syndrome using cross-sectional data worked fairly well, so cross-sectional data were employed in this study with improved measurement precision. Each child was assigned a status rating for comprehension and production relative to his or her own nonverbal cognitive age. This procedure used each child as his or her own control in the sense that cognitive skills determined the rating of language performance. At each of the four assessment intervals, two factors were measured: Each child's comprehension status was categorized as advanced, equivalent, or delayed relative to the child's cognitive skills; and each child's production skills were categorized as high, equivalent, or low relative to the child's cognitive skills. For the specific criteria employed, see the list in the next paragraph. The outcomes of this process could produce nine different profiles for each child ($N = 43$) at each testing time ($N = 4$). This process is referred to as the Profile Discovery Process (PDP).

Criteria for determining accelerated, equivalent, or delayed language performance were established as follows:

Mental ages at or below 24 months: Language plus or minus 3 months
Mental ages at or above 25 months: Language plus or minus 6 months

The rationale here was that 3 months was a significant difference in developmental progress for the first 2 years of life while 6 months was required for the remainder of the developmental period studied. The down side of this decision is the relative precision and the variety of the measures used. We should think of these data as descriptive of performance change rather than reflecting absolute values, even though the measures employed were the best available for children who are difficult to test.

Results of the Profile Discovery Process

The first step was to use the data to discover what profile types would characterize the language performance of this group. A language profile was calculated for each subject at each of their four visits, for a total of 172 profiles (43 subjects $\times$ 4 visits = 172). There were nine possible profile types that could have resulted from this analysis (Status [3]: accelerated, equal, delayed $\times$ Process [3]: cognition, comprehension, production = 9). The results revealed that only three profile types accounted for all 172 profiles out of a possible nine profile types for this analysis (see Table 3).

These results are significant on several grounds. First, even when using different measures over time for the same process, the data reveal consistent responses. Second, the results follow what is known about the language production performance of children with Down syndrome from previous research. Third, not all of these children exhibited the same profile. This finding is unique to this analysis because what was of interest in the study was how each individual's profile compared with the others in the group rather than how these individuals' production scores as a group compared with their comprehension or cognition scores as a group. The distinction may seem small, but the

Table 3.   Number of individuals studied by profile type

Profile type	n	Portion of N (%)
Mental age = Comprehension = Production	58	34
Mental age = Comprehension > Production	110	64
Mental age > Comprehension > Production	4	2

n, subsample; N, total number of individuals studied.

PDP allows children's scores to be compared as the scores relate to one another.

What do these data mean with regard to describing the developmental progress of language and communication skills in children with Down syndrome? First, it is significant that only three of nine possible profiles described the language performance of the group at all four visits. This means that, as a group, these children's language development is fairly consistent in the sense that the relationship between their language comprehension and language production relative to cognitive skills can be described in only three ways. Furthermore, although one might expect the majority of children with cognitive impairments to exhibit language consistent with their cognitive skills, reflecting a slow-motion version of typical development, the results of this analysis reveal that most children with Down syndrome exhibit a unique pattern of performance. The most frequent profile type is Profile Type 2, MA equal to language comprehension with language production delayed. This profile type accounts for 64% of all of the profiles. Why do two profiles account for 98% of the children in this study? Are the children exhibiting language skills consistent with their cognitive ability early in development and only later failing to keep pace with other cognitive skills? Alternatively, are children consistent in their individual profiles? The latter would suggest that profiles are a reflection of individual language-learning abilities, whereas the former would suggest that individual abilities are modified by environmental events. To address this question, profile changes in these children need to be evaluated.

Profile Change over Time

Next examined was the question of profile change over time. Are these profiles consistent for individual children? Alternatively, are they subject to change as children progress through the various stages of development in the acquisition of their language skills? The change data are explored in Table 4, which documents the number of individuals with each profile type at each of the four visits. Table 4 documents the change in profile types (i.e., the change in language status relative to MA) during 24 months of development. These data clearly document a shift in language status for these children from about 50% showing delays in language production at Time 1 to 72% showing such delays at Time 4. By the fourth visit to the laboratory, only 9 of the 43 children's language skills were commensurate with their other cognitive abilities. Also note that the majority of children exhibited delays in only language production; only three children had delays in both comprehension and production. These three children's delays did not be-

Table 4. Number of individuals of each profile type at each data point

Profile type	Time 1	Time 2	Time 3	Time 4
1	21 (49%)	15 (35%)	1 (2%)	9 (21%)
2	21 (49%)	28 (65%)	30 (70%)	3 (7%)
3	1 (2%)	0	0	3 (7%)

Profile Type 1: Mental age is equal to language comprehension is equal to language production; Profile Type 2: Mental age is equal to language comprehension, which exceeds language production; Profile Type 3: Mental age exceeds language comprehension, which exceeds language production.

come apparent until their fourth visit. Perhaps this pattern takes time to emerge, or perhaps these measurements are not sensitive enough to document children's failure to progress early, or perhaps the reason was that early development is quite varied among typical children. It is likely that all of these played a part and, though early development is variable, thus limiting the sensitivity of measurement, it is possible to examine the age issue with these data to see whether profile change is related to advancing MA. Table 4 reveals that Profile Type 2 describes the pattern of development for most children with Down syndrome. An examination of the children with this profile will determine the role that MA plays in changing profile type.

Table 5 shows the nature of the profile shift as MA advances in these children. It organizes the individuals with language production delays (Profile 2) by MA across the four visits. If advancing MA plays a role in the appearance of delayed language performance, it should be apparent in Table 5, which presents the percentage of individuals with Profile 2 (i.e., delayed language production relative to MA and language comprehension) by MA for each visit.

The pattern of these data is quite clear. As MA increases, the productive language gains of children with Down syndrome are slower

Table 5. Percentage of individuals delayed in language production at each visit, by mental age

Mental age (in months)	Time 1	Time 2	Time 3	Time 4
Birth–12	0	0	0	0
13–24	54	61	58	55
25–36	100	91	90	83
37–48	—	—	100	92
49–60	—	—	—	100

than their gains in language comprehension. The data confirm that by the time children with Down syndrome reach MA 36 months, the majority of them have significant impairments in their language production skills. The CA of these children was roughly twice their MA. Remember that syntactic production cannot be evaluated until much later than vocabulary production. Children are producing one-word utterances for some time before they produce two-word utterances. Furthermore, many of the children with Down syndrome had significant language production delays, requiring the use of a range of criteria to establish age at language production (see Table 2). As a result, language production scores were more likely to include measures of syntax as children's MA and language production advanced. One interpretation is that the impairments that children exhibited as their MA advanced were due to their failure to acquire syntax rather than to their experiencing a sudden onset of specific language impairment. The data clearly show that not all children with Down syndrome have the same LDP and that the changes in profile type may be associated with learning the syntax of the language. Those children who exhibited language production impairments early in development certainly had broad-based language-learning problems. The data in Table 5 clearly demonstrate that the 90%–100% of children with an MA of more than 37 months have impairments in language production. This research suggests that interventions should target prevention of these problems through aggressive language production remediation programs.

What Have We Learned from This Work? More than 65% of the total individual profiles reflect greater impairments in language production than in language comprehension and cognitive skills. The percentage of individuals exhibiting language impairment profiles (Profiles 2 and 3) increases at each data point: 51% at Time 1, 65% at Time 2, 69% at Time 3, and 79% at Time 4. This may mean that as these children get older, they are more likely to experience difficulty with productive language. Alternatively, it may mean that the pace of their language development is slower than that for their other cognitive skills and that this pace declines with advancing age. As these data are explored further, it is important to examine why children with Down syndrome experience more difficulty with language production than they experience with other equally complex cognitive skills. For example, is the problem with a specific feature of the language system (i.e., syntax)?

The children in the present study did not improve their productive language skills through the course of the research, even though all of the children were in special education programs. Children with profiles of productive language impairments at Time 1 continue to exhibit those impairments at Times 2, 3, and 4. The intervention programs provided for the children were quite diverse because the children came from different school districts across the state of Wisconsin. This does not mean that language intervention programs provided for these children are not effective. It is unknown what their language skill levels would be without intervention, so all that can be said is that problems in their language skills remain even with their participation in special education programs. Perhaps there is not enough emphasis placed on the development of oral communication skills in special education classrooms.

Impairments in language production are associated with advances in MA. Among children below MA 24 months, 54%–61% have impairments in language production and 83%–100% of the children above MA 25 months have language production impairments. These changes may reflect children's difficulty with the syntax of language, an aspect of language that usually appears at about 20–24 months of MA development. If these data reflect the difference between vocabulary skills and the mastery of English syntax, then one would expect to find that 54%–61% of children with Down syndrome acquire vocabulary at a slower rate than their cognitive skills would predict. That is, vocabulary development fails to keep pace with other cognitive abilities in almost one third of the population of children with Down syndrome. If this result can be confirmed, it suggests that the majority of children with Down syndrome have a generalized impairment in developing oral communication skills. Can this result be validated? Researchers are in the final stages of completing a longitudinal study of vocabulary acquisition in young children with Down syndrome at The Waisman Center. The results of the new vocabulary studies confirm the conclusions of the early work reported, suggesting that there is a group of children with Down syndrome who will have early language skills that are comparable to their MA; but they will develop more advanced language skills at a slower pace than they will develop other cognitive skills. At issue is whether this represents an overall rate slowdown for the acquisition of language skills with advancing MA or a specific problem with the acquisition of vocabulary or the syntax of the language. The results of vocabulary acquisition are studied in more detail in the next section.

VOCABULARY ACQUISITION IN CHILDREN WITH DOWN SYNDROME

Does the development of lexical skills in children with Down syndrome differ from that of children with the same cognitive skills who are developing typically? Or does language development progress at the same rate as other cognitive skills among children with Down syndrome and those developing typically early in the developmental period? These questions can be asked from several points of view; but the fact remains that, during the early stages of language learning, vocabulary is children's focus, and words become their currency of message exchange with the adults, siblings, and peers in their world. The discussion in the previous section on whether children with Down syndrome have the same language-learning skills as other children classified as having mental retardation concluded that language-learning patterns, not just the outcome of depressed cognitive advancement, among children with Down syndrome are unique. Their language production is uniquely affected, limiting the range of messages that they can communicate through oral language.

The profile data suggested that a detailed study of early vocabulary development might provide a window into the nature of the language-learning abilities of children with Down syndrome. The first problem faced is how to measure vocabulary growth when investigating similarities or differences in performance. Typically, performance is measured on a language test, which may ask the individual for definitions or recognition of word meaning, or the number of different words that the individual produces in a language sample may be counted, or parents may be asked to complete a checklist of words that their children use to communicate. Researchers have also begun to examine the types of words that children are learning early in development, the range of meanings that the words represent, and grammatical categories of words learned to gain insight into the similarities and differences in strategies that children use in acquiring their language.

Research on Early Vocabulary Development in Children with Down Syndrome

Previous studies investigating vocabulary development confronted the problem of how to gain access to the words children were able to produce when communicating in everyday situations. Young children do not talk readily to unfamiliar people such as researchers, and they do not talk much at all when first producing single words (seven to nine words per hour for children ages 12–18 months). These data persuaded the present author to experiment with parent report measures in addition to traditional language sample methods in which the child and parent are tape recorded during a play session of a standard length with a standard set of toys. Innovations in parent report measures of language development offer improved access to the early vocabulary of all children. The new parent report measures have overcome the problems of older measures such as retrospective memory and recall of words and sentences by asking parents to report what their child is saying at this moment and offering a list of more than 600 words that research has shown children typically learn early. The parents' task is simply to check off those words that their child is using in spontaneous conversation. The report is filled out at home by parents over several days and usually takes about 20–30 minutes. Research on these measures has found high reliability and validity with other measures of language performance. The present author's research has documented the validity of these measures with children with Down syndrome. Parents of children with Down syndrome report their children's vocabulary production as accurately as parents of children who are developing typically. Correlations between the number of words produced in a language sample recorded in the laboratory and the parent report vocabulary measure were $r = .82$ and $r = .75$, respectively. The additional advantage of parent report measures is that parent report allows researchers access to more of the child's total vocabulary. Language samples in the present author's studies produce vocabularies of 120–150 words at MA 30 months, whereas parent report measures typically provide vocabularies in the 350- to 500-word range. Given the validity of parent report measures, the larger vocabularies that parent report measures produce may help document true vocabulary-learning rates in children with Down syndrome rather than methodological limitations of laboratory methods.

The first study of vocabulary development using parent report measures used a cross-sectional design to evaluate rates of vocabulary development in children MA 12–30 months. A group of children with Down syndrome ($n = 43$) was matched with a group of children who were developing typically ($n = 46$) with regard to MA and socioeconomic status (SES). The results revealed that children who were developing typically were acquiring significantly more words than the children with Down syndrome at the same MA levels. The differences increased as MA increased, suggesting that children with Down syndrome have particular difficulty in learning language that is not accounted for by their general cognitive status. Because cross-sectional studies measure growth across children at different ages, it was necessary to confirm these results with a second longitudinal study following the same children through this developmental period.

The second study followed the youngest children from the first study, those who were MA 12–17 months. There were 20 children with Down syndrome and 23 children who were developing typically participating in this second study. In an effort to accommodate differences in their rates of cognitive growth, the children with Down syndrome were evaluated every 6 months, and the children who were developing typically were evaluated every 3 months. The study followed the children with Down syndrome for 2 years and the children who were developing typically for 1 year. The children's parents completed parent report measures of vocabulary development prior to each visit to the laboratory. The results of this study were similar to those of the first study: Children with Down syndrome produced fewer different words than children who were typically developing for MA 15–30 months. The gap between the two groups widened with their increasing MA. At the end of the study, the children who were typically developing had vocabularies four times larger than the children with Down syndrome. These data suggest a difference in the rate of vocabulary learning that is consistent with the research on acquiring the syntax of the language.

As a first step in investigating possible differences in the type of vocabulary acquired by each group, each word produced by each child was categorized according to two grammatical categories: Nouns and Other. It has been hypothesized that children with mental retardation are more concrete in their use of language. If that is true, then children with Down syndrome should acquire more nouns and words of other grammatical categories. It has also been suggested that one of the reasons why children with Down syndrome do not acquire syntax as rapidly as their MA-matched peers is that they have not acquired a vocabulary that contains verbs and adjectives that lead directly to two-word combinations. Both of these hypotheses predict that children with Down syndrome should have vocabularies containing mostly nouns, and children who are typically developing should have vocabularies that represent broad grammatical categorization. The results of the present analysis found no differences in the distribution of vocabulary in these two categories. One might argue that using more categories might have better distinguished the groups. However, because we did not find a preponderance of nouns in the vocabularies of the children with Down syndrome, there appears to be little reason to investigate this issue further.

Rate of Progress in Vocabulary Learning Relative to Other Cognitive Skills

The rate of vocabulary learning in children experiencing typical development is consistent with their MA progress. As MA increases, lexicon size increases. The children with Down syndrome did exhibit the same pattern, but their rate of acquiring new words was significantly slower. The equations describing both learning curves are quite different in slope. Although the children with Down syndrome do continue to learn new words, their rate of progress does not match their rate of acquiring other cognitive skills. The gap continues to widen with their increasing age.

Individual Differences in the Rate of Vocabulary Acquisition Among Children with Down Syndrome

Are there individual differences in the rate of vocabulary acquisition? There are several ways to answer this question. First, data for each child can be plotted, and the individual functions can be compared with the group mean. If the data are consistent, then most of the line describing the individuals should be close to the group mean. The degree of difference can be described in standard deviations (*SD*) or the standard error of measurement. The problem with these quantitative measures is that the variability of the individuals increases with their age. Transforming the data with the log or square root of each value equalizes this difference in variability, making standard scores more meaningful. This method of comparison is limited to a comparison of the experimental subjects to the control subjects and is therefore a relative comparison. It is unknown how representative of the population at large the children in the control group are, even though care was taken to select children who were typical.

The second method of evaluating these data for individual differences compares the experimental data with the norms of the test procedure to overcome the limitation of the limited control sample. The parent report measure used (the MacArthur Child Development Inventory [CDI] [Fenson et al., 1993]) was normed with more than 1,800 children, and the test manual provides percentile scores for children through age 30 months on the vocabulary checklist. Fenson and colleagues (1993) suggested that children who fall below the 10th percentile are at risk for delays in language development. Recall that the tenth percentile is 1.33 *SD*.

Each child was placed into one of three categories using the CDI data:

1. Below the 10th percentile
2. Between the 11th and 89th percentiles
3. Above the 90th percentile

The sample total was 43 children in this study. The 23 children who were developing typically were categorized as follows: 4 children below the 10th percentile, 12 children between the 11th and 89th percentiles, and 7 children above the 90th percentile. The children with Down syndrome (n = 20) included 13 children below the 10th percentile, 7 children between the 11th and 89th percentiles, and 0 children above the 90th percentile. These data suggest, on the one hand, that children with Down syndrome are significantly slower than their MA- and SES-matched peers who are developing typically and that 65% of them are below the 10th percentile in their rate of vocabulary learning. On the other hand, 35% of children with Down syndrome are learning vocabulary at a rate consistent with 80% of their MA-matched peers who are developing typically. Is this normal variation or significant individual variation? The data from this study are not sufficient to answer this question with any authority, but they are sufficient to test the trends found in the group data against the individuals' performance. In particular, one can investigate whether the children whose vocabulary is developing more slowly are slower in all cognitive functions, which is not likely, because the group matches are so close that variability is small. How can the slow rates of vocabulary learning be explained if they are not the result of these individuals' general cognitive impairments? The next phase of this research is aimed directly at answering that question. Exploration of some areas of explanation, including hearing loss and family interaction style, has begun, though it has not yet provided a satisfactory explanation.

Summary

Investigators who are interested in cognition and language problems as they relate to the study of asynchronous development of vocabulary and syntax in language production relative to comprehension and cognitive status will find that children with Down syndrome are an interesting sample population. The work to date at The Waisman Center has documented consistent differences in the rate of vocabulary learning in children with Down syndrome relative to their MA-matched peers. These impairments increase with advancing age, indicating that the learning rate of the group with Down syndrome is significantly slower than that of the group of children who are developing typically. Although the rate of vocabulary acquisition is significantly slower for the children with Down syndrome, not all of the children studied exhibited similar rates of learning. Of the children studied, 35% had rates of vocabulary growth consistent with MA expectations. These data suggest that neither the syndrome alone nor the cognitive impairment associated with Down syndrome can explain the differences observed in vocabulary growth. The next series of studies will evaluate a variety of causal constructs to explain the significant asynchronies in language learning compared with other cognitive abilities.

CONCLUSIONS

Three important conclusions can be drawn from this work:

1. A profile of productive language impairment relative to language comprehension and cognitive skill characterizes the majority of children with Down syndrome.
2. The profile changes observed over time were the result of language production skills' failing to keep pace with advancing MA.
3. The individuals with Down syndrome in this study appeared to fall into two groups relative to their language-learning progress. One group has production skills that were impaired from the onset of first words. The proportion of children falling into this profile was consistent across the two studies reported here at 65%–70% (see Table 4). No child was identified as delayed in language relative to other cognitive skills under age 12 months (see Table 5). The primary measurement used for children in the 12- to 24-month age range was vocabulary. Table 5 reveals that 54%–61% of the children in that age range were delayed, which is further support for the 65% identified as delayed in vocabulary development in the second study. It appears from both studies on 63 children that 48%–65% were delayed in vocabulary development during the initial stages of language learning. A second group of children appeared to have mastered sufficient vocabulary through the second year of life but fell behind in learning more advanced aspects of language production (e.g., syntax). The second group may be experiencing a specific problem with the syntax of the language. Virtually 100% of the children in the first study exhibited delayed production skills by the time they entered their third year of life. These studies suggest that there are language-learning differences evident early in development that may have a biological origin. Furthermore, the profile changes noted as children advanced in MA may have an environmental component associated with reduced expectations for communication, reduced speech intelligibility limiting effective communicative practice, or less effective adaptation of language input strategies necessary to foster optimum language and communication development.

The following are implications of this work for language intervention services:

1. These data suggest that school systems should alter their eligibility criteria for speech and language services. Because language production impairments are likely to be a part of the learning impair-

ments associated with Down syndrome, eligibility should be automatic rather than waiting to document the inevitable language
delay when children's MA reach 25 months, usually when they
are ages 4–5 years. This strategy would focus on prevention of
productive language impairments rather than waiting for them to
be documented and then trying to play catch-up. If the service
programs provided for the children (Study 1) are an example of
what is available, language production skills are not going to catch
up with their language comprehension or their other cognitive
abilities.

2. It would be prudent to use intervention methods that focus on
oral motor integrity during the early periods of development
while encouraging communication attempts regardless of the
mode of communication used. The goal here is to stimulate communicative attempts rather than to worry about the child's producing intelligible utterances. Gestural or vocal signs or pointing
are acceptable. If parents and others can understand what the
child wants or is attempting to say, then they should respond enthusiastically. Our experience suggests that children continue to
learn the most efficient mode of getting their message across, and
that mode is speech. A great many of the children participating in
the research projects reported here used American Sign Language
and other gestures to produce messages early in development. All
of these children have moved to exclusive use of speech, dropping
the signs when their speech became more intelligible. Parents and
teachers should focus on communicating messages to these children. The goal of communication is to exchange messages, not to
produce messages of perfect form.

Individual variations in the language and communication skills of
children with Down syndrome precludes giving a standard intervention sequence. Children with Down syndrome seem to enjoy visual
stimulation and are particularly attracted to computers and televised
or videotaped presentations (Iacano & Miller, 1989). This fact is supported by the successes in literacy training for children with Down
syndrome (Buckley, 1995). Language interventions that incorporate
print material have shown significant gains in these children's oral language skills and in their learning to read. These data should help us to
approach the language-learning task from a broader perspective, helping children with Down syndrome to new levels of communicative
effectiveness. Remember—talk, talk, talk. Children with Down syndrome understand far more than they are able to say. Reducing messages to the level of their language production skills seriously limits the

language models available for their continued language learning. Remember also that families that talk more have children with more advanced language skills (Hart & Risley, 1995).

REFERENCES

Bayley, N. (1969). *Bayley Scales of Infant Development.* New York: The Psychological Corporation.

Buckley, S. (1995). Teaching children with Down syndrome to read and write. In L. Nadel & D. Rosenthal (Eds.), *Down syndrome: Living and learning in the community* (pp. 158–169). New York: Wiley-Liss.

Carrow-Woolfolk, E. (1985). *Test for Auditory Comprehension of Language–Revised* (TACL–R). Chicago: Riverside.

Chapman, R.S. (1995). Language development in children and adolescents with Down syndrome. In P. Fletcher & B. MacWhinney (Eds.), *The handbook of child language* (pp. 641–663). Cambridge, England: Basil Blackwell.

Chapman, R.S., & Miller, J.F. (1980). Analyzing language and communication in the child. In R.L. Schiefelbusch (Ed.), *Language intervention series: Vol. IV. Nonspeech language and communication: Analysis and intervention* (pp. 159–196). Baltimore: University Park Press.

Cole, K., Dale, P., & Mills, P. (1992). Stability of the intelligence quotient–language quotient relation: Is discrepancy modeling based on a myth? *American Journal of Mental Retardation, 97,* 131–143.

Cromer, R. (1974). The development of language and cognition: The cognition hypothesis. In R.L. Schiefelbusch & L. Lloyd (Eds.), *Language perspectives: Acquisition, retardation, and intervention* (pp. 98–141). Baltimore: University Park Press.

Cromer, R. (1991). *Language and thought in normal and handicapped children.* Cambridge, England: Basil Blackwell.

Dunn, L.M., & Dunn, L.M. (1981). *Peabody Picture Vocabulary Test–Revised* (PPVT–R). Circle Pines, MN: American Guidance Service.

Fenson, L., Dale, P.S., Reznick, J.S., Thal, D.J., Bates, E., Hartung, J., Pethick, S., & Reilly, J. (1993). *MacArthur Communicative Development Inventories* (CDI). San Diego: Singular Publishing Group.

Grossman, H. (Ed.). (1983). *Classification in mental retardation.* Washington, DC: American Association on Mental Deficiency.

Hart, B., & Risley, T.R. (1995). *Meaningful differences in the everyday experience of young American children.* Baltimore: Paul H. Brookes Publishing Co.

Hedrick, D., Prather, E., & Tobin, A. (1984). *Sequenced Inventory of Communication Development* (Rev. ed.). Seattle: University of Washington Press.

Iacono, T., & Miller, J.F. (1989, March). Can microcomputers be used to teach communication skills to students with mental retardation? *Education and Training of the Mentally Retarded,* 32–44.

Lowe, M., & Costello, A. (1988). *Symbolic Play Test* (2nd ed.). Berkshire, England: Nfer-Nelson Publishing Co.

Luckasson, R., Coulter, D.L., Polloway, E.A., Reiss, S., Schalock, R.L., Snell, M.E., Spitalnik, D.M., & Stark, J.A. (1992). *Mental retardation: Definition, classification and systems of supports* (Special 9th ed.). Washington, DC: American Association on Mental Retardation.

McLean, J., & Snyder-McLean, L. (1978). *A transactional approach to early language training.* Columbus, OH: Charles E. Merrill.

Miller, J.F. (1978). Assessing children's language behavior: A developmental process approach. In R.L. Schiefelbusch (Ed.), *The basis of language intervention* (pp. 269–318). Baltimore: University Park Press.

Miller, J.F. (1981). *Assessing language production in children: Experimental procedures.* Baltimore: University Park Press.

Miller, J.F. (1987). Language and communication characteristics of children with Down syndrome. In S.M. Pueschel, C. Tingey, J.E. Rynders, A.C. Crocker, & D.M. Crutcher (Eds.), *New perspectives on Down syndrome* (pp. 233–262). Baltimore: Paul H. Brookes Publishing Co.

Miller, J.F. (1988). The developmental asynchrony of language development in children with Down syndrome. In L. Nadel (Ed.), *The psychobiology of Down syndrome* (pp. 167–198). Cambridge, MA: MIT Press.

Miller, J.F. (1990). *The reference database.* Madison: University of Wisconsin–Madison, The Waisman Center, Language Analysis Laboratory.

Miller, J.F. (Ed.). (1991). *Research on child language disorders: A decade of progress.* Boston: College-Hill Press.

Miller, J.F. (1995). Individual differences in vocabulary acquisition in children with Down syndrome. In C. Epstein, T. Hassold, I. Lott, L. Nadel, & D. Patterson (Eds.), *Etiology and pathogenesis of Down syndrome: Proceedings of the International Down Syndrome Research Conference* (pp. 93–103). New York: Wiley-Liss.

Miller, J.F. (1997). The search for a phenotype of disordered language performance. In M.L. Rice (Ed.), *Toward a genetics of language* (pp. 297–314). Mahwah, NJ: Lawrence Erlbaum Associates.

Miller, J.F., & Chapman, R.S. (1981). The relation between age and mean length of utterance in morphemes. *Journal of Speech and Hearing Research, 24*(2), 154–161.

Miller, J.F., & Chapman, R.S. (1993). *SALT: Systematic Analysis of Language Transcripts* (DOS Version 3.0) [Software program]. Madison: University of Wisconsin–Madison, The Waisman Center, Language Analysis Laboratory.

Miller, J.F., Chapman, R.S., Branston, M., & Reichle, J. (1980). Language comprehension in sensorimotor Stages 5 and 6. *Journal of Speech and Hearing Research, 23*(2), 284–311.

Miller, J.F., & Paul, R. (1995). *The clinical assessment of language comprehension.* Baltimore: Paul H. Brookes Publishing Co.

Miller, J.F., Rosin, M., Pierce, K., Miolo, G., & Sedey, A. (1989, November). *Language profile stability in children with Down syndrome.* Paper presented at the annual convention of the American Speech-Language-Hearing Association, St. Louis.

Miller, J.F., Streit, G., Salmon, D., & Lafollette, L. (1987, November). *Developmental synchrony in children with Down syndrome.* Paper presented at the annual convention of the American Speech-Language-Hearing Association, New Orleans, LA.

Thorndike, R.L., Hagen, E.P., & Sattler, J.M. (1986). *Stanford-Binet Intelligence Scale* (4th ed.). Chicago: Riverside.

3

Language Development in Children and Adolescents with Down Syndrome

Robin S. Chapman

This chapter summarizes cross-sectional research on language development in older children and adolescents with Down syndrome.

HISTORICAL BACKGROUND

Rosenberg's (1982) review of research supported six conclusions about the course of language development in children with Down syndrome:

1. The language performance of children with Down syndrome was predicted better by their nonverbal mental age (MA) than by their chronological age (CA).
2. Home environments were associated with better language outcomes than institutional environments.

This chapter was supported in part by Grant R01 HD23353 from the National Institutes of Health to the author and in part by Core Support Grant 5 P30 HD03352 to The Waisman Center, University of Wisconsin–Madison. The help of the participants and parents is gratefully acknowledged, as is the research assistance of Elizabeth Kay-Raining Bird, Denise Maybach, Scott E. Schwartz, Hye-Kyeung Seung, and Laura Wagner. Portions of this chapter were presented at the Wisconsin Symposium on Child Language Disorders, Madison, June 5, 1992; at the International Association for the Scientific Study of Mental Deficiency, The Gold Coast, Australia, August 5, 1992; at the International Conference on Language and Cognition in Down Syndrome, University of Portsmouth, England, September 24, 1994; and at the Rosenstadt Lecture in Medical Education, Faculty of Medicine, University of Toronto, Ontario, Canada, May 26, 1995.

3. Mothers' language input was appropriately adjusted to their children's language levels, as indexed by mean length of utterance (MLU).
4. The language of children with Down syndrome, in comparison with CA-matched controls, appeared developmentally delayed, with their comprehension and production developing at similar rates.
5. In limited evidence from MLU comparisons, the language acquisition strategies of individuals with Down syndrome appeared similar to those of controls.
6. The diagnosis of Down syndrome did not predict children's patterns of linguistic performance, except in the area of articulation, and then only to a limited extent.

In contrast to Rosenberg's findings, research reviewed since that time (Chapman, 1997, in press; Fowler, 1990; Hartley, 1986; Miller, 1988) and my own work has suggested that all but the first two conclusions just listed can be revised. The evidence is summarized in this chapter. It indicates that the diagnosis of Down syndrome is associated with a characteristic pattern of strengths and weaknesses in the language development of adolescents, including 1) differential rates of development in language comprehension and production, with comprehension being a strength and production being an area of specific delay, relative to individuals' nonverbal MA; and 2) differential rates of acquisition of vocabulary and syntax within each of those process domains, with vocabulary being a particular strength in comprehension and syntax being a particular deficit in production.

These findings mean that development is differentially delayed in different domains and increasingly so with individuals' increasing CA and MA. The finding of better comprehension than production in older individuals also suggests that language input geared particularly to MLU becomes increasingly less appropriately adapted to older children's lexical and syntactic comprehension skills. Predictors of individual differences in comprehension performance exist, including MA, hearing, and CA. Comprehension scores in turn predict individual variation in more limited production skills. Finally, some differences in the details of language acquisition strategies compared with MA and MLU-matched controls can be identified. These can be related to the greater nonverbal understanding that is available to individuals with Down syndrome than their MLU-matched controls as well as to auditory short-term memory that is more restricted than that of MA-matched controls.

The studies on which these revised conclusions are based were carried out at Time 1 of a study of children and adolescents ages 5–20 years initially (Chapman, Schwartz, & Kay-Raining Bird, 1991; Chapman, Seung, Schwartz, & Kay-Raining Bird, in press). That cross-sectional work focuses on three general questions related to these conclusions:

1. Do children with Down syndrome have a characteristic pattern of specific language impairment (SLI) relative to expectations based on their MA?
2. Does the gap between the language comprehension skills and language production skills of children with Down syndrome widen with age?
3. What processes of language acquisition are associated with individual variations in language skills among children with Down syndrome?

DESCRIPTION OF RESEARCH

To answer the questions posed at the end of the preceding section, a study was undertaken comparing the language and cognitive skills of children and adolescents with Down syndrome with those of MA-matched children who were typically developing (Chapman, Schwartz, et al., 1991; Chapman et al., in press).

Participants

The participants at Time 1 were 48 children and adolescents with Down syndrome ages 5 years, 6 months, to 20 years, 6 months, and 48 children ages 2–6 years who were developing typically (see Table 1). The control group mean and variance were matched to the group with Down syndrome on nonverbal MA, as determined by mean age–equivalent scores on the Bead Memory and Pattern Analysis subtests of the Stanford-Binet Intelligence Scale (Thorndike, Hagen, & Sattler, 1986). The groups were also matched with regard to their mothers' years of education.

The children with Down syndrome were recruited from Wisconsin and northern Illinois. All children who used speech as their primary means of communication and whose hearing showed no more than a mild loss were included in the study.

The children in the control group were recruited from Madison, Wisconsin, and its surrounding small communities, and ranged in CA from 2 to 6 years. These CAs corresponded to the main range of MA scores of children with Down syndrome.

Procedures   All children participated in a 3-hour protocol that included, in order, a hearing screening; picture descriptions; story re-

Table 1. Children participating in study: Characteristics by group

Characteristic	Children with Down syndrome (N = 48)			Controls (N = 48)			
	n	M	SD	n	M	SD	p*
Boys	30			23			
Chronological age (Years)		12.54	(4.50)		4.16	(1.16)	< .05
Nonverbal mental age (Years)ª		4.58	(1.45)		4.71	(1.43)	NS
Mothers' levels of education (Years)		13.33	(1.87)		13.88	(2.27)	NS

From Chapman, R.S., Schwartz, S.E., & Kay-Raining Bird, E. (1991). Language skills of children and adolescents with Down syndrome: I. Comprehension. *Journal of Speech and Hearing Research, 34,* 1108; reprinted by permission.

ª Based on mean of Bead Memory and Pattern Analysis subtests of the Stanford-Binet Intelligence Scale (Fourth Edition) (Thorndike, Hagen, & Sattler, 1986).

*p < .05, t-test of group difference.

n, subsample; N, total sample population; M, mean; SD, standard deviation.

telling; the Peabody Picture Vocabulary Test–Revised (PPVT–R) (Dunn & Dunn, 1981); conversation and narration with the examiner; an object-hiding task (Chapman, Kay-Raining Bird, & Schwartz, 1990); the Expressive Vocabulary, Bead Memory, and Pattern Analysis subtests of the Stanford-Binet Intelligence Scale; conversation and snack with a parent; a speech motor evaluation; delayed story recall; event narration; the Test for Auditory Comprehension of Language–Revised (TACL–R) (Carrow-Woolfolk, 1985); and the delay condition of the object-hiding task. Breaks were incorporated at frequent intervals. Interviews with the children's parents elicited background data on the children's hearing history, the children's educational and intervention histories, and the parents' education and occupation.

Narrative Language Sample Children's expressive language skills were assessed through a 12-minute narrative free speech sample with the examiner, which included a request of the child to tell about a favorite story, to describe family photographs (brought from home) of recent events, to complete three story beginnings, and (if necessary to complete the 12 minutes) descriptions of complex pictures and videotaped events drawn from other parts of the protocol.

Conversation Sample A 6-minute conversation sample with the experimenter was tape recorded and transcribed.

Transcription Children's conversations and narratives were transcribed as computer files using *SALT: Systematic Analysis of Language Transcripts* conventions (Miller & Chapman, 1993), including the marking of bound morphemes, disfluencies, omissions of bound morphemes or words, and indications of unintelligible syllables.

Scoring Transcripts were checked for reliability, corrected, and analyzed with the SALT program. MLU in morphemes was computed on complete and intelligible utterances in each child's narrative and conversation samples. For the narrative sample, the distribution of utterance length in morphemes for complete and intelligible utterances was also computed for each child.

Reliability Reliability was established by tallying, during checking of transcripts, the number of disagreements in which morphemes were added, deleted, changed, or put into or taken out of mazes; or in which utterance segmentation changed. These changes averaged 6.1 per 456 words of narrative transcript for the controls and 7.8 per 367 words for the group with Down syndrome.

FINDINGS

The language testing revealed, overall, no significant difference between the group with Down syndrome and the group without for comprehension; and significant differences ($p < .05$) in every case for differences in language production based on the 12-minute narrative sample (see Table 2). Relationships between the variables across ages are discussed in the subsections that follow.

Table 2. Vocabulary and syntactic comprehension measures for children with Down syndrome and controls: Mean age-equivalent scores and standard deviations

Measure	Children with Down syndrome		Controls		
	M	SD	M	SD	p*
Vocabulary comprehension					
PPVT–R	5.27	2.41	4.71	1.56	NS
Syntax comprehension					
TACL–R Total	4.33	1.41	4.65	1.28	NS
TACL–R subtest I	4.81	1.79	5.16	1.54	NS
TACL–R subtest II	4.15	1.51	4.50	1.38	NS
TACL–R subtest III	4.31	1.75	4.62	1.64	NS
Difference between PPVT–R and Total TACL–R	.94	1.18	.06	.77	<.01

From Chapman, R.S., Schwartz, S.E., & Kay-Raining Bird, E. (1991). Language skills of children and adolescents with Down syndrome: I. Comprehension. *Journal of Speech and Hearing Research, 34,* 1109; reprinted by permission.

PPVT–R, Peabody Picture Vocabulary Test–Revised (Dunn & Dunn, 1981); TACL–R, Test for Auditory Comprehension of Language–Revised (Carrow-Woolfolk, 1985)

*$p < .05$, *t*-test.

M, mean; *SD*, standard deviation; NS, not significant.

n = 48 for each group.

Language Comprehension

Strikingly, differences between vocabulary and syntax comprehension were greater for children with Down syndrome than for those without, revealing their greater strength in lexical comprehension.

Vocabulary Comprehension of vocabulary is reported to be equivalent to that of MA-matched controls not only in the younger children with Down syndrome whom Miller studied (see Chapter 2) but also in comparisons of children in later childhood (Chapman, Schwartz, et al., 1991). Among the adolescents studied, however, comprehension vocabulary exceeded expectations based on MA. We have attributed the larger vocabulary in adolescents to the greater diversity of educational and vocational experiences available to adolescents with Down syndrome in the study (Chapman, Schwartz, et al., 1991).

Syntax Comprehension In contrast with vocabulary comprehension, syntax comprehension among the adolescents with Down syndrome was equivalent to their MAs. Thus, in adolescence, a gap emerged between individuals' vocabulary comprehension and their syntax comprehension that was not present for MA-matched controls; and this gap widened with age. This finding is consistent with Hartley's (1982) report of poorer performance on syntactic comprehension tasks among children with Down syndrome than among children with mental retardation of other origin who were matched on vocabulary comprehension. Taken together, these findings suggest a pattern of acquisition that is specific to children with Down syndrome of a divergence, increasing with age, between lexical and syntactic comprehension, with vocabulary comprehension being a special strength.

Implications for Research The finding of divergent lexical and syntactic comprehension in adolescents with Down syndrome raises a methodological question about much of the cognitive research carried out on the group, in which MA matching has often been carried out in actuality through PPVT–R (Vocabulary Comprehension) matching. For younger individuals with Down syndrome, such a match might effectively equate to nonverbal MA and syntax comprehension as well. For adolescents and older individuals, however, such a match might create a control group that is significantly more advanced than the group of children with Down syndrome in both nonverbal MA and syntax comprehension—a disparity that would alter the interpretation of any differences found.

Cognition

With regard to the findings discussed in the previous section, Rosin, Swift, Bless, and Vetter (1988) reported a similar split in lexical and syntactic comprehension for adolescents. They reported a somewhat different set of findings, however, with respect to MA: Vocabulary comprehension was equivalent to MA expectations, and syntactic comprehension fell below them. Their study used the Columbia Test of Mental Maturities to operationalize MA (Burgemeister, Blum, & Lorge, 1972). The Columbia Test is a test of children's ability to notice perceptual and conceptual relationships that does not require memory for the forms shown. As such, it is more similar to the Pattern Analysis subtest than the Bead Memory subtest of the Stanford-Binet Intelligence Scale. The Bead Memory subtest depends on individuals' short-term memory of visual sequences. The study reported in this chapter used the averaged age equivalent on the two subtests.

When the performance of individuals on the two Stanford-Binet subtests was examined, a clear difference emerged for older children. If syntax comprehension had been compared with Pattern Analysis alone, it would fall below MA, the same conclusion as that reached by Rosin et al. (1988). The children who were studied as MA controls, in contrast, did not show such a divergence in performance on the two subtests. The divergence in the older children with Down syndrome suggested a more complex picture of nonverbal cognitive functioning than a simple overall delay, unless the source of the divergence resided in verbal labeling and rehearsal strategies, which would reflect the slower expressive language development of the group of older children.

Pervasive Sequencing Impairment   It was important to include a task that tapped visual memory as well as visual analytic skill in the operationalization of nonverbal cognition. Performance on the bead memory, auditory short-term memory, and story recall tasks was examined (Kay-Raining Bird & Chapman, 1994) to see if it contained evidence of a pervasive sequencing impairment, which Rosin and colleagues (1988) suggested might be the underlying source of the problems that they observed. We asked whether memory for item order is selectively impaired in individuals with Down syndrome. The ability to recall the correct order of items, given that the items had been recalled, was examined for Time 1 recall of the propositions of a narrative, Time 2 digit span, and Time 2 memory for bead order. The individuals with Down syndrome recalled significantly less information than MA-matched controls on both auditory tasks, replicating previous findings of auditory memory span deficits. No differences in the ordering of recalled information were found, and the groups did not differ in the relative frequency of ordering errors in the visual task when span was matched. Thus, no evidence was found to support a pervasive impairment in sequential processing across modalities, and no specific difficulty was found in individuals' recall of the order of information within the auditory modality (Kay-Raining Bird & Chapman, 1994).

Auditory Short-Term Memory Impairment In contrast, a specific impairment in auditory memory is clearly characteristic of the children with Down syndrome (see Chapman, 1995). Sentence memory and story recall show similar limitations (Kay-Raining Bird & Chapman, 1994). The possibility that auditory short-term memory limits syntactic comprehension in children with Down syndrome is consistent with Marcell and Weeks's (1988) report that comprehension of grammatically difficult syntactic structures on the TACL–R, in particular those that require attention to word order, is significantly associated with auditory short-term memory when CA and IQ score are partialed out in individuals with Down syndrome. Those individuals with the shortest auditory memory spans were also those who failed to fast-map new vocabulary in comprehension (see page 56 for a description of fast mapping).

Hearing Status

Hearing status is another important potential limiter of comprehension, and thus, in order to make the present study more fully representative of the population with Down syndrome, individuals with mild hearing loss were included. The study attempted to find out how well children's comprehension skills can be predicted on the basis of multiple regression analyses using the best predictors from each of the following six areas: CA, sex, cognitive level, socioeconomic status, hearing status, and educational history (Chapman, Schwartz, et al., 1991). Stepwise multiple analyses showed that CA and mean MA collectively accounted for 78% of the variability in vocabulary comprehension and 80% of the variability in syntax comprehension in the group with Down syndrome, with total passes on a hearing screening accounting for an additional 3%–4%. Few children who were developing typically had hearing loss; in analyses of their data, CA, mother's education, and mean MA collectively accounted for 90% of the variance in their vocabulary comprehension. Mean MA accounted for 78% of the variance in their syntax comprehension, with the history of presence or absence of tubes for otitis media accounting for an additional 3%.

Language Production

Impairments in the development of language production, relative to expectations based on nonverbal MA or comprehension skill, have frequently been reported for children and adolescents with Down syndrome. Productive syntax has been cited as the locus of particular impairment in older children with Down syndrome (see Chapman, 1995, 1997; Fowler, 1990; Hartley, 1986; Miller, 1988).

Expressive Language Impairments Specific impairments in narrative language production have been confirmed relative to controls matched for nonverbal MA and socioeconomic status for the individuals studied (Chapman, Kay-Raining Bird, & Schwartz, 1991) (see Table 3). The pattern of development in syntax production was then examined more closely in the narrative language samples (Chapman et al., in press). At least three hypotheses about the nature of this expressive syntax impairment have been proposed in the literature (see Fowler, 1990): the Critical Period Hypothesis, the Syntactic Ceiling Hypothesis, and the Grammatical Morpheme Deficit Hypothesis. These are described and evaluated in turn in the following section.

Critical Period Hypothesis Two versions of the hypothesis that language learning can take place only within a restricted age range have been proposed. Lenneberg (1967), on the basis of a 3-year longitudinal study of 62 children with Down syndrome, proposed the Critical Period Hypothesis to account for the fact that those who had attained puberty had failed to make any discernible progress in acquiring language structure in contrast to younger children. Fowler (1990) suggested that evidence for a maturational limit to language learning would place the end of the critical language-learning period earlier, at around 7 years of age. Either version of this maturational

Table 3. Lexical, syntax, pragmatic, and intelligibility production measures from 12-minute narratives by group

Measure	Children with Down syndrome (N = 48)		Controls (N = 48)		
	M	SD	M	SD	p*
Lexical:					
Number of different words	132.79	56.07	155.44	60.55	<.05
Total words	365.58	202.31	462.73	215.49	<.05
Syntactic:					
Mean length of utterance in morphemes	2.98	1.44	4.70	1.72	<.01
Pragmatic:					
Total utterances	160.77	42.41	120.00	33.94	<.01
Intelligibility:					
Number of complete and intelligible utterances	132.73	40.84	108.38	33.63	<.01
Proportion of complete and intelligible utterances	.83	.11	.90	.07	<.01

N, total number of individuals in sample; M, mean; SD, standard deviation.

* One-tailed *t*-test for all variables except total utterances and number of complete and intelligible utterances.

hypothesis leads to the prediction that substantive progress in syntax development is not to be expected in adolescence for children with Down syndrome.

Does the rate of language acquisition decrease with the onset of adolescence, cross-sectionally? MLU in narratives increased from an average of 2.00 (standard deviation [SD] = .67), or Brown's Late Stage I, for children ages 5–8 years; to 2.47 (SD = .83), Stage II, at ages 8–12 years; to 3.05 (SD = .89), Stage III–Early Stage IV, at ages 12–16 years; to 4.3 (SD = 1.82), or late Stage V, at ages 16–20 years. Group 4 (ages 16–20 years) showed a significant (p < .05) increase relative to the younger groups in MLU for both narrative and conversational samples. The cross-sectional evidence argued against views that syntax acquisition is restricted to a critical preadolescent or preschool period (Chapman et al., in press).

Potential sources of conflicting findings are suggested by the results. Increasingly, with age, narrative speech samples tap longer average utterances than conversational samples, as Miller and Leadholm (1992) showed for language-learning children ages 3–13 years. Had the age range of participants with Down syndrome in this study been restricted to conversational samples between ages 5 and 16 years, my colleagues and I might have concluded, as Fowler did, that language acquisition plateaued for most individuals with Down syndrome. The narrative samples across a broader age range reveal the reverse—that is, that substantial progress in syntax production might be expected in late adolescence. Regardless of whether the superior performance of the oldest group is a cohort effect or an increase replicable in the longitudinal study, the MLU results do not support the Critical Period Hypothesis in either of its versions.

Syntactic Ceiling at Simple Sentences   Fowler (1988) proposed that apart from or in interaction with maturational factors, there may simply be a ceiling on the level of syntax that most children with Down syndrome can acquire. This ceiling would exist at roughly the level of simple syntax, or Brown's Linguistic Stage III, with departures from typical acquisition patterns occurring thereafter. If children with Down syndrome in fact fail to acquire complex syntax, one would expect that the distribution pattern of their number of utterances of each utterance length would differ from those of MA- or MLU-matched controls in having relatively fewer long utterances and that those longer utterances that occurred would prove to be syntactically simple in structure. In addition, children with Down syndrome might achieve their increasing MLU through fewer instances of one-word utterances. If they did, one might expect to see a relatively truncated tail to the utterance length distributions for each age group and differing shapes to the distribution when groups matched for MLU were compared; this, however, does not occur (Chapman et al., in press). The two oldest groups with Down syndrome did not differ in terms of MLU from the two youngest groups of preschoolers, with values of 3.0 (Brown's Stage III) and 4.3 (Brown's late Stage V), respectively. These values corresponded to the last stage of simple sentences and the stage of embedded and conjoined structures.

The distributions of utterance lengths for the Stage III group with Down syndrome and controls were similar, as were the distributions for the late Stage V groups. If anything, the speakers with Down syndrome gave more one-morpheme responses than controls did in the MLU-matched groups. Concerned that the experimenters may have addressed yes-or-no and one-word-response questions to the groups with Down syndrome, the transcripts were reviewed. The source of increased one-word responses by individuals with Down syndrome turned out to be a product of their more advanced comprehension and social understanding. They were more likely to be pragmatically appropriate in acknowledging requests and confirming examiners' repetitions of what they had said than the MLU-matched preschoolers, who were only 2 or 3 years old and of significantly lower MA.

Were the longer utterances observed in the oldest group with Down syndrome actually complex, or had they been formed through phrasal additions or elaborations? Again, reading the transcripts revealed the answer to be yes. The longer sentences were likely to be complex. The following are examples from individuals whose MLUs were nearest the mean of the two age groups:

#44: I got that one for Christmas because they didn't drill holes in it.
    (Age group 3, speaking of a bowling ball)
#26: Rocky's manager died when Mister T was mad at something he said about him. (Age group 4)

All utterances of five morphemes or more were coded in all transcripts for the presence (and type) of complex sentence constructions. This analysis revealed no significant differences in percentage of complex utterances when those age groups equivalent in MLU were matched (see Table 4). Not surprising, analyses indicated that the probability of children with Down syndrome producing a complex sentence increased with utterance length. For example, in the oldest age group, the person with Down syndrome whose MLU was the longest, 7.24, produced complex sentences—that is, sentences containing an embedded or conjoined clause—the following percentage of times as a function of utterance length: of the 7- and 8-morpheme sentences, 24%; of the 8- and 10-morpheme sentences, 48%; of the 11-

Table 4. Mean percentage of complex sentences in complete and intelligible utterances in the two older age groups with Down syndrome and two groups of younger preschool-age children that are equivalent in mean length of utterance

Mean length of utterance	Children with Down syndrome	Preschool-age children
3.0	12% ($n = 11$)	12% ($n = 11$)
4.3	28% ($n = 13$)	25% ($n = 11$)

n, subsample population.

and 12-morpheme sentences, 89%; of the 13-and-greater-morpheme utterances, 100%.

When individual variations in this 16- to 20-year-old group were examined, six of the children had MLUs above 4.5, though no younger ones did. Clearly, some individuals with Down syndrome acquire complex syntax. This age group also included individuals, however, whose mean MLUs ranged down to 2.0 and whose transcripts did not include complex sentence structure. The acquisition of complex syntax also represented a dimension of individual differences among people with Down syndrome. Small-sample studies may have actively misled researchers about the range of outcomes for syntax acquisition that can be encountered.

What Predicts MLU? The same six predictor domains as examined in the previous sections were evaluated for comprehension data: CA, sex, cognitive level, socioeconomic status, hearing status, and educational history, choosing the best predictor from each domain; and syntactic comprehension was added as a seventh predictor of syntactic production (Chapman et al., in press). Syntactic comprehension entered the stepwise regression equation first, accounting for approximately 78% of the variability in MLU; occupational index, MA as indicated by pattern analysis, and CA accounted for successive 3% increments of variability, 86% in all. Thus, individual differences in syntactic production are associated with individual differences in comprehension (and the additional predictors); but the level of performance is lower and the gap widens with age and increasing cognitive level.

Implications for Defining the Behavioral Phenotype These findings lead to two recommended changes in the language assessment protocol recommended for genetic studies establishing the behavioral phenotype of Down syndrome (Epstein et al., 1991): 1) Use of a narrative, rather than conversational, free speech sample in older children and adolescents with Down syndrome offers a developmentally more sensitive index of expressive syntax; and 2) language comprehension and language production skills should be evaluated separately in establishing the profile of language skill in children with Down syndrome.

Grammatical Morpheme Impairment In children without mental retardation but with specific impairment in language acquisition, their overall delay in achieving developmental milestones has been accompanied by additional impairment in the acquisition of grammatical morphology (Leonard, 1992). Do children with Down syndrome, who also have SLI, show additional impairment with regard to MLU in acquisition of grammatical morphemes? Fowler, Gelman, and Gleitman (1994) compared four children with Down syndrome ages 10–13 years with four children age 2 years, 6 months, who were matched for MLU level and found no difference in the overall percentage of grammatical morphemes supplied in obligatory contexts; but all of these children were functioning at Stage III, a level of simple syntax in which few grammatical morphemes are produced. Evidence of impairment in grammatical morphology would be clearer at later linguistic stages, however, when later-emerging grammatical morphemes could be expected.

The two older groups with Down syndrome were compared with the two younger preschool groups, who functioned as MLU matches (Chapman et al., in press). (The corresponding groups did not differ in MLU or total words.) Eight indices of bound morpheme omission and two indices of word omission were compared.

The omitted grammatical morphemes in the Stage III group include omissions of contracted "will," contracted "am," contracted "is," third-person singular inflection of regular verbs, regular past-tense "-ed" endings, present progressive "-ing" endings, noun plural "-s" endings, and noun possessive endings. The variability in frequency of omissions is great enough that none of the differences between the group of children with Down syndrome and the control group is significant; rather, they are dimensions of individual difference. The fact that mainly the sibilant morphophonemes are affected raises the question of whether this is a morphological or articulatory dimension of difference.

A similar result for the oldest group with Down syndrome again revealed differences that did not prove, on a *t*-test, to be statistically significant, given the wide variation; however, the pattern of difference suggested morphological as well as phonological contributions to the dimension of individual difference.

When the same groups were compared with regard to omitted words, significantly more omitted words were contained in the narrative transcripts from the groups with Down syndrome. This was true for total omitted words ($p < .01$, one-tailed, for the younger age group comparison) and for number of different word types omitted ($p < .01$, one-tailed, for the older age group comparison).

Did these omitted words belong to closed grammatical classes? All instances of omitted words were pulled from the transcripts for the two older groups with Down syndrome (see Table 5). With the exception of one verb in the younger group, all instances of omitted words were from closed grammatical classes. Note that copula, auxiliary, and modal auxiliary omissions could have been augmented by the contracted bound-morpheme omissions for those categories, or they could themselves have been omissions of bound morphemes, with few exceptions. In addition, note that errors of agreement and subject inclusion occurred frequently in the transcripts and are not reflected, aside from pronoun omission, in this summary. Thus, there is evidence that the SLI in productive syntax includes not only delay relative to nonverbal cognitive development but also specific additional impairments in grammatical morpheme mastery. With narrative language samples, cross-sectional evidence against the Critical Period and Syntactic Ceiling hypotheses in support of the Grammatical Morphology impairment was found. Language acquisition does not stop with adolescence in individuals with Down syndrome, nor is it confined to simple syntax. Evidence of unusual difficulty with use of closed-form class items suggested problems in grammatical morphology as more complex syntax was acquired.

Table 5. Omitted words by syntactic category in 12-minute narratives from adolescents with Down syndrome

Group	Mean length of utterance	Omitted words by syntactic category
People with Down syndrome ages 12–16 years	3.0	Copula: is, are, am, were, be Auxiliaries: is, are, am, does Modal auxiliaries: can, will Articles: a, an, the Prepositions: with, at, for, to, of, in Pronouns: she, it, I, they, what, where Conjunctions: and Other: said
People with Down syndrome ages 16–20 years	4.3	Copula: is, are, am, was, were Auxiliaries: is, are, were, did Articles: a, the Prepositions: with, at, to, of, in, over Pronouns: she, they, my, that, who Pro-form for place adjunct: there Conjunctions: and Infinitive: to

Language Acquisition Processes

The work on the language acquisition of children and adolescents with Down syndrome discussed in this chapter was carried out within the context of a model called Child Talk (Chapman et al., 1992) that emphasizes contextual contributions to the child's learning of language comprehension and production skills. In the Child Talk model, language learning is viewed as the outcome of a large, accumulating database of language experienced or used in communicative contexts in which the speaker's meaning is clear or in which expectations can be confirmed or disconfirmed. Children as listeners are viewed in this model as acquiring expectations for a given environment about what communicative goals the speaker is likely to have, how the speaker feels, how action is likely to unfold in the event taking place, who will be spoken to, what will be talked about, and the words and phrases or the gestures likely to be used in the talk. For example, a child listening to a bedtime story has expectations about who gets to choose the book and the reader's commitment to pointing to every picture or reading every page and every word of the story; and, if it is a frequently told story, the child can often detect departures from the expected text, such as a page skipped or a sentence omitted. The same child may later take over the parent's voice in the bedtime ritual, pointing to pictures and asking the parent "What's that?" or providing the same comment about the dinosaur that the parent had offered nightly months earlier.

In the Child Talk model's view, what is connected in memory modules that can be activated relatively independently of one another and develop further complexity is not initially a system of linguistic rules or a growing dictionary of words, though this is often how researchers test children's later linguistic knowledge. Rather, modularity is a property of event representations within the knowledge network—that is, the degree to which talk and context have or have not co-occurred in the child's experiences. The child's own communicative goals of continuing interaction, of drawing the parent's attention to him- or herself or to the world, of obtaining a desirable object, or of protesting an undesirable action are strongly linked to the child's early word use. Thus, event representations and their generalization (Nelson, 1986), particularly with regard to communicative events, are an early source of modularity and govern the language likely to be used and understood by the child in that context, including word choice and syntax.

From the viewpoint of the Child Talk model, then, a wide variety of cognitive skills feed into the acquisition of language skill, including social understanding of speakers, speakers' intentions and feelings, and the interactional events taking place; understanding of the physical world of objects, including the relationship of cause and effect; and memory of the acoustic patterns of sounds encountered and the speech-motor means of reproducing those sound patterns. The rate and typicality of development in each of these domains affect representation of events and the language embedded in them. Thus, delays in the development of social and spatial cognition are associated with delays in the acquisition of language that encoded those aspects of meaning for the child. Such delays in language acquisition are typically encountered in children with cognitive challenges generally. Learning how to put words together, or syntax, offers additional challenges to one's memory for the acoustic patterns, or sentences, encountered.

The following are among the predictions that can be derived from a contextualized, distributed model of language learning such as Child Talk. First, learning of a new word can occur rapidly, on a single trial, within a context in which the child can easily infer meaning and remember a word's form; this is called the "fast mapping" phase of word acquisition. Acquisition of words and utterance frames occurs more slowly in contexts in which processing demands are greater, such as discourse contexts, or in contexts in which learning must take place across events, such as learning grammatical morphemes. If auditory memory were more limited than other cognitive skills, as is the case in children with Down syndrome, these rapid phases of meaning acquisition might be selectively impaired for the discourse and multiple event contexts that challenged auditory short-term memory (Gathercole & Baddeley, 1993).

Children's ability to fast-map word meaning and form during a simple hiding game (Chapman et al., 1990; Kay-Raining Bird & Chapman, 1998) and while listening to stories (Chapman, Kay-Raining Bird, et al., 1991) was examined. Equivalent performance was found in the simple event context for simple consonant-vowel-consonant novel words. Overall, comprehension averaged 73%, and production averaged 40%. Both the group with Down syndrome and the control group functioning at preschool levels encountered difficulty, however, in fast mapping the production of novel words in story contexts (10% correct performance overall on production), in contrast to findings for event contexts. In story contexts, the children with Down syndrome were as poor as those without Down syndrome in the fast mapping of production forms and in inferring the likely referent of the novel word; but these children encountered additional and specific difficulties in memory for the story's gist and in particular for the text associated with the novel words. Thus, the discourse comprehension demands of online story processing appeared to limit the elaboration of the knowledge network associated with novel words for children and adolescents with Down syndrome to a greater degree than one would predict from their cognitive skills or vocabulary comprehension.

A possible consequence of more limited short-term memory for auditory information, over time, is that lexical learning may progress at rates faster than the comprehension and storage of longer utterances, or discourse stretches, whose pattern can serve as the basis for expressive language. According to this view, the standardized comprehension tests used in the present study fail to tap the processing rates and short-term memory limitations that may operate in ordinary discourse processing and experimental story tasks. (For a review of the literature on specific patterns of language divergence in children with Down syndrome and auditory short-term memory as one potential mechanism of SLI, see Chapman, 1995.)

To the extent that standard picture-pointing sentence comprehension tasks permit listeners long processing times for response and depend on lexical rather than word order aspects of sentence processing, the assessment procedures used may conceal the true extent of discourse comprehension impairment for individuals with Down syndrome. Some portion of the expressive language impairment may ultimately be attributable to the consequently reduced database of more complex language encountered and understood in context. If this is so, the success of interventions based on visual representation—including signing, reading, and writing—or on specific expansions of language produced within a situational context become doubly significant.

CONCLUSIONS

The findings of the cross-sectional study reported in this chapter have important implications for intervention. First, they suggest that continuation of language therapy into late adolescence is likely to be beneficial for individuals with Down syndrome because continued language acquisition can be expected in terms of both comprehension and production for at least some individuals (see, e.g., Buckley, 1993; Cossu, Rossini, & Marshall, 1993; Shepperdson, 1994). In addition, intelligibility gains were seen in the oldest adolescent group. Second, these findings suggest that the potential targets of later interventions should include grammatical morphology and complex sentence structure when a developmental approach to target selection is used.

The model of the acquisition process used also has implications for intervention. In the Child Talk model, language learning can be most surely achieved and used when the intervention context is similar in all of these respects to later contexts of use. Generalization of learning for all children arises in the Child Talk model from links learned across speakers, environments, situations, and communicative goals through the elaboration of knowledge of the world. Thus, interventions that use script-based or routine event contexts to support communicative learning are expected to be especially effective.

If auditory short-term memory is a particular source of difficulty in the acquisition of language for children with Down syndrome, then reduction of short-term memory demands should enhance their learning. For example, routine communicative contexts should increase expectations about the language to be encountered. The repeated reading of favorite stories—especially those predictable in format and content—should similarly support children's learning. Repeated dictation of one's own stories, elaborating what was said before, may support discourse production development. Support for meaning within the context—such as through enactment, videotapes, pictures, and printed text—should enhance children's word recognition and sentence comprehension. The use of augmentative or alternative communication systems to support communicative success should not be ignored, including signing, reading, and writing (Buckley, 1993).

The intervention techniques successful for children with language impairments should also be considered. These include provision of processing time, such as waiting 3 seconds before speaking (Ellis Weismer & Schraeder, 1993), slower speaking rates for input (Ellis Weismer & Hesketh, 1993), and inclusion of elicited production for developmentally appropriate models (Ellis Weismer, Murray-Branch, & Miller, 1993). For older individuals, these techniques also include deliberate strategies to increase communicative effectiveness.

Finally, the intervention techniques adopted might usefully draw from the teaching literature on creativity, instruction for the gifted and talented, whole language, and reading intervention. Everything that is known about the acquisition of language for powerful expression in symbolic play, sociodramatic play, drama, story, poetry, and song; for problem analysis and solution; and for social interaction (e.g., making friends, persuading people) is relevant to the choice of intervention contexts.

REFERENCES

Buckley, S. (1993). Developing the speech and language skills of teenagers with Down's syndrome. *Down's Syndrome: Research and Practice, 1,* 63–71.

Burgemeister, B., Blum, L.H., & Lorge, I. (1972). *Columbia Mental Maturity Scale* (3rd ed.). Orlando, FL: Harcourt Brace & Co.

Carrow-Woolfolk, E. (1985). *Test for Auditory Comprehension of Language–Revised* (TACL–R). Allen, TX: DLM Teaching Resources.

Chapman, R.S. (1995). Language development in children and adolescents with Down syndrome. In P. Fletcher & B. MacWhinney (Eds.), *Handbook of child language* (pp. 641–663). Oxford, England: Blackwell Publishers.

Chapman, R.S. (1997). Language development in children and adolescents with Down syndrome. *Mental Retardation and Developmental Disabilities Research Reviews, 3,* 307–312.

Chapman, R.S. (in press). Semantic deficits in childhood language disorders. In R.G. Schwartz (Ed.), *Linguistics, cognitive science, and childhood language disorders.* Mahwah, NJ: Lawrence Erlbaum Associates.

Chapman, R.S., Kay-Raining Bird, E., & Schwartz, S.E. (1990). Fast mapping of words in event contexts by children with Down syndrome. *Journal of Speech and Hearing Disorders, 55,* 761–770.

Chapman, R.S., Kay-Raining Bird, E., & Schwartz, S.E. (1991, November). *Fast mapping in stories: Deficits in Down syndrome.* Paper presented at the annual convention of the American-Speech-Language-Hearing Association, Atlanta, GA. (From *ASHA Abstracts, 33*[10], 107)

Chapman, R.S., Schwartz, S.E., & Kay-Raining Bird, E. (1991). Language skills of children and adolescents with Down syndrome: I. Comprehension. *Journal of Speech and Hearing Research, 34,* 1106–1120.

Chapman, R.S., Seung, H.-K., Schwartz, S.E., & Kay-Raining Bird, E. (in press). Language skills of children and adolescents with Down syndrome: II. Production deficits. *Journal of Speech, Language, and Hearing Research.*

Chapman, R.S., Streim, N., Crais, E., Salmon, D., Negri, N., & Strand, E. (1992). Child talk: Assumptions of a developmental process model for early language learning. In R.S. Chapman (Ed.), *Processes in language acquisition and disorders* (pp. 3–19). Chicago: Mosby–Year Book.

Cossu, G., Rossini, F., & Marshall, J.C. (1993). When reading is acquired but phonemic awareness is not: A study of literacy in Down's syndrome. *Cognition, 46,* 129–138.

Dunn, L.M., & Dunn, L.M. (1981). *Peabody Picture Vocabulary Test–Revised* (PPVT-R). Circle Pines, MN: American Guidance Service.

Ellis Weismer, S., & Hesketh, L.J. (1993). The influence of prosodic and gestural cues on novel word acquisition by children with specific language impairment. *Journal of Speech and Hearing Research, 36,* 1013–1025.

Ellis Weismer, S., Murray-Branch, J., & Miller, J.F. (1993). Comparison of two methods for promoting productive vocabulary in late talkers. *Journal of Speech and Hearing Research, 36,* 1037–1050.

Ellis Weismer, S., & Schraeder, T. (1993). Discourse characteristics and verbal reasoning: Wait time effects on the performance of children with language learning disabilities. *Exceptionality Education Canada, 3,* 71–92.

Epstein, C., Korenberg, J., Anneren, G., Antonarakis, S., Ayme, S., Courchesne, E., Epstein, L., Fowler, A., Groner, Y., Huret, J., Kemper, T., Lott, I., Lubin, B., Magenis, E., Opitz, J., Patterson, D., Priest, J., Pueschel, S.M., Rapoport, S., Sinet, P.-M., Tanzi, R., & de la Cruz, F. (1991). Protocols to establish genotype-phenotype correlations in Down syndrome. *American Journal of Human Genetics, 49,* 207–235.

Fowler, A. (1988). Determinants of rate of language growth in children with Down syndrome. In L. Nadel (Ed.), *The psychobiology of Down syndrome* (pp. 217–246). Cambridge, MA: MIT Press.

Fowler, A. (1990). Language abilities in children with Down syndrome: Evidence for a specific syntactic delay. In D. Cicchetti & M. Beeghly (Eds.), *Chil-*

dren with Down syndrome (pp. 302–328). Cambridge, England: Cambridge University Press.

Fowler, A.E., Gelman, R., & Gleitman, L.R. (1994). The course of language learning in children with Down syndrome. In H. Tager-Flusberg (Ed.), *Constraints on language acquisition* (pp. 91–140). Mahwah, NJ: Lawrence Erlbaum Associates.

Gathercole, S.E., & Baddeley, A.D. (1993). *Working memory and language.* Mahwah, NJ: Lawrence Erlbaum Associates.

Hartley, X.Y. (1982). Receptive language processing of Down's syndrome children. *Journal of Mental Deficiency Research, 26,* 263–269.

Hartley, X.Y. (1986). A summary of recent research into the development of children with Down's syndrome. *Journal of Mental Deficiency Research, 30,* 1–14.

Kay-Raining Bird, E., & Chapman, R.S. (1994). Sequential recall in individuals with Down syndrome. *Journal of Speech and Hearing Research, 37,* 1369–1380.

Kay-Raining Bird, E., & Chapman, R.S. (1998). Partial representation and phonological selectivity in the comprehension of 13- to 16-month-olds. *First Language, 18,* 105–127.

Lenneberg, E. (1967). *Biological foundations of language.* New York: John Wiley & Sons.

Leonard, L.B. (1992). The use of morphology by children with specific language impairment: Evidence from three languages. In R.S. Chapman (Ed.), *Processes in language acquisition and disorders* (pp. 186–201). St. Louis: Mosby–Year Book.

Marcell, M., & Weeks, S.L. (1988). Short-term memory difficulties in Down's syndrome. *Journal of Mental Deficiency Research, 32,* 153–162.

Miller, J.F. (1988). The developmental asynchrony of language development in children with Down syndrome. In L. Nadel (Ed.), *The psychobiology of Down syndrome* (pp. 167–198). Cambridge, MA: MIT Press.

Miller, J.F., & Chapman, R.S. (1993). *SALT: Systematic Analysis of Language Transcripts* (DOS version 3.0) [Software program]. Madison: University of Wisconsin–Madison, The Waisman Center, Language Analysis Laboratory.

Miller, J.F., & Leadholm, B.J. (1992). *Language sample analysis: The Wisconsin guide.* Madison: Wisconsin Department of Public Instruction, Bureau for Exceptional Children.

Nelson, K.E. (Ed.). (1986). *Event knowledge: Structure and function in development.* Mahwah, NJ: Lawrence Erlbaum Associates.

Rosenberg, S. (1982). The language of the mentally retarded: Development, processes, and intervention. In S. Rosenberg (Ed.), *Handbook of applied psycholinguistics* (pp. 329–392). Mahwah, NJ: Lawrence Erlbaum Associates.

Rosin, M.M., Swift, E., Bless, D., & Vetter, D.K. (1988). Communication profiles of adolescents with Down syndrome. *Journal of Childhood Communication Disorders, 12,* 49–64.

Shepperdson, B. (1994). Attainments in reading and number of teenagers and young adults with Down's syndrome. *Down's Syndrome: Research and Practice, 2,* 97–101.

Thorndike, R.L., Hagen, E.P., & Sattler, J.M. (1986). *Stanford-Binet Intelligence Scale* (4th ed.). Chicago: Riverside.

4

The Biological Bases of Speech in People with Down Syndrome

Mark Leddy

A survey of 937 parents found that 95% of their children with Down syndrome sometimes or frequently had difficulty being understood and that only 5% of them never or rarely had such trouble (Kumin, 1994). Given that most people with Down syndrome have some difficulty in speaking intelligibly, researchers and professionals who work with people with Down syndrome must seek to understand the possible causes and the nature of this challenge as well as the implications that it has for their language production and successful communication. This chapter explores the biological bases for the speech intelligibility challenges that people with Down syndrome face.

Human beings communicate ideas, thoughts, and feelings through a series of complex biological systems. People use their ears to hear what others say to them. They use their nervous systems to perceive and understand what they hear, to think and generate language, and to signal their bodies to generate speech and nonspoken communication. People also use their lungs to generate the power for speech and their vocal cords and mouths to produce speech sounds. It is the integration of these different systems that produces successful communication. When one system fails or when multiple systems function inefficiently, communication falters. For example, if someone cannot hear speech clearly, then that person will have difficulty in understanding the meaning of what other people say. The person's hearing problem will cause him or her to have difficulty in generating an appropriate response to people's communications simply because he or she does not understand what speakers are saying.

People with Down syndrome, like all other human beings, communicate by using complex biological systems, and sometimes these systems do not function at their best. Some people with Down syndrome may experience a disruption in one of their biological systems, or they may have multiple systems functioning inefficiently. These systemic failures may result in communication failure. For example, if the nervous system is severely disrupted, the result may be difficulties in perceiving and understanding what people say or trouble in generating thoughts and language, and then signaling the body to generate speech movements. This disruption in a single biological system is just one example of how speech may fail; it is important to realize, however, that multiple systems functioning inefficiently may also restrict speech production.

There are many reasons beyond just biological causes for why reduced speech intelligibility limits language production and interferes with successful communication. These include how the person with Down syndrome alters his or her speaking style and content so that a communicative partner will understand him or her, how the communicative partner responds and interacts with him or her, and the levels of hearing and speech skills of the person with Down syndrome and that person's communicative partner. The following fictitious case study illustrates this point.

BILL

Bill wants to communicate his desire to go to the store to buy a chocolate candy bar. After years of unsuccessfully pronouncing many speech sounds and experiencing communication failure time and again, Bill has learned to use fewer words to communicate his message. He says to his sister Suzanne, "Go buy candy." This short and simple statement yields him greater success than attempting to clearly say, "Suzanne, let's go to the store so I can buy a chocolate candy bar." His speech-language pathologist, Ms. Wiz, is always disappointed when she observes Bill modifying his speech while talking with his family. Ms. Wiz has established situations and routines at school in which Bill produces lengthy and complex statements effectively with a variety of staff and students. Bill wants his biological system to function efficiently and effectively, so he has learned to simplify his speech so that Suzanne will understand him. In addition, Bill has learned to say the words that are easiest for him to pronounce and that most people seem to understand. Bill is displaying a common human phenomenon: He is self-correcting his biological systems for successful communication. This phenomenon is evident when most people communicate. For example, when people ask someone a question and that person does not understand, they quickly modify what they have said, either rewording the question or saying it louder. Although Bill is not instantaneously modifying his communication, he is showing how he has learned to successfully alter his biological systems to get his needs met, indicating his potential to make successful alterations in his communication in various contexts.

Bill has learned to communicate his ideas effectively, though not elegantly; but those who communicate with him, such as his sister Suzanne, have learned to phrase questions that do not require lengthy answers. For example, Suzanne responds to Bill with a question that is likely to elicit only a yes-or-no response: "Where do you want to go buy candy? At the mall?" Bill has also learned that Suzanne usually asks these closed-ended questions and that she expects only a simple one-word response. Again, Bill modifies his communication to function efficiently and effectively when he answers, "Okay."

This cycle of communication limits Bill's opportunities to produce a variety of speech sounds and to generate complex words and grammar. He also misses the opportunity to match language understanding and production with his thoughts, ideas, and feelings. Are these communication issues the result of limited speech production and intelligibility? Bill's speech problem does interfere to some extent with what he says. Remember that Bill is a human being who has learned to communicate efficiently and effectively by simplifying his language and using fewer speech sounds, the sounds that are easier for people to understand when he talks.

Most people—including, in this case, Suzanne and Ms. Wiz as well as Bill himself—want people like Bill to have opportunities to hear and generate complex language and to practice producing many different speech sounds. In order to understand ways to help Bill and others communicate more effectively, it is necessary to understand the nature of the speech problems with which people with Down syndrome live every day. The reasons why reduced speech intelligibility is a major hurdle that people with Down syndrome face must also be examined.

Parents, clinicians, and researchers have proposed biological, behavioral, and environmental explanations for the speech production patterns of people with Down syndrome. Speech development and maturation occur in a unique biological system—that is, in a human with complex biological mechanisms. Furthermore, the person's biology interacts with the output of that system; that is, the individual's biology interacts with the individual's behavior. Finally, environmental factors such as the behaviors of other people influence both the biology and the behavior of the person with Down syndrome. Although each factor is often proposed as an independent cause, the interaction among all three factors contributes to a person's ability to talk.

The focus of this chapter is speech production, which is the outcome of speech physiology, which is the regulation of and interactions among anatomical speech structures. The first part of this chapter includes a review of the speech characteristics and speech patterns of people with Down syndrome, including speech sound articulation, fluency, voice quality, and speech intelligibility. The biological factors thought to influence speech production in people with Down syndrome are discussed in the second section of this chapter, and several hypotheses about the anatomical and physiological bases for these speech patterns are proposed. The primary reason for discussing the distinct speech anatomy and physiology of people with Down syndrome is to identify what is known about the nature of speech-related systems as a starting point for assessing and improving speech production.

SPEECH CHARACTERISTICS

Parents and speech-language pathologists often report that people of all ages with Down syndrome have trouble talking and articulating speech sounds. In their accounts, however, the description and the severity of the speech problems of people with Down syndrome differ greatly. In addition, there is some disagreement in these reports about the type of speech problems that people with Down syndrome evidence. For explanations of common speech terminology, including speech intelligibility, speech sound articulation, fluency, and voice production, see Table 1.

Speech Intelligibility

Speech intelligibility refers to how clearly a person speaks so that his or her speech is comprehensible to a listener. Although Kumin's (1994) study found that reduced intelligibility is often a concern of parents and other family members, it also compromises communication between people with Down syndrome and educators, health care providers, and community service workers. Bodine (1974) suggested that

Table 1.   Speech characteristic terminology

Speech characteristic	Description
Speech intelligibility	This term refers to how clearly a person speaks so that his or her speech is comprehensible to a listener. Speech articulation, fluency, and voice production all contribute to speech intelligibility. When you cannot understand what a person is saying to you because of that person's speech, the speaker has a speech intelligibility problem.
Speech sound articulation	When people speak, they articulate speech sounds using the structures of the face, mouth, and throat. If a person has a problem in articulating speech sounds, then a sound might be absent, distorted, or replaced by another sound. In addition, the person's speech might sound slurred.
Fluency	This term refers to the rhythm or flow of a person's speech. This includes the rate at which someone speaks; if there is a problem, then the rate might be fast or slow. The rhythm of speech means how smoothly the person's speech flows. If there are long pauses while the person is speaking, including interruptions with "ah"s and "um"s, or prolonged speech sounds such as "sssssss," then rhythm is disrupted.
Voice production	The pitch, loudness, and quality of a person's voice constitute *voice production. Pitch* refers to how high or low the voice is produced; *loudness* refers to how loud or soft the voice is produced; and *quality* refers to how pleasant and/or clear the person's voice is. If a person speaks with any extreme in pitch, loudness, or quality, then there is a problem with voice production.

when a speaker with Down syndrome speaks to a physician, psychologist, or speech-language pathologist, the speaker's reduced speech intelligibility, coupled with his or her characteristic physical traits, may lead the health care professional to develop decreased expectations for interventions. This is consistent with the views of numerous researchers who reported that a listener negatively perceives an individual with speech production impairment (Blood & Hyman, 1977; Love, 1981; Mowrer, Wahl, & Doolan, 1978; Ruscello & Lass, 1992; Silverman, 1976; Woods & Williams, 1976).

Several clinical and research reports in the literature have suggested that people with Down syndrome have speech intelligibility problems (Chapman, Schwartz, & Kay-Raining Bird, 1991; Horstmeier, 1990; Miller & Leddy, 1998; Rosin, Swift, Bless, & Vetter, 1988; Willcox, 1988), but very few clinical investigators have studied speech intelligibility in people with Down syndrome. The speech intelligibility studies that have been completed were conducted while researchers were investigating other issues about communication. For example, Chapman and her colleagues (1991) studied speech intelligibility while investigating the language skills of children with Down syndrome ages 5–20 years. They found that intelligibility increased with chronological age, a finding that is similarly found in the population that is developing typically. Chapman and colleagues also found that 30% of the variability in speech intelligibility was accounted for by individuals' chronological age and hearing status, which is consistent with many clinical reports that children with Down syndrome who have fluctuating hearing problems and whose hearing improves with age show improvements in speech production and intelligibility.

Other investigators have examined the speech intelligibility of people with Down syndrome while studying other communication characteristics. Willcox (1988), for example, investigated speech intelligibility in adolescents while examining factors influencing the fluency of speech; and Rosin and her colleagues (Rosin, Swift, Bless, & Vetter, 1988) studied speech intelligibility in adolescents as part of the larger pattern of communication seen in people with Down syndrome. Both Rosin and colleagues (1988) and Willcox (1988) found poor speech intelligibility performance in groups of older children and adolescents. *Poor intelligibility* in this context means that about 65% of the time speech was understandable, but about 35% of the time it was not. Willcox related this poor speech intelligibility to how fluently or smoothly speech was produced. Rosin and colleagues provided a different interpretation; they hypothesized that the intelligibility performance was related to possible impairments in sequential information processing. Kay-Raining Bird and Chapman (1994) challenged Rosin's hypothesis, however, when they found no differences in the order in which information was recalled by people with Down syndrome and those who were typically developing. Miller and Leddy (1998) argued that people with Down syndrome have intelligibility impairments that are due to both biological speech factors and specific linguistic production problems affecting fluent speech. The biological factors affecting speech production and intelligibility are detailed in the following sections of this chapter.

Speech Sound Articulation

The term *speech sound articulation* refers to the production of speech sounds using the physical structures of the face, mouth, and throat. The majority of speech studies about people with Down syndrome have been about speech sound articulation. The earlier investigations found a prevalence rate of 95%–100% for deviant, or impaired, articulation among individuals with Down syndrome (Blanchard, 1964; Schlanger & Gottsleben, 1957), a significantly higher prevalence rate than that found among individuals with other developmental disabilities or people who are developing typically. More recent investigations have also found a higher incidence of speech sound errors in people with Down syndrome (Dodd, 1976; Rosin et al., 1988), and parents have reported that speech sound errors are a greater problem than speaking rate, stuttering, or voice production (Kumin, 1994). These studies suggested that many people with Down syndrome have speech sound articulation impairments. However, many people with Down syndrome clearly produce well-articulated speech sounds. This great variability probably exists because the articulation patterns of people with Down syndrome can be attributed to a variety of influencing factors: cognitive impairments, muscle hypotonia, cerebellar abnormalities, fine motor coordination impairments, and oral anatomical-structural abnormalities (see Blager, 1980; Miller, Leddy, Miolo, & Sedey, 1995; Miller, Stoel-Gammon, Leddy, Lynch, & Miolo, 1992; Yarter, 1980). Regardless of whether the cause of these impairments is neurological in nature or is due to a combination of anatomical and physiological differences, biological influences likely restrict speech production, causing articulation errors and ultimately reducing effective communication.

Fluency

Fluency refers to the smoothness or rhythmicity of speech production and is influenced by the rate of speech. There is a higher prevalence of stuttering, or disfluent speech, found in groups of people with Down syndrome compared with other people with developmental disabilities and compared with individuals who are developing typically (Van Riper, 1982). Whereas stuttering occurs in approximately 1% of the population who are typically developing and in about 10% of people with developmental disabilities, it occurs in about 45%–53% of the population with Down syndrome (see Devenny & Silverman, 1990; Preus, 1990). These speech behaviors primarily include sound prolongations; interjections; pauses; and repetitions of sounds, syllables, parts of words, and whole words (Devenny & Silverman, 1990; Evans, 1977; Willcox, 1988).

There are two competing views of the disfluent behavior of people with Down syndrome. The first is that disfluent behavior resembles classic stuttering behavior in that it is characterized by blocks, tremors, and vocal spasms and in that these events are the results of speech motor dysfunction. The second view is that the disfluencies of this group are language based and are associated with an utterance formulation or word-finding impairment. (For a summary of the linguistic production argument, see Chapter 5.) In summary, investigators have attributed the higher prevalence of disfluent speech to both linguistic influences (Preus, 1990; Willcox, 1988)—to the point of calling the disorder *cluttering* instead of *stuttering* (Cabanas, 1954)—and impairments in the speech motor control system (Devenny & Silverman, 1990; Farmer & Brayton, 1979; Van Riper, 1982).

Voice Production

Voice production refers to the pitch, loudness, and quality of the speaker's voice. When speakers have difficulty in producing appropriate pitch, loudness, or quality, this difficulty contributes to reduced intelligibility and how listeners perceive them. When Ruscello and Lass (1992) examined listeners' attitudes toward speakers with and without voice problems, they found that listeners rated speakers with voice problems more negatively than they rated speakers without voice problems. Similarly, Moran, LaBarge, and Haynes (1988) found that people listening to the voice production of children with Down syndrome and of children who were developing typically viewed the speakers with Down syndrome as being less confident and less capable. Moran and colleagues suggested that such findings negatively influence educational and social planning for people with Down syndrome. People with Down syndrome and their family members generally do not report that voice production is a significant concern, however, and Kumin (1994) found that only about 13% of parents surveyed indicated that they were concerned about the voice production of their children with Down syndrome.

Nonetheless, clinicians and researchers have long recognized that the voice production of people with Down syndrome is characterized by a hoarse quality (Bergendal, 1976; Cabanas, 1954; Montague & Hollien, 1973; Moran & Gilbert, 1982; Novak, 1972; Schlanger, 1962; Strazulla, 1953; West, Kennedy, & Carr, 1947). Several investigators (Moran & Gilbert, 1982; Novak, 1972; Novak, Sedlackova, Klajman, & Betlejewski, 1967; Pentz & Gilbert, 1983; Rosin, Swift, Khidr, & Bless, 1992) examined the acoustic correlates of hoarse voice production in individuals with Down syndrome. These researchers established that acoustic correlates of hoarse voice production differentiate people with Down syndrome from those with developmental disabilities or those who are typically developing.

While studying the acoustic correlates of hoarseness in people with Down syndrome, investigators have identified several factors that may contribute to their hoarse voice production:

1. Anatomical skull anomalies
2. Endocrine dysfunction
3. Abnormal vocal fold structure

In 1949, Benda identified anatomical anomalies of the skull (i.e., absence or poor development of sinuses) as a possible reason why the voices of people with Down syndrome sound different from those of people who are typically developing (see also Benda, 1960). Although many people with phenotypic characteristics of Down syndrome are missing frontal sinuses (Benda, 1941; Roche, Seward, & Sutherland, 1961; Spitzer & Quilliam, 1958; Spitzer & Robinson, 1955) and have poorly developed sphenoid sinuses (Benda, 1941; Spitzer, Rabinowitch, & Wybar, 1961), the significant contribution of the sinuses to the perception of hoarse voice production is unlikely because hoarse voice production reflects how the larynx, or vocal cords, functions. Thus, the absence of frontal sinuses and/or the poor development of sphenoid sinuses in people with Down syndrome is unlikely to have a strong impact on listeners' perceptions of hoarse voice production, though there may be a relationship between the presence of these sinuses and listeners' perceptions of other speech and voice characteristics such as nasality.

Strazulla (1953) suggested that another factor, endocrine dysfunction, contributes to the hoarse voice production characteristics of people with Down syndrome. She suggested that thyroid hypofunction in people with Down syndrome produces laryngeal myxedema—that is, tissue swelling in the larynx—resulting in hoarse voice production. Strazulla reported that in a group of 17 children with Down syndrome who were receiving thyroid medication, only 5 had voices that were appropriate for their age and gender. Thus, her findings suggested that despite interventions provided for thyroid hypofunction, individuals with Down syndrome have dysphonic voice production. Unfortunately, Strazulla's study group selection was biased; that is, the individuals she observed all had hypothyroidism. Her suggestion that people with Down syndrome have hoarse voice production as a result of hypothyroidism is not substantiated by the data she collected. In addition, Pozzan and colleagues (1990) reported that only 5% of people with Down syndrome have hypothyroidism, raising questions about the possibility that more than a small percentage of individuals with Down syndrome have hoarse voice production related to hypothyroidism.

In addition to the suggestions that abnormal voice production in people with Down syndrome might be related to hypothyroidism or the absence of facial sinuses, there are reports in the literature suggesting that abnormal laryngeal structures may account for the hoarse voice production of this population. Benda reported observing the larynxes of several people with Down syndrome and finding "the mucosa thickened and fibrotic" (1949, p. 21). Two decades later, Novak and his colleagues reported that when they used direct laryngoscopy to examine the laryngeal structure of 32 children, adolescents, and young adults with Down syndrome, they found "a light thickness of the mucosa of the vocal cords . . . [but] . . . did not find thickened vocal folds" (1972, p. 184). Novak and his colleagues did not relate these findings to laryngeal myxedema secondary to hypothyroidism but hypothesized that their findings were due to vocal cord edema secondary to excessive and forceful use of the larynx. Leddy (1996) concurred with the hypothesis of Novak and colleagues, having found evidence of laryngeal structure thickening and hyperfunction in a small group of adult males with Down syndrome. Leddy attributed his findings to multiple causal factors, including asymptomatic subclinical hypothyroidism, excessive and forceful use of the larynx, gastroesophageal reflux entering the larynx, and other biological factors such as differences found in the neurological systems of people with Down syndrome.

BIOLOGICAL SYSTEMS AFFECTING SPEECH

People with Down syndrome are biologically unique. The most easily observable features of their unique biology have historically been described as the cardinal signs of Down syndrome (Benda, 1941). Experts working with individuals who have Down syndrome have found great variability in these phenotypic characteristics (Pueschel, 1990), identifying more than 300 different signs. Pueschel (1992) suggested that an individual with Down syndrome be considered a human being first and a person with unique clinical characteristics second. Despite the attempt to humanize individuals with Down syndrome, researchers are using contemporary molecular and cytogenetic methods of investigation to map the phenotypic characteristics of people with Down syndrome to regions on the long arm of chromosome 21 (Korenberg, Paulst, & Gerwehr, 1992). The features of the trisomy 21 phenotype that have been mapped in select individuals include mental retardation, congenital heart disease, duodenal stenosis, and facial features such as epicanthal folds, a flat nasal bridge, up-slanting palpebral fissures, and a flat facial profile. Consistent with these unique characteristics is evidence that biomedical and anatomical variability are found in nearly every body system of people with Down syndrome (see Lott & McCoy, 1992; Van Dyke, Lang, Heide, van Duyne, & Soucek, 1990), including considerably notable differences in specific systems that affect speech production, such as the musculoskeletal, central and peripheral nervous, and respiratory systems (Bersu, 1976, 1980).

Anatomical-structural differences in the skeletal, muscular, and nervous systems are found in a high percentage of, but not all, people with Down syndrome, and many of these differences are treated surgically or pharmaceutically early in life. In addition, differences in these systems do not always cause speech production impairments or reduced speech intelligibility. Human physiology has a great capacity to accommodate structural variations, and some people with Down syndrome may adapt to system differences to produce acceptably intelligible speech. Other people with Down syndrome who have more serious nervous system exceptions may have a greater difficulty in accommodating these skeletal, muscular, and respiratory structural differences. Miller and Leddy (1998) hypothesized that it is primarily the neurological system that influences speech production in people with Down syndrome and that this affects their ability to adapt to unique speech structures. The purpose of discussing these distinct biological variations is not to distance people with Down syndrome from other people with developmental disabilities or from people who are typically developing; rather, it is to identify what is known about the nature of speech-related systems as a starting point for assessing and improving the speech production of people with Down syndrome.

Skeletal System

Variations in the skeletal systems of some people with Down syndrome include absent and/or reduced bone growth. These differences are found in the bones of the head and face, which are structures designed to support speech as well as the muscles used to produce speech. People with Down syndrome often have smaller skulls than people without Down syndrome; missing or poorly developed midfacial bones; and smaller, wider jaws (Frostad, Cleall, & Melosky, 1971; Kisling, 1966; Roche, Roche, & Lewis, 1972; Sanger, 1975). Although not directly influencing speech production, these variations may create a smaller mouth and throat (Ardran, Harker, & Kemp, 1972), which may influence how speech sounds travel through those spaces and how voice quality is produced (Pentz, 1987).

The structural differences in the skeletal system contribute to the smaller oral cavities of people with Down syndrome, a characteristic that may limit the distance and range of movements for a typical-size tongue. Clinicians have reported observing a high palate in children with Down syndrome; but careful examination of the palate in children with Down syndrome reveals that it is actually equal in height to the palate of people who are typically developing, though it is narrow (Redman, Shapiro, & Gorlin, 1965; Shapiro, Gorlin, Redman, & Bruhl, 1967; Shapiro, Redman, & Gorlin, 1963). Figure 1 illustrates these findings. Given that individuals with Down syndrome have difficulty in producing sounds that require the tongue to make contact with the palate (Borghi, 1990; Van Borsal, 1988), it is possible that these speech production difficulties stem from limited tongue movement in the presence of a narrower, not a higher, palate. Rosin, Swift, Khidr, and Bless (1992) found that adolescents with Down syndrome actually produce the vowel sound "ee" (as in "key") with a lower and more posterior tongue placement. This difference might be an indirect result of the tongue's moving in a mouth that is smaller than that found in adolescents who are developing typically. Some people with Down syndrome have multiple variations in their nervous systems, however; and these differences, coupled with the variations in skeletal structures, probably make tongue control and positioning for speech sounds difficult.

Muscular System

People with Down syndrome are known to have absent and extra muscles throughout their bodies (Bersu, 1976, 1980). In the facial re-

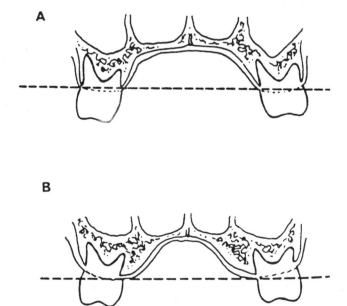

Figure 1.   Cross-sections through the normal palate (A) and "steeple" palate often associated with Down syndrome (B) at the level of permanent first molars. Palatal heights from horizontal plane are equal. The distance between teeth is less in (B). Shelflike palatal alveolar processes may be noted in (B). These last factors contribute to the illusion of increased height and decreased width of palates in people with Down syndrome. (From Shapiro, B.L., Gorlin, R.J., Redman, R.S., & Bruhl, H.H. [1967]. The palate and Down's syndrome. *New England Journal of Medicine, 276,* 1462; reprinted by permission.)

gion, these include poorly differentiated midfacial muscles and an additional facial muscle (see Figure 2). The extra muscle, the platysma occipitalis, runs from the corner of the mouth to the back of the head. This muscle likely contributes to lateral lip retraction such as those movements used when smiling and in producing some lip movements for speech sounds such as the "ee" in "key." This muscle may serve to increase oral opening for facial expression and feeding, but it likely has minimal effects on speech production. Rather than disrupting the speech of people with Down syndrome, the fusion of the midfacial muscles probably limits the elevation of their upper lips and the corners of their mouths for facial expressions such as sneering or smiling. Nonetheless, there are a few individuals with Down syndrome who may experience more specific speech production problems as a result of these facial structural variations. Additional speech problems may be the result of as yet undetermined anatomical anomalies of the facial, head, and neck muscles. An assumption may be made that deeper muscles of the face, head, and neck will evidence differences in morphology, given that Bersu (1976, 1980) found differences in the superficial facial muscles. Further investigations are necessary to examine this hypothesis.

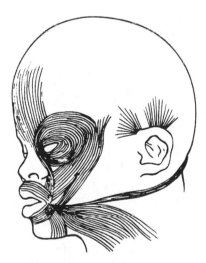

Figure 2.   Variations of the muscles of facial expression. The muscles of the midface region consist of a single muscle sheet that is continuous laterally with orbicularis oculi. The extra muscle slip extends between the occipital attachment of the trapezius muscle and the platysma muscle at the corner of the mouth. (From Bersu, E.T. [1980]. Anatomical analysis of the developmental effects of aneuploidy in man: The Down syndrome. *American Journal of Medical Genetics, 5,* 406. Copyright © 1980 by John Wiley & Sons. Reprinted by permission of Wiley-Liss, Inc., a subsidiary of John Wiley & Sons, Inc.)

People with Down syndrome have a relatively larger, more muscular tongue (Ardran et al., 1972) that protrudes from the oral cavity. Parents and clinicians have suspected for many years that this relatively larger tongue interferes with articulatory placements for both vowel and consonant productions, contributing to reduced speech intelligibility (Gibson, 1978; Miller & Leddy, 1998). These observations have resulted in some children with Down syndrome undergoing partial tongue resections to reduce tongue size. Carefully conducted studies have shown almost no speech improvement as a result of this procedure (Katz & Kravitz, 1989; Parsons, Iacono, & Rozner, 1987), though numerous parents have reported improvements in the speech of their children with Down syndrome following their children's surgery. As of 1999, no clear explanation for the tongue size has been offered other than the observation that people with Down syndrome have a larger tongue in relation to a smaller oral cavity (Ardran et al., 1972). This may explain several speech distortions that people with Down syndrome produce.

Nervous System

Anatomical variability in the central and peripheral nervous systems of people with Down syndrome likely influence speech production, probably disrupting the sequencing and timing of speech movements. Researchers examining the gross structure of the central nervous system in individuals with Down syndrome have found reduced brain size and weight, smaller and fewer sulci and gyri, a narrower superior temporal gyrus, and a smaller cerebellum than what is typically found in people without Down syndrome (see Flórez, 1992). In Kemper's (1988) review of the neurology literature, he reported that people with Down syndrome have fewer cortical neurons and a decreased neuronal density as compared with individuals who are developing typically (see Figure 3). In addition, investigators have found that people with Down syndrome have delayed neural myelination, atypical dendrite structures, and altered cellular membranes (see Flórez, 1992; Scott, Becker, & Petit, 1983). These anatomical differences may affect speech production, probably disrupting the accuracy, speed, consistency, and economy of their speech movements and thus altering the sequencing and timing of their speech.

Variations in speech, specifically in speech timing characteristics, are evident in the disfluent productions, or stuttering behaviors, of people with Down syndrome. Additional examples of these neurological speech problems include 1) greater difficulties in producing voiced speech sounds than in producing unvoiced speech sounds and 2) difficulties in maintaining air pressure in the mouth for speech (Swift,

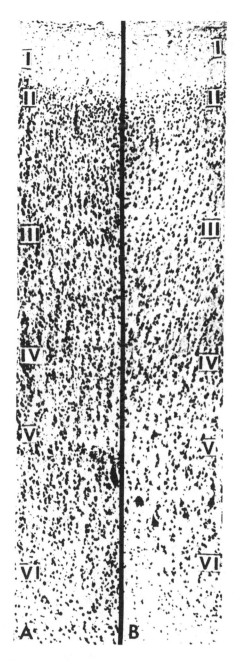

Figure 3. Low-power photomicrographs of primary motor cortex in the brain of a typical individual (A) and the brain of an age- and sex-matched individual with Down syndrome (B). Note the diminution of small neurons in Down syndrome. (From Ross, M.H., Galaburda, A.M., & Kemper, T.L. [1984]. Down's syndrome: Is there a decreased population of neurons? *Neurology, 34*, 912; reprinted by permission.)

Rosin, Khidr, & Bless, 1992). Hesselwood, Bray, and Crookston (1995) described speech rhythm errors of an adult with Down syndrome; these investigators suggested that the speech intelligibility problems of people with Down syndrome stem from speech-planning impairments. It is plausible that these speech-planning differences may stem from the underlying nervous system variations found in people with Down syndrome and that they may act in combination with the previously described annotated features to restrict speech production.

CONCLUSIONS

People with Down syndrome can improve communication and speech production in a variety of ways (see Chapters 8 and 9). Speech improvement among people with Down syndrome is the result of a well-designed therapy plan that includes not just the person with Down syndrome and the speech-language pathologist but also family members, educators, and members of the community. This team must understand that biological subsystems affect speech and that the unique biology of a person with Down syndrome can alter how these systems operate. This chapter summarizes the speech characteristics of people with Down syndrome, identifying how biological systems function related to speech. Because speech production is limited among some people with Down syndrome because of biological problems such as neuromuscular difficulties, speech-language pathologists and the families of individuals with Down syndrome must understand the biological bases of these speech production challenges, considering them during speech evaluations and when developing interventions. For example, if a person with Down syndrome experiences disfluent speech production, the speech-language pathologist must not focus just on the speech behavior but must also consider the underlying neuromuscular difficulties and speech-planning impairments that may exist. These must be considered when designing therapy so that if other impairments in motor planning exist, they are treated in combination with the speech-planning problem. People with Down syndrome must be viewed as people first and as biological systems that work to function to the best of their ability to produce behaviors such as speech second. By viewing people with Down syndrome in this way, parents and professionals can better help them improve their speech production and communicate effectively.

REFERENCES

Ardran, G.M., Harker, P., & Kemp, F.H. (1972). Tongue size in Down syndrome. *Journal of Mental Deficiency Research, 16,* 160–166.

Benda, C.E. (1941). Observations on the malformation of the head in mongoloid deficiency. *Journal of Pediatrics, 19,* 800–816.

Benda, C.E. (1949). *Mongolism and cretinism.* New York: Grune & Stratton.

Benda, C.E. (1960). *The child with Mongolism (congenital acromicria).* New York: Grune & Stratton.

Bergendal, B. (1976). Language and voice in mongoloid children. In E. Loebel (Ed.), *Proceedings of the 16th International Congress of Logopedics and Phoniatrics* (pp. 28–32). Basel, Switzerland: S. Karger.

Bersu, E.T. (1976). *An analysis of the anatomic variations in human trisomy based on dissections of 21- and 18-trisomies.* Unpublished doctoral dissertation, University of Wisconsin, Madison.

Bersu, E.T. (1980). Anatomical analysis of the developmental effects of aneuploidy in man: The Down syndrome. *American Journal of Medical Genetics, 5,* 399–420.

Blager, F.B. (1980). Speech and language development of Down's syndrome children. *Seminars in Speech, Language, and Hearing, 1,* 63–72.

Blanchard, I.B. (1964). Speech patterns and etiology in mental retardation. *American Journal of Mental Deficiency, 68,* 613–617.

Blood, G., & Hyman, M. (1977). Children's perception of nasal resonance. *Journal of Speech and Hearing Disorders, 42,* 446–448.

Bodine, A. (1974). A phonological analysis of the speech of two Mongoloid (Down's syndrome) boys. *Anthropological Linguistics, 16*(1), 1–24.

Borghi, R.W. (1990). Consonant phoneme and distinctive feature error patterns in speech. In D.C. Van Dyke, D.J. Lang, F. Heide, S. van Duyne, & M.J. Soucck (Eds.), *Clinical perspectives in the management of Down syndrome* (pp. 147–152). New York: Springer-Verlag New York.

Cabanas, R. (1954). Some findings in speech and voice therapy among mentally deficient children. *Folia Phoniatrica, 6,* 34–37.

Chapman, R.S., Schwartz, S.E., & Kay-Raining Bird, E. (1991). Language skills of children and adolescents with Down syndrome: I. Comprehension. *Journal of Speech and Hearing Research, 34,* 1106–1120.

Devenny, D.A., & Silverman, W.P. (1990). Speech dysfluency and manual specialization in Down's syndrome. *Journal of Mental Deficiency Research, 34,* 253–260.

Dodd, B.J. (1976). A comparison of the phonological systems of mental age matched, normal, severely subnormal and Down's syndrome children. *British Journal of Communication, 11,* 27–42.

Evans, D. (1977). The development of language abilities in Mongols: A correlational study. *Journal of Mental Deficiency Research, 21,* 103–117.

Farmer, A., & Brayton, E.R. (1979). Speech characteristics of fluent and dysfluent Down's syndrome adults. *Folia Phoniatrica, 31,* 284–290.

Flórez, J. (1992). Neurological abnormalities. In S.M. Pueschel & J.K. Pueschel (Eds.), *Biomedical concerns in persons with Down syndrome* (pp. 159–173). Baltimore: Paul H. Brookes Publishing Co.

Frostad, N.A., Cleall, J.F., & Melosky, L.C. (1971). Craniofacial complex in the trisomy 21 syndrome (Down's syndrome). *Archives of Oral Biology, 16,* 707–722.

Gibson, D. (1978). *Down's syndrome: The psychology of Mongolism.* Cambridge, England: Cambridge University Press.

Hesselwood, B.C., Bray, M., & Crookston, I. (1995). Juncture, rhythm and planning in the speech of an adult with Down's syndrome. *Clinical Linguistics and Phonetics, 9,* 121–137.

Horstmeier, D. (1990). Communication. In S.M. Pueschel, *A parent's guide to Down syndrome: Toward a brighter future* (pp. 233–257). Baltimore: Paul H. Brookes Publishing Co.

Katz, S., & Kravitz, S. (1989). Facial plastic surgery for persons with Down syndrome: Research findings and their professional and social implications. *American Journal on Mental Retardation, 94,* 101–110.

Kay-Raining Bird, E., & Chapman, R.S. (1994). Sequential recall in individuals with Down syndrome. *Journal of Speech and Hearing Research, 37,* 1319–1380.

Kemper, T.L. (1988). Neuropathology of down syndrome. In L. Nadel (Ed.), *The psychobiology of Down syndrome* (pp. 269–289). Cambridge, MA: MIT Press.

Kisling, E. (1966). *Cranial morphology in Down's syndrome: A comparative roentgenocephalometric study in adult males.* Copenhagen: Munksgaard.

Korenberg, J., Paulst, S., & Gerwehr, S. (1992). Advances in the understanding of chromosome 21 and Down syndrome. In I. Lott & E. McCoy (Eds.), *Down syndrome: Advances in medical care* (pp. 3–12). New York: Wiley-Liss.

Kumin, L. (1994). Intelligibility of speech in children with Down syndrome in natural settings: Parents' perspective. *Perceptual and Motor Skills, 78*(1), 307–313.

Leddy, M. (1996). *The relations among select vocal function characteristics of adult males with Down syndrome.* Unpublished doctoral dissertation, University of Wisconsin, Madison.

Lott, I.T., & McCoy, E.E. (Eds.). (1992). *Down syndrome: Advances in medical care.* New York: Wiley-Liss.

Love, R. (1981). A forgotten minority: The communicatively disabled. *Asha, 23,* 485–489.

Miller, J.F., & Leddy, M. (1998). Down syndrome: The impact of speech production on language development. In R. Paul (Ed.), *Communication and language intervention series: Vol. 8. Exploring the speech–language connection* (pp. 163–177). Baltimore: Paul H. Brookes Publishing Co.

Miller, J.F., Leddy, M., Miolo, G., & Sedey, A. (1995). The development of early language skills in children with Down syndrome. In L. Nadel & D. Rosenthal (Eds.), *Down syndrome: Living and learning in the community* (pp. 115–120). New York: Wiley-Liss.

Miller, J.F., Stoel-Gammon, C., Leddy, M., Lynch, M., & Miolo, G., (1992, November). *Factors limiting speech development in children with Down syndrome.* Miniseminar presented at the annual convention of the American Speech-Language-Hearing Association, San Antonio, TX.

Montague, J.C., & Hollien, H. (1973). Perceived voice quality disorders in Down's syndrome children. *Journal of Communication Disorders, 6,* 76.

Moran, M.J., & Gilbert, H.R. (1982). Selected acoustic characteristics and listener judgments of the voice of Down syndrome adults. *American Journal of Mental Deficiency, 86,* 553–556.

Moran, M.J., Labarge, J.M., & Haynes, W.O. (1988). Effect of voice quality on adults' perceptions of Down's syndrome children. *Folia Phoniatrica, 40,* 157–161.

Mowrer, D.E., Wahl, P., & Doolan, S.J. (1978). Effects of lisping on audience evaluation of male speakers. *Journal of Speech and Hearing Disorders, 43,* 140–148.

Novak, A. (1972). The voice of children with Down's syndrome. *Folia Phoniatrica, 24,* 182–194.

Novak, A., Sedlackova, E., Klajman, S., & Betlejewski, S. (1967). Acoustic analysis of the voice of children suffering from the Down-syndrome. *Cs. Otolaryngologie [Czechoslovakian Otalaryngology]*, 16, 26–31.

Parsons, C.L., Iacono, T.A., & Rozner, L. (1987). Effect of tongue reduction on articulation in children with Down syndrome. *American Journal of Mental Deficiency*, 91, 328–332.

Pentz, A.L. (1987). Formant amplitude of children with Down syndrome. *American Journal of Mental Deficiency*, 92, 230–233.

Pentz, A.L., & Gilbert, H.R. (1983). Relation of selected acoustical parameters and perceptual ratings to voice quality of Down syndrome children. *American Journal of Mental Deficiency*, 88(2), 203–210.

Pozzan, G.B., Rigon, F., Girelli, M.E., Rubello, D., Busnardo, B., & Baccichetti, C. (1990). Thyroid function in patients with Down syndrome: Preliminary results from non-institutionalized patients in the Veneto region. *American Journal of Medical Genetics*, 7, 57–58.

Preus, A. (1990). Treatment of mentally retarded stutterers. *Journal of Fluency Disorders*, 15, 223–233.

Pueschel, S.M. (1990). Clinical aspects of Down syndrome from infancy to adulthood. *American Journal of Medical Genetics*, 7, 52–56.

Pueschel, S.M. (1992). The person with Down's syndrome: Medical concerns and educational strategies. In I.T. Lott & E.E. McCoy (Eds.), *Down syndrome: Advances in medical care* (pp. 53–60). New York: Wiley-Liss.

Redman, R.S., Shapiro, B.L., & Gorlin, R.J. (1965). Measurement of normal and reportedly malformed palatal vaults: III. Down's syndrome (trisomy 21, Mongolism). *Journal of Pediatrics*, 67, 162–165.

Roche, A.F., Roche, J.P., & Lewis, A.B. (1972). The cranial base in trisomy 21. *Journal of Mental Deficiency Research*, 16, 7–20.

Roche, A.F., Seward, F.S., & Sutherland, S. (1961). Nonmetrical observations on cranial roentgenograms in mongolism. *American Journal of Roentgenology*, 85, 659–662.

Rosin, M.M., Swift, E., Bless, D., & Vetter, D.K. (1988). Communication profiles of adolescents with Down syndrome. *Journal of Childhood Communication Disorders*, 12, 49–64.

Rosin, M.M., Swift, E., Khidr, A., & Bless, D. (1992, November). *Acoustic manifestations of voice production in adult males with Down syndrome*. Poster presented at the annual convention of the American Speech-Language-Hearing Association, San Antonio, TX.

Ross, M.H., Galaburda, A.M., & Kemper, T.L. (1984). Down's syndrome: Is there a decreased population of neurons? *Neurology*, 34, 909–916.

Ruscello, D.M., & Lass, N.J. (1992, November). *Attitudes of three age groups toward individuals with voice disorders*. Paper presented at the annual convention of the American Speech-Language-Hearing Association, San Antonio, TX.

Sanger, R.G. (1975). Facial and oral manifestations of Down's syndrome. In R. Koch & F.F. de la Cruz (Eds.), *Down's syndrome (Mongolism): Research, prevention and management* (pp. 32–46). New York: Brunner/Mazel.

Schlanger, B.B. (1962). Brain injury, mental retardation, aphasia and emotional maladjustment in delayed and defective speech. In N.M. Levin (Ed.), *Voice and speech disorders: Medical aspects* (pp. 557–603). Springfield, IL: Charles C Thomas.

Schlanger, B.B., & Gottsleben, R.H. (1957). Analysis of speech defects among the institutionalized mentally retarded. *Journal of Speech and Hearing Disorders, 22,* 98–104.

Scott, B.S., Becker, L.E., & Petit, T.L. (1983). Neurobiology of Down's syndrome. *Progress in Neurobiology, 21,* 199–237.

Shapiro, B.L., Gorlin, R.J., Redman, R.S., & Bruhl, H.H. (1967). The palate and Down's syndrome. *New England Journal of Medicine, 276,* 1460–1463.

Shapiro, B.L., Redman, R.S., & Gorlin, R.J. (1963). Measurements of normal and reportedly malformed palatal vaults: 1. Normal adult measurements. *Journal of Dental Research, 42,* 1039.

Silverman, E. (1976). Listeners' impressions of speakers with lateral lisps. *Journal of Speech and Hearing Disorders, 41,* 547–552.

Spitzer, R., & Quilliam, R.L. (1958). Observations on congenital anomalies in teeth and skull in two groups of mental defectives (a comparative study). *British Journal of Radiology, 31,* 596–604.

Spitzer, R., Rabinowitch, J.Y., & Wybar, K.C. (1961). A study of the abnormalities of the skull, teeth, and lenses in Mongolism. *Canadian Medical Association Journal, 84*(11), 567–572.

Spitzer, R., & Robinson, M.I. (1955). Radiological changes in teeth and skull in mental defectives. *British Journal of Radiology, 28,* 117.

Strazulla, M. (1953). Speech problems of the Mongoloid child. *Quarterly Review of Pediatrics, 8,* 268–273.

Swift, E., Rosin, M., Khidr, A., & Bless, D. (1992, November). *Aerodynamic properties of speech in adult males with Down syndrome.* Poster presented at the annual convention of the American Speech-Language-Hearing Association, San Antonio, TX.

Van Borsal, J. (1988). An analysis of the speech of five Down's syndrome adolescents. *Journal of Communication Disorders, 21,* 409–421.

Van Dyke, D.C., Lang, D.J., Heide, F., van Duyne, S., & Soucek, M.J. (Eds.). (1990). *Clinical perspectives in the management of Down syndrome.* New York: Springer-Verlag New York.

Van Riper, C. (1982). *The nature of stuttering.* Upper Saddle River, NJ: Prentice-Hall.

West, R., Kennedy, L., & Carr, A. (1947). *The rehabilitation of speech* (Rev. ed.). New York: Harper & Brothers.

Willcox, A. (1988). An investigation into non-fluency in Down's syndrome. *British Journal of Disorders of Communication, 23,* 153–170.

Woods, C., & Williams, D. (1976). Speech clinicians' conceptions of boys and men who stutter. *Journal of Speech and Hearing Disorders, 36,* 225–234.

Yarter, B.H. (1980). Speech and language programs for the Down's population. *Seminars in Speech, Language and Hearing, 1,* 49–60.

5

Verbal Fluency, Speech Intelligibility, and Communicative Effectiveness

Jon F. Miller and Mark Leddy

Communicating with children with Down syndrome requires the listener to work hard to grasp the messages that are being expressed. It is readily apparent that the listener must initially resolve two kinds of information to understand the message. First is the speech pattern or the clarity of production of each word, and second is the message or coherence of the word combinations, which is greatly influenced by the fluency of production. This chapter briefly reviews what is known about the speech intelligibility and fluency of children with Down syndrome.

Developing the ability to produce the individual sounds of language clearly and to combine those sounds into intelligible words has been a challenge for people with Down syndrome. Although the literature has documented this fact, the mechanisms responsible for the unintelligible speech of these individuals have not been studied. In considering how researchers might go about improving the speech intelligibility of these individuals, knowledge of these speech mechanisms is important. In Chapter 4, Leddy documents differences in several systems—skeletal, nervous, and muscular—that may be associated with speech intelligibility. Do they all contribute to speech intelligibility? Is one system more at fault than the others? Is each of them of equal concern for each individual, or can some individuals have more difficulty with one or two systems?

Fluency problems pose serious difficulties for listeners who are attempting to work out the intended message of the speaker. Fluency problems may involve long pauses within or between utterances, partial word or phrase repetition, or word and phrase revisions. These behaviors disrupt the communication process. The traditional literature on stuttering has been concerned primarily with speech production issues involving timing, respiration, and muscle tension. Theory suggests that stuttering may be a disruption of the motor planning at the neurological level. Does this literature have any relevance to the fluency impairments observed in children with Down syndrome? An alternative assertion is based on linguistic performance and argues that the fluency problems that they experience are associated with difficulties in finding the proper word to communicate an idea or the appropriate syntactic structure to formulate a sentence. This chapter reviews what is known about these two arguments and posits some rules of thumb that may help researchers to understand the speech production of individuals with Down syndrome.

The two prominent speech production impairments observed in people with Down syndrome, reduced speech intelligibility and disfluency, are discussed relative to possible neurological limitations, in the context of anatomically different vocal tract structures, that may affect sequencing and speech timing. The association between the anatomical and physiological differences and speech intelligibility or fluency impairments can only be speculated on. There is a great deal of support for future research to test several hypotheses put forward in this chapter, however.

SPEECH PRODUCTION MECHANISMS

Children with Down syndrome are biologically different from typically developing children. Abnormal anatomical structures have been found in all of the body systems of people with Down syndrome, including the skeletal, muscular, nervous, cardiovascular, digestive, respiratory, urogenital, and endocrine systems. Those systems that are thought to have the strongest association with speech production include the skeletal, muscular, nervous, and respiratory mechanisms. These are discussed in detail in Chapter 4. Anatomical-structural abnormalities in the skeletal, muscular, and nervous systems are found in a high percentage of children with Down syndrome, but they are not found in every child. In addition, differences in these systems do not always cause speech production deficits or reduced speech intelligibility. Human physiology has a great capacity to accommodate structural deviations, and some children with Down syndrome may adapt to structural anomalies to produce acceptably intelligible speech. Other children with Down syndrome who have more serious nervous system anomalies may have greater difficulty with accommodating these skeletal, muscular, and respiratory structural differences. We propose that neurological impairments mediated by motor constraints influence the precision of speech production in people with Down syndrome and that these impairments affect children's ability to adapt to their unique vocal tract structures.

Disfluent Speech Production: A Motor or Linguistic Dysfunction

There is a higher prevalence of stuttering, or disfluent speech, in people with Down syndrome compared with people with developmental disabilities and individuals who are developing typically (Van Riper, 1982). Whereas stuttering occurs in approximately 1% of individuals who are developing typically and in approximately 10% of those with developmental disabilities, it occurs in about 45%–53% of people with Down syndrome (see Devenny & Silverman, 1990; Preus, 1990). Although there is a higher prevalence of disfluent speech production in people with Down syndrome, there is disagreement about whether the speech behaviors they exhibit are the same as those observed in speakers with disfluent speech who are typically developing. These speech behaviors primarily include sound prolongations, interjections, pauses, and repetitions of sounds, syllables, parts of words and whole words (Devenny & Silverman, 1990; Evans, 1977; Willcox, 1988).

There are two competing views of the disfluent behavior of people with Down syndrome. The first is that this behavior resembles the classic stuttering behavior in the speech pathology literature, which is characterized by blocks, tremors, and vocal spasms and that these events are the result of speech motor dysfunction. The second view is that the disfluencies of this group are language based and are associated with an utterance formulation or word-finding impairment. Investigators have attributed the higher disfluency prevalence to linguistic influences (Preus, 1990; Willcox, 1988), to the point of calling the disorder *cluttering* instead of *stuttering* (Cabanas, 1954), and to impairments in the speech motor control system (Devenny & Silverman, 1990; Farmer & Brayton, 1979; Van Riper, 1982).

A SPEECH MOTOR BASIS FOR STUTTERING

The argument that disfluent speech is due to a motor control impairment gains support from other investigations that address non–speech motor coordination and timing impairments in people with Down syndrome (Frith & Frith, 1974; Henderson, Morris, & Frith, 1981; Henderson, Morris, & Ray, 1981). In addition, the results of several studies (e.g., Dembowski & Watson, 1991; Nudelman, Herbich, Hess, Hoyt, & Rosenfield, 1992) on laryngeal reaction time and vocal tracking behavior involving disfluent speakers suggested that stutterers have specific speech motor control impairments that could be the result of neural processing difficulties that negatively influence early stages of preparatory speech motor control programming.

When Otto and Yairi (1974) compared the disfluent speech patterns of people with Down syndrome with those of people who were developing typically, these investigators found that besides repeating parts of words and whole words more frequently, speakers with Down syndrome also had more dysrhythmic phonations. These disruptions might be due to speech motor control impairments that are secondary to different neurophysiological mechanisms.

Because people with Down syndrome have cognitive-linguistic impairments as well as gross, fine, and speech motor impairments, it is unlikely that only one specific and abnormally functioning system explains the underlying basis for their disfluent speech behavior. In fact, theories and models of stuttering recognize multifactorial influences (i.e., the combined effects of several factors including cognitive-linguistic and motor control parameters) on disfluent speech production (Conture, 1990; Nudelman et al., 1992; Smith, 1990).

The Cluttering or Language-Based Hypothesis

There is a long history of research and clinical reports contrasting stuttering as a speech production–based fluency problem with cluttering, which is a language-based fluency problem. The behaviors defining each disorder have been debated for some years with more heat than light. The classical definition of stuttering includes sound and syllable repetitions and blocking—that is, the lack of vocalization associated with tension in the speech system, tremors, and facial tics. Cluttering, however, is associated with rapid speech rate, word repetition, and phrase revision and repetition.

Since the late 1980s, word and phrase repetition and revision behaviors have been cited as evidence for word-finding problems in children with language-learning disabilities (German, 1992). In the 1990s, work aimed at defining different types of language disorders among children diagnosed with specific language impairment (SLI) has suggested that these disfluent behaviors may be indicative of two different language production impairments: word finding and utterance formulation (Miller, 1987; Miller & Leadholm, 1992). For some children, the repetitions and revisions are primarily of phrase units indicating that they are struggling with units longer than single words. These children may be struggling with learning complex syntax in order to express more than one proposition at a time or may be having difficulty in coordinating utterance content either within the utterance or with previous utterances. Word-level repetitions and revisions are more likely associated with word-finding problems.

There are measures that reflect a general class of verbal fluency behaviors as an index of language formulation load (Miller, 1991). Loban (1976) was first to describe these measures, referred to as *mazes*. Mazes were characterized as false starts, repetitions, and reformulations, which Loban used to describe children's progress toward adult language competence. Miller (1991) showed that mazes are an index of formulation load in that the number of mazes that children produce in utterances increases in narrative speaking contexts compared with conversational contexts. Narratives place a greater burden on utterance formulation and discourse cohesion for the speaker than does conversation, in which these duties are shared. Mazes also increase when children attempt longer utterances rather than shorter utterances, supporting the hypothesis that formulation load is greater when message content is increased.

These data suggest that mazes can be used to differentiate between stuttering and language-based fluency impairments. Mazes are the key to identifying the nature of the fluency problems in children with Down syndrome. Recording and transcribing a language sample provides the data needed to document the nature of the disfluencies in an individual child. Valuable indices of disfluent speech are provided when a sample is analyzed for several maze measures, including the nature of the maze (filled pause, repetition, or revision), the size of the maze (part word, word, or phrase), and the proportion of words in mazes to the total words in the sample. Further analysis of where the mazes occur in the utterance help to identify specific linguistic features with which the child is having difficulty.

When maze data are combined with the visual observation of tension, facial tics, and/or other blocking behaviors associated with stuttering, investigators and clinicians have the information necessary to differentiate speech-based stuttering from language-based fluency problems. Speech-based problems probably result from the same causal mechanisms as stuttering in children who are developing typically: primarily the environmental pressure to speak, which they feel is being thrust on them. Whether real or imagined, this pressure must be reduced so that these children feel that their speech is accepted at any level.

SPEECH INTELLIGIBILITY

The majority of children with Down syndrome experience a prolonged period of unintelligible speech that has a significant impact on their establishing competent communicative interactions with their families. In reviewing the early period of language production, one expects children who are developing typically to begin to indicate their wants and needs by ages 8–10 months and children with Down syndrome to do so as late as age 24 months. Their communications at those ages are not words but communications by gestures, vocalizations, or both produced simultaneously. Imagine a child who wants a drink standing in front of a refrigerator pointing and yelling, "Ahh, ahh, ahh." As children practice such gestures, they improve as others get better at interpreting what they mean by those gestures. First words appear when others understand an infant's or young child's consistent vocalization as a word (e.g., "Dada" meaning *Daddy*). When one is not successful in understanding what the child intends to communicate, two things happen: The child and the child's parents become frustrated, and the parents may fail to appreciate the communication value of the child's attempt while focusing on the form (i.e., clear articulation of the word).

Most children do not produce adultlike words for a number of years; but as long as children have been labeled *typical,* adults are not overly concerned. When children with Down syndrome are not producing clear speech at age 2 years, adults become much more agitated, wondering whether the child will ever be understood. Children with Down syndrome take much longer to develop the ability to produce clear speech, and some have more difficulty than others in developing this ability. Researchers need to focus first on the child's message and to expect clear speech to emerge at ages 5–6 years. There are a number of supports to help one understand the early speech production of children with Down syndrome. The most common support is sign language, with 75% of children participating in our research having had sign language introduced during the first 3–6 years of life. Signs representing single words give the listener an alternative source of information about the child's message. Clearly, both the child and the child's conversation partner need to be familiar with the sign system the child uses. Parents and teachers frequently report that the use of signs improves communication effectiveness, reduces frustration, and seems to help the child recognize that gestures as well as speech represent objects, actions, and relationships in their environment. That is, the signs help children develop representational skills. The most frequently asked question about introducing signs is, Won't teaching signs inhibit children's learning to speak? After all, if children can sign, why would they learn to talk? Children who are taught 20–50 signs and use them for communication stop using them as soon as their speech intelligibility improves. Speech is simply a more efficient mode of communication than signs. Everyone knows speech, but not everyone knows signs.

Alternatively, one can introduce a picture communication system rather than signs or questions. Chapter 10 provides a detailed account of this strategy. Basically, the picture symbols are used instead of signs. A graphic symbol system is used rather than the gesture symbol system. The advantage of graphic systems is that they are permanent, not fleeting like gestures. So, the graphic symbols can be attached to objects around the house and the classroom to facilitate learning. N. Marriner (personal communication, November 1990), a Seattle-based speech-language pathologist, found these systems to be successful. She argued that children with Down syndrome show a preference for visual learning styles. She noted that the vocabulary skills of children with Down syndrome show accelerated growth when symbols are introduced. Of course, signs are visual as well; but the permanence of the graphic symbols appears to be advantageous.

These observations are consistent with the research of Buckley (1994) in England in teaching children with Down syndrome to read. In reading, the word is the symbol, though it is constructed from individual letters. Children with Down syndrome seem to be able to read whole words as early as 3 years of age. Although there is some debate about the validity of the reading ability of children with Down syndrome, there is no argument about the positive effect of language-based reading such as that which Buckley studied with regard to overall language and communication performance. Intelligibility may not be improved, but other means exist by which to understand the child with Down syndrome. Many of children's behavior problems stem from their inability to communicate, resulting in their feeling frustrated and acting out inappropriately (Reichle & Wacker, 1993).

Speech Production Impairments Influence Communicative Effectiveness

Speech Intelligibility The relationship between speech intelligibility impairments and language and communication performance among people with Down syndrome requires some discussion, as does the relationship between verbal fluency impairments and communication proficiency. Is the impact of speech intelligibility impairments on productive language development and communicative efficiency any different in people with Down syndrome than in individuals who are developing typically? Can intervention improve speech intelligibility in this population? There are three areas in which the impact of speech intelligibility on language learning and communication can be demonstrated. First, impairments in speech intelligibility interfere with message understanding, which may cause children with Down syndrome to reduce their attempts to speak and in turn limit the language production practice required for learning language.

A second effect of unintelligible speech is the child's increased frustration resulting from messages that are not understood. This frustration can lead to behavior problems if it is not dealt with early (Reichle & Wacker, 1993). Interventions that are designed to limit frustration and improve communicative effectiveness include the introduction of gestural communication by teaching 20–50 signs for frequently used vocabulary when children begin to indicate wants and needs through vocalizations and gestures at 12–18 months of age. Children with Down syndrome use signs until speech becomes more intelligible, which occurs at 3–4 years of age for many of these children, and then their use of signs fades. Signs should be taught as augmentative alternatives to speech and not as a second language. Children always opt for speech as the most efficient method of communicating their wants and needs.

The third effect of unintelligible speech on language and communication has to do with the complexity of messages attempted. Children choose to produce short, intelligible messages rather than long, unintelligible messages. This trade-off among length, intelligibility, and message complexity may be a resource allocation limitation; that is, if the child is focusing on the articulation of sounds and the clarity of speech, then the child's available resources for language formulation and message construction are reduced. Alternatively, the lack of practice with productive language may have limited the child's language learning to simple sentence patterns. There are data to support this hypothesis (Fowler, 1990).

Verbal Fluency Impairments What do the prevalence data about disfluent speech in people with Down syndrome tell us? The data do not differentiate stuttering from language-based fluency impairments. Thus, researchers do not have a clear understanding of how frequently disfluent behaviors constitute stuttering. The authors' experiences with several hundred children with Down syndrome suggest that the frequency of stuttering behaviors is far too high, and these observations are probably contaminated with typical developmental disfluencies. Data from children who are developing typically document that 20%–25% of utterances contain mazes in children ages 3–13 years in conversational contexts. In narrative samples, the percentages increase to 30%–45% over the same age range (Miller, 1994). Given these high rates of disfluent behavior, it is not inconceivable that the majority of these children were exhibiting typical nonfluent behavior. Do children with Down syndrome have similar rates of language-based disfluencies?

Are mazes the cause or a consequence of productive language disorders? If mazes were the cause of productive language disorders, one would have to argue that somehow the disfluent behavior prevented the child from practicing or trying new language forms to express increasingly complex messages. This certainly could happen, but it is far more likely that mazes are the consequence of a specific linguistic impairment such as word-finding or utterance formulation problems.

If one considers related behaviors when evaluating this hypothesis, one finds support for this point of view. Two types of behavior suggest themselves: pauses, which can occur either between or within utterances, and abandon utterances, which occur when the child makes repeated attempts to repair an utterance, producing several mazes in succession, and fails to complete the utterance. Pauses may be simply a silent version of a maze resulting from the same source: The child cannot find the right word or utterance form to express a thought. Pauses may be substituted for mazes, which represent just one method by which a child may gain time to get his or her message sorted out. Therefore, mazes and pauses may not be distributed together. Data on 256 children with SLI confirm this view: Children usually produced mazes or pauses but rarely both (Miller, 1996).

Abandon utterances could be considered unresolved mazes in which the child could not pull enough of the utterance together to finish it. Abandon utterances should increase as the number of mazes increases, particularly when the mazes are predominate at the phrase level. This is exactly the pattern found in children with SLI. A high frequency of mazes in children with Down syndrome may be associated with their limited syntactic skills or with their short-term memory impairments, making finding the right word difficult. It is safe to say that these disfluencies provide a valuable insight into the productive language impairments of this group. Further research is necessary to document the impact of these disfluencies on the language development and communication proficiency of children with Down syndrome.

CONCLUSIONS

Both unintelligible speech and disfluent speech have adverse effects on the language and communication performance of children with Down syndrome. It is important to continue investigating these speech behaviors to determine whether they are causing or contributing to SLI or communication problems and whether they are the result of cognitive-linguistic impairments in children with Down syndrome. Both behaviors are amenable to intervention in children and adults with Down syndrome. Leddy and Gill (1996) showed that, as a result of clinical speech and language interventions, adults with Down syndrome make significant improvements in speech intelligibility and use these improvements to repair communication breakdowns. These findings provide hope for improving the communication skills of people with Down syndrome and suggest the need for intervention studies of this population.

REFERENCES

Buckley, S. (1994). Teaching children with Down syndrome to read and write. In L. Nadel & D. Rosenthal (Eds.), *Down syndrome: Living and learning in the community* (pp. 158–169). New York: Wiley-Liss.

Cabanas, R. (1954). Some findings in speech and voice therapy among mentally deficient children. *Folia Phoniatrica, 6,* 34–37.

Conture, E.G. (1990). *Stuttering* (2nd ed.). Upper Saddle River, NJ: Prentice-Hall.

Dembowski, J., & Watson, B.C. (1991). Preparation time and response complexity effects on stutterers' and nonstutterers' acoustic LRT. *Journal of Speech and Hearing Research, 34,* 49–59.

Devenny, D.A., & Silverman, W.P. (1990). Speech dysfluency and manual specialization in Down's syndrome. *Journal of Mental Deficiency Research, 34,* 253–260.

Evans, D. (1977). The development of language abilities in Mongols: A correlational study. *Journal of Mental Deficiency Research, 21,* 103–117.

Farmer, A., & Brayton, E.R. (1979). Speech characteristics of fluent and disfluent Down's syndrome adults. *Folia Phoniatrica, 31,* 284–290.

Fowler, A. (1990). Language abilities in children with Down syndrome: Evidence for a specific syntactic delay. In D. Cicchetti & M. Beeghly (Eds.), *Children with Down syndrome: A developmental perspective* (pp. 302–328). Cambridge, England: Cambridge University Press.

Frith, U., & Frith, C.D. (1974). Specific motor disabilities in Down's syndrome. *Journal of Child Psychology and Psychiatry, 15,* 293–301.

German, D. (1992). Diagnosis of word finding disorders in children with learning disabilities. *Journal of Learning Disabilities, 17,* 353–358.

Henderson, S.E., Morris, J., & Frith, U. (1981). The motor deficit in Down's syndrome children: A problem of timing? *Journal of Child Psychology and Psychiatry, 22,* 233–245.

Henderson, S.E., Morris, J., & Ray, S. (1981). Performance of Down syndrome and other retarded children on the Cratty Gross-Motor Test. *American Journal of Mental Deficiency, 85,* 416–424.

Leddy, M., & Gill, G. (1996, July). *Speech and language skills of adolescents and adults with Down syndrome: Enhancing communication.* Paper presented at the National Down Syndrome Congress Annual Convention, Miami Beach, FL.

Loban, W. (1976). *Language development: Kindergarten through grade 12* (No. 18). Urbana, IL: National Council of Teachers of English.

Miller, J.F. (1987). A grammatical characterization of language disorder. In *Proceedings of the First International Symposium on Specific Speech and Language Disorders in Children*. London: AFASIC Press.

Miller, J.F. (1991). Quantifying productive language disorder. In J.F. Miller (Ed.), *Research on child language disorders: A decade of progress* (pp. 211–220). Boston: College-Hill.

Miller, J.F. (1994, April). *Documenting rate and verbal facility deficits in children with language disorders*. Invited paper presented at the University of Amsterdam, the Netherlands.

Miller, J.F. (1996). Progress in assessing, describing and defining child language disorder. In K.N. Cole, P.S. Dale, & D.J. Thal (Eds.), *Communication and language intervention series: Vol. 6. Assessment of communication and language* (pp. 309–324). Baltimore: Paul H. Brookes Publishing Co.

Miller, J.F., & Leadholm, B. (1992). *Language sample analysis guide: The Wisconsin guide for the identification and description of language impairment in children*. Madison: Wisconsin Department of Public Instruction.

Nudelman, H.B., Herbich, K.E., Hess, K.R., Hoyt, B.D., & Rosenfield, D.B. (1992). A model of the phonatory response time of stutterers and fluent speakers to frequency-modulated tones. *Journal of the Acoustical Society of America, 92*, 1882–1888.

Otto, F.M., & Yairi, E. (1974). An analysis of speech disfluencies in Down's syndrome and in normally intelligent subjects. *Journal of Fluency Disorders, 1*, 26–32.

Preus, A. (1990). Treatment of mentally retarded stutterers. *Journal of Fluency Disorders, 15*, 223–233.

Reichle, J., & Wacker, D.P. (Eds.). (1993). *Communication and language intervention series: Vol. 3. Communicative alternatives to challenging behavior: Integrating functional assessment and intervention strategies*. Baltimore: Paul H. Brookes Publishing Co.

Smith, A. (1990). Factors in the etiology of stuttering. *American Speech-Language-Hearing Association Reports: Research Needs in Stuttering: Roadblocks and Future Directions, 18*, 39–47.

Van Riper, C. (1982). *The nature of stuttering*. Upper Saddle River, NJ: Prentice-Hall.

Willcox, A. (1988). An investigation into non-fluency in Down's syndrome. *British Journal of Disorders of Communication, 23*, 153–170.

6

Individual Differences in Mothers' Communication with Their Young Children with Down Syndrome

Mary A. Roach,
Marguerite Stevenson Barratt, and Lewis A. Leavitt

Communication between mothers and their young children is a reciprocal process that requires each participant to produce and receive signals that are mutually understandable. Within this interactive system, mothers are instrumental in encouraging their children's vocal and nonvocal play and maintaining their children's play within typical limits (Bell & Harper, 1977). Mothers' interactions with their children are shaped by their perceptions of their children (Donovan & Leavitt, 1991) as well as by the signals they receive from their young children (Barratt, Roach, & Leavitt, 1992). In the case of young children with Down syndrome (trisomy 21), the pattern of interactive signals may be different from that evident in most young children who are developing typically (see Hodapp, 1995). Authors in this book (this chapter as well as Chapters 7 and 8) address the unique language patterns of

The research described in this chapter was made possible in part by a Biomedical Research grant, a grant from the Graduate School, University of Wisconsin–Madison, and Grant R01-28094 from the U.S. Department of Health and Human Services to the second author; Grant R01-22393 from the U.S. Department of Health and Human Services to Jon F. Miller; March of Dimes Grant 12-197 to Jon F. Miller and Lewis A. Leavitt; and Grant HD03352 from the U.S. Department of Health and Human Services to The Waisman Center, University of Wisconsin–Madison.

young children with Down syndrome as well as associations between the language patterns of young children with Down syndrome and their development in motor and cognitive domains (see Chapter 2). This chapter focuses on individual differences in mothers' patterns of communication with their young children with Down syndrome.

Caregiving that is reciprocal and responsive to children's signals is thought to be key to optimal development (Girolametto, 1988; Maccoby & Martin, 1983; Marfo, 1990). Reciprocity and responsiveness between mothers and their young children with Down syndrome may be particularly difficult to achieve, however. Impairments in the interactive and communicative capacities of young children with Down syndrome may lead to reduced opportunities for appropriate and contingent feedback from their mothers. Mothers of children with Down syndrome are particularly concerned about delays in the communicative development of their young children (Hodapp, Dykens, Evans, & Merighi, 1992). Yet, they adapt their communication styles to cope with their young children who may provide signals that are difficult to read and who may respond less readily than expected or desired. Access to reciprocal and responsive maternal caregiving may be particularly critical for children with Down syndrome to moderate the effects of their disabling conditions (Girolametto, 1988; Jasnow et al., 1988; Marfo, 1991).

This chapter reviews research on young children with Down syndrome, with a particular emphasis on individual differences in mothers' patterns of communication. Factors influencing the ways in which mothers of young children with Down syndrome uniquely structure their vocal interactions and respond to the early vocal efforts of their young language-learning children are identified. Specifically examined is the extent to which children's developmental status, interactive vocal and play behaviors, and family background characteristics may influence the language input mothers provide for their young children with Down syndrome.

GROUP DIFFERENCES IN MOTHERS' COMMUNICATION

Considerable research on mothers' communication with their children with Down syndrome has involved comparisons of the communication styles of mothers of preschool-age children with Down syndrome and those of mothers of children who are developing typically (see Hodapp, 1995; Marfo, 1990). The results of these comparative studies have led to the well-established conclusion that mothers of young children with Down syndrome rely more frequently on the use of directive behaviors designed to guide and channel their young children's play than do mothers of children who are typically developing (e.g., Roach, Barratt,

Miller, & Leavitt, 1998). Thus, the vocalizations of mothers of young children with Down syndrome tend to be characterized by numerous implicit or explicit requests such as "Find the blue block," "Go get the ball," and "Put it in." In a 1998 study, mothers of children with Down syndrome exhibited an average of almost 25% more of these types of directives during naturalistic free play than did mothers of 10- to 17-month-old developmentally and socioeconomically matched children who were typically developing (Roach et al., 1998). Using a variety of measures and diverse populations, studies consistently have shown a high prevalence of mother–child interactions in which mothers of children who are atypically developing use directiveness to manipulate their children's behavior (see Marfo, 1992). The overall robustness of this finding suggests that the frequency of maternal directiveness may be of some clinical significance. A description of our definition of *maternal directiveness* is outlined in Table 1.

A preponderance of directives by mothers of young children with Down syndrome as compared with mothers of children who are typically developing was once assumed to occur at the expense of responsiveness (Berger & Cunningham, 1983; Mash & Terdal, 1973; Petersen & Sherrod, 1982). That is, mothers' directiveness was thought to interfere with their abilities to sensitively respond to their children's interactive signals. Responsive mothers are skilled at noticing and responding to signals from their young children. Mothers who are preoccupied with teaching, directing, and encouraging their young children to play with toys may fail to notice and respond to their children's vocalizations or successes during play.

Research exploring the role of responsiveness in mothers' interactions with their young children with Down syndrome has yielded inconclusive results. Various investigations have indicated that mothers of children with Down syndrome are less responsive (Brooks-Gunn & Lewis, 1984), more responsive (Fischer, 1987), or equally responsive (Davis, Stroud, & Green, 1988; Mahoney & Robenalt, 1986; Marfo & Kysela, 1988; Tannock, 1988) relative to mothers of children who

Table 1.   Categorization of maternal directive behavior

Maternal directive	Explicit example	Implicit example
Request for action	"Put it in." "Shake it hard."	"Can you find it?" "Why don't you hold it?"
Request for object	"Give me the ball." "Roll it to Mommy."	"Can I have the ball?" "Can you bring it here?"
Request for information	"What is this?" "Where did Ernie go?"	"Do you know what that is?" "Do you know his name?"

are typically developing. Lack of consistency in the findings from a broad set of investigations suggests that a more sensitive indicator of responsiveness may be needed before the role of responsiveness in early parent–child interactions with children with Down syndrome can be determined accurately.

The results of a comparative study (Roach et al., 1998) indicated that mothers of children with Down syndrome effectively balance their directiveness with supportive behaviors by, for example, using significantly higher levels of praise relative to mothers of children who are typically developing (see Figure 1). In addition, mothers of children with Down syndrome temper their directiveness with high levels of responsiveness to their children's communicative signals. That is, mothers of young children with Down syndrome sensitively paced their directive interventions to systematically follow and reinforce their children's early attempts at social play and generally accomplished the goal of optimizing their children's play without sacrificing responsiveness (Roach et al., 1998). Faced with different task de-

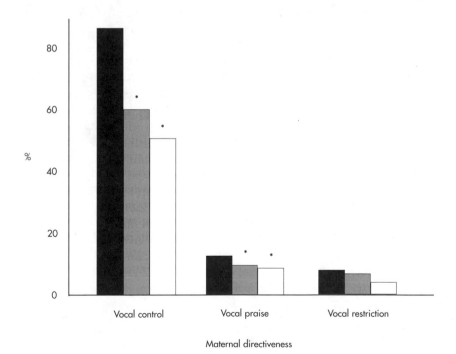

Figure 1.   Summary of maternal directiveness in comparative study of children with Down syndrome and children who were typically developing. (*, significantly different from mothers of children with Down syndrome; ■, children with Down syndrome; ▨, mental age–matched children who were typically developing; ☐, chronological age–matched children who were typically developing.)

mands (Boyce & Barnett, 1991; Crnic, Friedrich, & Greenberg, 1983; Rodrigue, Morgan, & Geffken, 1990), mothers of children with Down syndrome evidence impressive sensitivity to their children's behavioral signals and confirm researchers' confidence in the skills of mothers to adapt their parenting when confronted with children who are developing atypically.

INDIVIDUAL DIFFERENCES IN MOTHERS' PATTERNS OF COMMUNICATION

Consistent efforts to distinguish mothers of children with Down syndrome from mothers of children who are developing typically have tended to accentuate group differences while ignoring the vast individual differences that exist within groups of mothers of children with Down syndrome (Crawley & Spiker, 1983). Certainly, high rates of directive behavior by mothers of children with Down syndrome relative to mothers of children who are typically developing may result from these mothers' tendencies to interact with their children to some extent as a function of their developmental status as children with Down syndrome (Mahoney, 1988; Mahoney, Fors, & Wood, 1990; Marfo, 1992). That is, the mere diagnosis of a disabling condition may influence these mothers' vocal interactive strategies. Research (Caissie & Cole, 1993; Pellegrini, Brody, & Sigel, 1985; Wasserman, Smilansky, & Hahn, 1986) has suggested that mothers may have a tendency to be somewhat more directive with children who are developmentally younger and perhaps require more direction. Likewise, mothers' use of restrictions may increase over time as their children become increasingly competent and increasingly successful at challenging maternal regulations (Hart & Risley, 1992). Thus, the developmental status of children with Down syndrome clearly plays a role in mothers' communicative behavior. At the same time, children's actual behavior and family background characteristics are also likely to influence mothers' communicative efforts.

Children with Down syndrome are consistently found to show less active involvement with their environments than children who are developing typically (Fischer, 1987; Mundy, Sigman, Kasari, & Yirmiya, 1988; Tannock, 1988). Decreased involvement may encourage mothers to become particularly active in structuring their children's play (Landry, Garner, Pirie, & Swank, 1994; Schneider & Gearhart, 1988). Borrowing from the thermostat analogy in systems theory, maintaining a comfortable temperature in a poorly insulated home may require higher levels of energy than maintaining that same temperature in a well-insulated home. In a similar vein, achieving an optimal level of play behavior with young children with Down syndrome may require higher levels of maternal directiveness than what might be required to achieve that same level of play by children who are developing typically. Evidence from a comparative study (Roach et al., 1998) lends credence to this analogy. Roach and colleagues found overall similarity in the frequencies of simple and complex object play behavior by children who were developing typically as compared with a developmentally matched sample of young children with Down syndrome. Consistent with Cielinski, Vaughn, Seifer, and Contreras (1995), these findings suggested that comparable performance by children with Down syndrome and children who are developing typically may come about through different maternal pathways. Higher levels of direct assistance balanced by praise and an avoidance of restriction may be particularly beneficial to raise the level of play behavior of children with Down syndrome to a level comparable to that of children who are developing typically.

Research suggests that maternal education and social class are positively related to the richness of social experiences provided for school-age children with Down syndrome (Sloper, Turner, Knussen, & Cunningham, 1990). However, the role of family background in influencing mothers' speech directed at their young children with Down syndrome has received minimal empirical attention. Within the literature on mothers' speech to their children who are typically developing, however, distinctively different maternal communicative styles have been shown to be associated with mothers' demographic and sociocultural characteristics (Bradley & Caldwell, 1984; Hart & Risley, 1992). Specifically, less-educated mothers from less-advantaged backgrounds tend to talk to their children less frequently (Gottfried, 1984), ask fewer questions (Schieffelin & Ochs, 1983), and use more restrictions (Hart & Risley, 1992) than do their more-educated and socially advantaged counterparts. Likewise, maternal age has been found to be positively associated with more optimal parenting within samples including both adolescent and adult mothers (McKenry, Kotch, & Browne, 1991; Ragozin, Basham, Crnic, Greenberg, & Robinson, 1982; Reis & Herz, 1987; Schilmoeller & Baranowski, 1985). This study examined whether similar associations existed between mothers' communicative styles and their family background characteristics such as maternal age, education, and social status in families of children with Down syndrome.

Parents, clinicians, and researchers are interested in understanding mothers' patterns of communication with their children with Down syndrome and recognizing some of the factors that potentially influence these patterns. This chapter not only explores the range of variability that exists in the communication patterns of mothers of children with Down syndrome but also assesses the role of children's developmental status, vocal and nonvocal play behavior, and background characteristics on maternal patterns of communication. Observations of mother–child interactions inevitably yield variations in mothers' propensities to structure their children's play (Bornstein & Tamis-LeMonda, 1990). The specific focus of this chapter is on variables influencing mothers' tendencies to use vocal directives to guide their children's behavior and their tendencies to use praise and restriction to mark their children's successes and transgressions, respectively.

An overriding challenge for mothers is to tailor their directive strategies and positive and negative feedback to the developmental capacities and interactive behavior of their young children while providing a mutually rewarding context of warmth and responsiveness to their children's interactive signals (Brazelton, 1988). In an effort to go beyond the assessment of simple frequencies of maternal vocalizations, this chapter examines mothers' tendencies to structure their children's play in a manner that is responsive to their children's communicative signals. A measure called *responsive vocal structuring* is used in an attempt to identify which mothers are most likely to use their young children's early vocal efforts at communication as opportunities to provide vocal guidance of their children's play. For example, one question the researchers attempted to answer by using this measure was whether mothers of young children with Down syndrome spontaneously follow their children's vocalizations with directive vocalizations in order to further encourage their children's vocal and play behavior. Individual differences in children's developmental status and behavior, together with individual differences in mothers' ages, education, and socioeconomic characteristics, are examined as potential contributors to mothers' use of responsive vocal structuring.

SAMPLE CHARACTERISTICS AND PROCEDURES OF THE STUDY

Children with Down syndrome and their mothers were recruited from an ongoing research and service program at The Waisman Center at the University of Wisconsin–Madison.

Sample Population

The sample included 28 young children with Down syndrome. The children's chronological ages ranged from 16 to 30 months (mean [*M*] age = 22.3 months) and their mental ages ranged from 10 to 17 months

(M age = 14.0 months). The sample included 15 male and 13 female children; 8 of the children were firstborns (see Table 2).

All of the families involved in the study were Caucasian. The sample was composed of two-parent families who had had some participation in intervention programs. Mothers' ages ranged from 22 to 42 years (M age = 33 years). Mothers' educational levels averaged 14 years (range = 12–18 years). Examination of families' socioeconomic status (Hollingshead, 1958) indicated that 21% of the families were classified as major business or professional, 46% were classified as minor professional or technical, and 28% were classified as skilled or semiskilled workers.

During a visit to the laboratory playroom, an experienced tester administered the Bayley Scale of Mental Development (Bayley, 1969) as the best available measure of children's developmental status. Because many of the children received Mental Development Index (MDI) scores below 50, scores were calculated for these children using extrapolated norms published by Naglieri (1981), as recommended by Crawley and Spiker (1983). The mean MDI score for this sample of children with Down syndrome was 48.3 (range = 25–74). Their delays in mental ability (chronological age minus mental age) ranged from 3 to 17 months (M = 8.3 months).

Following the Bayley assessment, mothers were asked to play with their children as they typically would if they had some free time at home. A large assortment of age-appropriate toys were made available to the children and their mothers. An unobtrusive camera in the corner of the playroom was used to record mother–child free-play interaction on videotape for 15 minutes.

Behavior Coding

Researchers at The Waisman Center laboratories have gone to great lengths over the years to develop a reliable videotape-coding system

Table 2. Sample characteristics

Characteristic	Mean	Range
Children		
Mental age	14.0	10–17 months
Chronological age	22.3	16–30 months
Developmental delay	8.3	3–17 months
Mental Development Index	48.3	25–74
Family		
Maternal age	33.3	22–42 years
Maternal education	14.6	12–18 years
Socioeconomic status	45.5	22–66

for collecting objective behavioral data from the naturalistic free-play observations of mothers and their young children (see Barratt et al., 1992; Roach et al., 1998; Stevenson, Ver Hoeve, Roach, & Leavitt, 1986). Because of these researchers' interest in both the frequency and the patterning of mothers' and children's behaviors, they developed a customized computer program that allowed them to independently record the behaviors of each communicative partner. Using this system, two viewings are made of each videotape. The first is used to code maternal vocalizations, and the second is used to code children's behaviors. As each maternal or child behavior is entered into the computer, custom software is used to record its precise time of occurrence. This procedure allows observations to be made in real time without requiring the observer to look away from the videotape to record behavior codes or to rewind the videotape to determine exact times of occurrence. The separate strings of behavior codes from the mother and child and their associated times of occurrence are synchronized and combined by computer to produce a sequential time-ordered record of the interaction. This allows us to summarize the data in three ways: 1) mothers' vocal communication (e.g., directives, praise, restrictions), 2) children's vocal and nonvocal play behavior, and 3) maternal responsive structuring (see Table 3).

To assess maternal responsive vocal structuring, the extent to which vocal signals from the young children with Down syndrome were followed by directive vocalizations from their mothers was examined. Because the measure of responsive vocal structuring used in the study, described in detail later, controlled both for frequencies of children's signaling and for frequencies of mothers' directiveness, it may represent a particularly appropriate means of gauging mothers' sensitivity to the communicative signals of their young children with Down syndrome.

Behavioral Measures

Data from the behavioral observations were summarized in three ways. Each of these measures is described in the subsections that follow.

Mothers' Vocal Communication On the first viewing of the videotapes, three measures of mothers' vocal communications with their young children with Down syndrome (see Table 4) were recorded:

1. Vocal directives included explicit or implicit requests for action (e.g., "Go get the ball," "Why don't you turn the page?"), requests for objects (e.g., "Give me the doggy," "Can Mommy have the spoon?"), or requests for information (e.g., "Who's on the telephone?" "What does the piggy say?").

Table 3. Behavior code definitions

Behavior	Definition
	Mothers' vocal communication
Directive	Vocalization in which the mother requests an action, an object, or information
	Directives that are explicit (e.g., "feed the baby") or implicit (e.g., "Can you make it go?")
Praise	Vocalization conveying praise or approval of the child's behavior or qualities (e.g., "such a good girl," "You did it!")
Restriction	Vocalization conveying rejection or disapproval of the child's behavior or qualities (e.g., "I don't want that," "Such a naughty girl")
	Children's vocal and play behavior
Vocalization	Vocalization that carries communicative meaning or expresses joy or amusement
Negative vocalization	Vocalization specifically conveying rejection, denial, or defiance; vocal objection or protest characterized by a vocal outburst
Simple object play	Any simple manipulative, functional, or exploratory play in which a child engages with a toy (e.g., roll the car, talk on the telephone)
Complex object play	Any relational, combinatorial, or symbolic play behavior that results in a positive outcome (e.g., put driver in the truck, stack blocks)
Oppositional play	Behavior that is aggressive or destructive and likely to bring a negative response from the mother (e.g., throwing or knocking down toys, hitting, kicking)

2. Vocal praise reflected mothers' approval of the child's behavior or qualities (e.g., "Good job!" "That's right," "You are really good at puzzles").
3. Vocal restrictions conveyed mothers' rejection or disapproval of their children's behavior or qualities (e.g., "Don't hit the dolly," "Take that out of your mouth," "That's not a toy").

Interobserver reliability averaged 84% for mothers' communication behaviors. A summary of the average frequencies and range of mothers' communication behaviors indicated that directive vocalizations were particularly common and that vocal restrictions were relatively rare (see Table 4).

Children's Vocal and Nonvocal Play Behavior On the second viewing of the videotapes, five children's behaviors were coded (see Table 5). Children's vocalizations consisted of any vocal effort to communicate with the mother. Vocal behaviors were coded either as *simple vocalizations* or as *negative vocalizations* if they conveyed objection, rejection, or protest. Children's play behaviors were coded as *simple object*

Table 4. Frequencies of mothers' vocal communication

Mothers' vocal behavior	Frequency measures		
	Mean	Minimum	Maximum
Directive	116.7	19.8	181.3
Praise	14.9	2.3	39.4
Restriction	8.0	0.0	27.0

Note: Measures are based on 15-minute observations of mother–child free play in a laboratory.

play, which referred to children's simple manipulative, functional, or exploratory play with the toys; *complex object play,* which referred to children's relational, combinatorial, or symbolic play behaviors that resulted in a successful outcome; and *oppositional play,* which referred to aggressive or destructive play behaviors. Interobserver reliability averaged 78% for the coding of children's vocal and play behaviors. A summary of the average and range of children's vocal and play behaviors indicated particularly high rates of children's simple vocalizations and relatively low rates of negative vocalizations and oppositional play (see Table 5).

Maternal Responsive Structuring   Event lag sequential analyses (Sackett, 1979) were used to assess the association between children's vocalizations and their mothers' vocal directive behavior. Specifically, mothers' tendencies to follow their children's vocalizations with a vocal directive (i.e., a request for some object, action, or information) served as the measure of responsive vocal structuring. This approach involves examining the sequence of mothers' and children's behaviors, finding each child's vocalization, and calculating the probability that the following behavior will be a maternal vocal directive. The strength of the association between the children's vocalizations and their mothers' directives was assessed by using beta, or the natural log

Table 5. Frequencies of children's behaviors

Children's behavior	Frequency measures		
	Mean	Minimum	Maximum
Vocalization	71.7	3.6	117.7
Negative vocalization	4.5	0.0	34.9
Simple object play	27.0	6.0	80.2
Complex object play	10.9	0.0	30.9
Oppositional play	1.7	0.0	6.0

Note: Measures are based on 15-minute observations of mother–child free play in a laboratory.

of the odds ratio (Fienberg, 1980; Wickens, 1989).[1] This contingency measure was used to reflect the likelihood that mothers would capitalize on their children's early communicative efforts as opportunities to provide further vocal guidance or structure.

INDIVIDUAL DIFFERENCES IN MATERNAL COMMUNICATION

In a comparative study (Roach et al., 1998), mothers of children with Down syndrome as a group were found to be more likely than mothers of children of a similar mental age who were typically developing to emit a directive vocal or nonvocal behavior following their children's vocalizations. This chapter focuses specifically on maternal vocal directives following children's vocalizations (i.e., responsive vocal structuring) in an attempt to explore factors that may be associated with these individual differences.

Maternal Directiveness

It is clear from the wide range of frequencies presented in Tables 4 and 5 that mothers of children with Down syndrome adopt diverse styles of communicating with their prelinguistic young children and that their children also exhibit a wide range of vocal and nonvocal play behaviors. During the course of a 15-minute free-play session, the 28 mothers varied considerably in their use of directives with their children with Down syndrome. The least directive mother emitted slightly more than one directive per minute, whereas the most directive mother issued an average of 12 directives per minute (i.e., one directive every 5 seconds). These data illustrate that mothers of children with Down syndrome do not universally adopt a directiveness strategy. Rather, mothers' levels of directiveness with their children with Down syndrome fall along a broad continuum from minimal to possibly excessive. Recall that directive communication included a range of both implicit and explicit vocal requests for specific objects, actions, or information from the children. Mothers sought to direct their children's attention to the toys and to encourage their children to play actively with the toys. Certain types of maternal directive behavior within a joint attentional context have been shown to be facilitative of communicative development in young children who are developing typically (Akhtar, Dunham, & Dunham, 1991; McCathren, Yoder, & Warren, 1995; Pine, 1992). Given the prevalence of research on the

---

[1]The odds ratio is calculated as the ratio of the relative likelihood that the child's vocalization will be followed by a maternal directive divided by the likelihood that other behaviors will be followed by maternal directives.

issue of maternal directiveness and the tendency in the literature to view high levels of maternal directiveness as inherently negative, however, it is imperative that attempts be made to determine why some mothers are prone to using this strategy so much more readily than other mothers (see Marfo, 1990, for a review).

Results of the correlational analyses (see Table 6) indicated that neither children's actual behaviors during the free-play session nor their family background characteristics were significantly related to their mothers' tendencies to direct or guide their children's play. However, maternal directiveness was significantly related to children's developmental status as assessed by their Bayley MDI scores. That is, within this group of children with Down syndrome, the children who were more developmentally advanced received more vocal direction from their mothers than did the children who were less developmentally advanced. Given the inability to infer causality from correlations, it is impossible to say whether higher levels of directiveness by these mothers may have spurred these children with Down syndrome toward greater developmental competence or whether children who were more developmentally advanced in fact elicited higher levels of directiveness from their mothers. Suffice it to say that in interactions with their children with Down syndrome who were relatively more cognitively advanced, mothers tended to direct and guide their chil-

Table 6. Correlations between maternal communication and children's characteristics

| Children's characteristics | Maternal communication | | | |
	Directive	Praise	Restriction	Responsive structuring
Developmental status				
Mental Development Index	.44*	.15	.42*	−.16
Children's behavior				
Vocalization	−.14	−.08	−.21	.21
Negative vocalization	.04	.05	.38*	−.08
Simple object play	−.30	.04	−.00	.46*
Complex object play	.18	.50**	.12	.10
Oppositional play	−.02	−.01	.36+	−.38*
Family background				
Mothers' age	−.07	−.25	−.23	.52**
Mothers' education	−.04	−.21	−.46*	.40*
Families' socioeconomic status	−.14	−.18	−.15	.39*

+ $p < .10$
* $p < .05$
** $p < .01$

dren toward increasingly higher goals. In interactions with their children who were less cognitively advanced and who perhaps failed to benefit from their mothers' directive strategies, mothers seemed to devise alternative, less directive, possibly less challenging communicative strategies in order to maintain a satisfying dyadic interaction with their young children.

These results are inconsistent both with those of Marfo (1992), who found that mothers tended to be more directive with their children who were less cognitively competent and developmentally delayed, and with those of Crawley and Spiker (1983), who found no significant relationship between maternal directiveness and the developmental competence of toddlers with Down syndrome. Mothers' reliance on the directiveness strategy, although generally adaptive and appropriate with children who are atypically developing, may also be dependent on some threshold above which mothers are able to recognize and appreciate the effectiveness of their guiding interventions. Mothers of young children with Down syndrome may gauge their levels of directiveness by the extent to which their children exhibit the cognitive potential to benefit from their maternal efforts. Thus, some mothers of children with Down syndrome may be more directive than other mothers of children with Down syndrome because some children with Down syndrome are relatively more cognitively competent than other children with Down syndrome and might thereby be more receptive to their mothers' guiding interventions.

Maternal Praise

The behavioral code for maternal praise included any attempts by the mothers studied to comment positively on their children's qualities or behaviors. Obviously, some mothers are more likely to use positive feedback to guide their young children than are other mothers. Overall frequencies in this sample ranged from two instances of praise in 15 minutes to almost three instances of praise per minute (see Table 4). One might predict that mothers' provision of positive verbal feedback in the form of praise would be in large measure dependent on the behavior of their children during the play session. In fact, children who exhibited more complex levels of play with the toys in the laboratory playroom had mothers who expressed more praise and encouragement (see Table 6). Given the bidirectional nature of this relationship, it is again unclear whether the mothers' praise provided the incentive for these children with Down syndrome to engage in more complex object play or whether these children's higher levels of complex object play simply warranted higher frequencies of praise. In any case, it is reassuring to note the positive association between these logically related events. Moreover, because neither the developmental status of the children nor the background characteristics of the family seemed to be significantly associated with mothers' tendencies to praise their young children, complex play with objects turned out to be the only variable among those assessed to be related to frequencies of positive feedback from these children's mothers.

Maternal Restriction

The code for restriction included a variety of negative verbal communications designed by the mothers to convey rejection, disapproval, or restriction. Overall, this was a somewhat infrequently occurring event, with a few mothers avoiding the use of restriction altogether, although the most restrictive mother engaged in almost two restrictions per minute over the course of the 15-minute play session (see Table 4).

Multiple determinants of negative feedback by these mothers of children with Down syndrome included the children's developmental status, the children's tendencies to engage in negative vocal and non-vocal play behaviors, and the mothers' levels of education (see Table 6). A positive link between mothers' frequencies of restriction and their children's developmental status indicated that children with Down syndrome who were more developmentally advanced were more frequently restricted by their mothers than were children with Down syndrome who were less developmentally advanced. These results suggested that more competent children may simply be more capable of getting into trouble and therefore require more negative feedback from their mothers. Alternatively, regular use of restrictive communication may be part of a larger teaching strategy that mothers reserve for children with Down syndrome who exhibit greater cognitive potential.

Correlations indicated that children who exhibited more negative vocalizations and engaged in more oppositional play had mothers who exhibited more restriction or disapproval. This rather consistent association between negative vocal and nonvocal behaviors by the children and negative communicative feedback from their mothers suggested a somewhat discouraging possibility that heightened levels of negativity by either communicative partner may be matched by heightened levels of negativity by the other communicative partner. A negative link between the frequency of maternal restriction and the number of maternal years of education indicated that more-educated mothers were less likely to rely on restriction or negative vocalizations as a strategy for shaping their children's behavior than were less-educated mothers. This finding is consistent with research with children who are developing typically and their mothers (e.g., Gottfried, 1984; Hart & Risley, 1992). Because less restriction has been linked with subsequently higher levels of intelligence in children who are typically developing (Hart & Risley, 1992), less-restrictive behavior by mothers of young children with Down syndrome may also be beneficial for the developmental outcomes of children with Down syndrome. Conversely, young children with Down syndrome in families in which the mother has less education may be at some risk for experiencing higher levels of restriction.

Responsive Vocal Structuring

In the study, *responsive vocal structuring* was used to refer to the likelihood of mothers' following their children's vocalizations with vocal directives. This measure reflects a more complex communicative capacity than what can be assessed with simple frequency data. The probability that mothers would follow their children's vocalizations with a vocal directive varied across mothers from 8% to 100%, with a mean of 25%. In other words, considerable variability was evident in mothers' tendencies to use responsive vocal structuring.

Correlations between the measure of responsive vocal structuring and the other measures suggested that mothers who responded to their children's early attempts at communication with vocal direction were more likely to have children who frequently demonstrated simple play with the toys and were less likely to have children who exhibited oppositional toy play (see Table 6). This assessment of the patterning rather than the simple frequency of mothers' directive behaviors suggested that mothers' selective use of directives following their children's vocalizations may represent a key strategy for enhancing children's positive participation in play.

Mothers' tendencies to use responsive vocal structuring were unrelated to their children's developmental status. This tendency suggested that mothers' levels of responsive vocal structuring were influenced more by the actual behaviors of their children than by the global measure of their children's cognitive capacities. Children who were positively engaged in toy play may have elicited more responsive vocal structuring from their mothers. By attending directly to their children's vocalizations, mothers who employed responsive vocal structuring may have been able to sensitively guide and enhance their children's positive engagement in toy play. Thus, maternal directives that followed children's vocalizations may have provided the essential structure to allow their children the freedom for greater engagement with the toys and less oppositional toy play.

Mothers' background characteristics were clearly related to maternal responsive vocal structuring or to mothers' tendencies to follow their children's vocalizations with vocal directives (see Table 6). Significant positive correlations indicated that children with older mothers, children with more-educated mothers, and children in families of higher socioeconomic status were likely to experience more maternal responsive vocal structuring than were children with younger, less-educated mothers from less-advantaged circumstances. Thus, it was the vocal interactions of the older, more-educated mothers from more-advantaged circumstances that were particularly likely to be characterized by responsive vocal structuring.

Consistent with previous research (Crawley & Spiker, 1983; Marfo, 1990), no significant correlation was found between mothers' frequencies of directiveness and their tendencies to use responsive vocal structuring. Whereas mothers' frequencies of directives were associated with the global measure of their children's developmental status (MDI), mothers' tendencies toward responsive vocal structuring were associated both with their children's actual behaviors and with their own background characteristics. In contrast, mothers' frequencies of restriction were found to be negatively associated with mothers' tendencies toward responsive vocal structuring. That is, mothers who used responsive vocal structuring were significantly less likely to be restrictive with their young children with Down syndrome than were mothers who did not use responsive vocal structuring.

Responsive vocal structuring, the measure of behavioral contingency employed in these analyses, was designed to reflect the likelihood that mothers would respond to the vocalizations of their young children with Down syndrome with vocal directives. Mothers who employed this strategy were essentially trying to build on the communicative efforts of their young children by encouraging even greater interactive contributions. Goldberg (1979) suggested that mothers may feel ineffective if their children are unresponsive to them. Research with mothers of children with Down syndrome has indicated that higher levels of maternal responsiveness have indeed been associated with higher levels of child involvement (Schneider & Gearhart, 1988). Mothers may increase their levels of responsiveness as their children show evidence of responding to their efforts to guide them (Lojkasek, Goldberg, Marcovitch, & MacGregor, 1990). Correspondingly, children with Down syndrome who are perceived to be less responsive to their mothers' initiatives may ultimately experience their mothers' being less responsive to their needs (see, e.g., Barrera, Watson, & Adelstein, 1987).

Children with Down syndrome who exhibit less simple object play or who choose to engage in oppositional play may limit their own opportunities for responsive maternal structuring. Furthermore, mothers who fail to display responsive vocal structuring in their interactions with their young children with Down syndrome may be missing opportunities to enhance their children's positive play behaviors. Because the multitude of factors that influence communication patterns are not yet well delineated even within the literature on parenting children who are typically developing (Gleason, 1988), further exploration of intrafamily and extrafamily sources of individual differences such as social support and maternal well-being (see Dunst & Trivette, 1986) could provide useful insight for future research and could be beneficial for guiding future intervention efforts.

CONCLUSIONS

Placing the results of this investigation into a larger context may make it possible to confirm what mothers of children with Down syndrome and mothers of children with other disabling conditions (Cahill & Glidden, 1996) have perhaps discovered naturally in their relationships with their young children. Communication involves the sending and receiving of signals, the exchange of information, and the give and take of ideas. Over time, as the cognitive and language delays of children with Down syndrome become increasingly evident, impairments in these children's skills as effective social partners become increasingly notable. Individual circumstances may vary, but mothers must ultimately adapt their patterns of communication in order to maintain effective communicative relationships with their young children with Down syndrome. Mothers clearly play an active role in structuring their children's play interactions (Bruner, 1983; Vygotsky, 1978). Aspects of children's developmental status, behavior, and family background seem to be related to their mothers' adaptations.

All of the children in the study discussed in this chapter participated in intervention programs to some extent, and, although little detail is available regarding the quantity and quality of information received by these families, one can assume that many received some guidance on parent–child interactions and communication from these intervention programs (Spiker & Hopmann, 1997). Either spontaneously or as a result of these intervention efforts, these mothers, relative to mothers of children who are typically developing, were more likely to use directiveness, praise, and restriction as tools for enhancing the play of their young children with Down syndrome. Although individual differences were clearly evident, these mothers seemed to adapt to the sometimes challenging task of parenting their children with Down syndrome and seemed to demonstrate competence in their abilities to provide direction and positive and negative feedback in a manner that was sensitive and responsive.

From a clinical standpoint, it is notable that these mothers of children with Down syndrome exhibited a range of sensitivity as measured by their tendencies to engage in responsive vocal structuring with their young children. That is, some mothers consistently followed their children's vocalizations with vocal directives, thus attempting to encourage greater interactive participation from their children. Other mothers were less likely to show this pattern of vocal responsiveness. Examination of individual differences revealed that this more complex communicative strategy was considerably more characteristic of the older, more-educated mothers from higher socioeconomic backgrounds than it was of younger, less-educated, and less socioeconomically advantaged mothers. Because responsive vocal structuring was closely linked to children's positive engagement with the toys in the laboratory playroom, it may prove beneficial to assist younger and less-educated mothers in adopting this strategy. Less-educated mothers of young children with Down syndrome may intuitively adapt their communicative strategies by becoming particularly directive in an effort to encourage their children's participation. Without recognition of the importance of responsive vocal structuring, however, their efforts at enhancing their children's play may fall short of achieving their ultimate purpose. Using interaction-based intervention approaches as a model (e.g., Tannock, Girolametto, & Siegel, 1992), mothers of children with Down syndrome in general, but especially the mothers who are more disadvantaged, may benefit from specific guidance to help them recognize the importance of and develop appropriate strategies for linking directiveness in their early communications with the early vocalizations of their young children with Down syndrome.

REFERENCES

Akhtar, N., Dunham, F., & Dunham, P.J. (1991). Directive interactions and early vocabulary development: The role of joint attentional focus. *Journal of Child Language, 18*, 41–49.

Barratt, M.S., Roach, M.A., & Leavitt, L.A. (1992). Early channels of mother–infant communication: Preterm and term infants. *Journal of Child Psychology and Psychiatry, 33*, 1193–1204.

Barrera, M.E., Watson, L.J., & Adelstein, A. (1987). Development of Down's syndrome infants with and without heart defects and changes in their caretaking environment. *Child: Care, Health and Development, 13*, 87–100.

Bayley, N. (1969). *Manual for the Bayley Scales of Infant Development.* San Antonio, TX: The Psychological Corporation.

Bell, R.Q., & Harper, L.V. (1977). *Child effects on adults.* Mahwah, NJ: Lawrence Erlbaum Associates.

Berger, J., & Cunningham, C.C. (1983). Development of early vocal behaviors and interactions in Down's syndrome and nonhandicapped infant–mother pairs. *Developmental Psychology, 19*, 322–331.

Bornstein, M.H., & Tamis-LeMonda, C.S. (1990, September). Activities and interactions of mothers and their firstborn infants in the first six months of life: Covariation, stability, continuity, correspondence, and prediction. *Child Development, 61,* 1206–1217.

Boyce, G.C., & Barnett, W.S. (1991, September). *Parenting children with Down syndrome: Do your activities and attitudes differ from parents of children without Down syndrome?* Paper presented at the 19th annual convention of the National Down Syndrome Congress, Boston.

Bradley, R.H., & Caldwell, B.M. (1984). 174 children: A study of the relationship between home environment and cognitive development during the first 5 years. In A.W. Gottfried (Ed.), *Home environment and early cognitive development: Longitudinal research* (pp. 5–56). San Diego: Academic Press.

Brazelton, T.B. (1988). Importance of early intervention. In E. Hibbs (Ed.), *Children and families: Studies in prevention and intervention* (pp. 107–120). Madison, CT: International Universities Press.

Brooks-Gunn, J., & Lewis, M. (1984). Maternal responsivity in interactions with handicapped infants. *Child Development, 55,* 782–793.

Bruner, J.S. (1983). *Child's talk: Learning to use language.* New York: W.W. Norton.

Cahill, B.M., & Glidden, L.M. (1996). Influence of child diagnosis on family and parental functioning: Down syndrome versus other disabilities. *American Journal on Mental Retardation, 101,* 149–160.

Caissie, R., & Cole, E.B. (1993). Mothers and hearing-impaired children: Directiveness reconsidered. *Volta Review, 95,* 49–59.

Cielinski, K.L., Vaughn, B.E., Seifer, R., & Contreras, S.J. (1995). Relationships among sustained engagement during play, quality of play, and mother–child interaction in samples of children with Down syndrome and normally developing toddlers. *Infant Behavior and Development, 18,* 163–176.

Crawley, S.B., & Spiker, D. (1983). Mother–child interactions involving two-year-olds with Down syndrome: A look at individual differences. *Child Development, 54,* 1312–1323.

Crnic, K.A., Friedrich, W.N., & Greenberg, M.T. (1983). Adaptation of families with mentally retarded children: A model of stress, coping, and family ecology. *American Journal of Mental Deficiency, 88,* 125–138.

Davis, H., Stroud, A., & Green, L. (1988). Maternal language environment of children with mental retardation. *American Journal on Mental Retardation, 93,* 144–153.

Donovan, W.L., & Leavitt, L.A. (1991). Maternal self-efficacy and response to stress: Laboratory studies of coping with a crying infant. In T. Field, P.M. McCabe, & N. Schneiderman (Eds.), *Stress and coping in infancy and childhood* (pp. 47–68). Mahwah, NJ: Lawrence Erlbaum Associates.

Dunst, C.J., & Trivette, C.M. (1986). Looking beyond the parent–child dyad for the determinants of maternal styles of interaction. *Infant Mental Health Journal, 7,* 69–80.

Fienberg, S.E. (1980). *The analysis of cross-classified categorical data* (2nd ed.). Cambridge, MA: MIT Press.

Fischer, M.A. (1987). Mother–child interaction in preverbal children with Down syndrome. *Journal of Speech and Hearing Disorders, 52,* 179–190.

Girolametto, L.E. (1988). Developing dialogue skills: The effects of a conversational model of language intervention. In K. Marfo (Ed.), *Parent–child interaction and developmental disabilities: Theory, research, and intervention* (pp. 162–180). New York: Praeger.

Gleason, J.B. (1988). Language and socialization. In F.S. Kessel (Ed.), *The development of language and language researchers: Essays in honor of Roger Brown* (pp. 269–280). Mahwah, NJ: Lawrence Erlbaum Associates.

Goldberg, S. (1979). Premature birth: Consequences for the parent–infant relationship. *American Scientist, 67,* 214–222.

Gottfried, A.W. (1984). Home environment and early cognitive development: Integration, meta-analysis, and conclusions. In A.W. Gottfried (Ed.), *Home environment and early cognitive development: Longitudinal research* (pp. 329–342). San Diego: Academic Press.

Hart, B., & Risley, T.R. (1992). American parenting of language-learning children: Persisting differences in family–child interactions observed in natural home environments. *Developmental Psychology, 28,* 1096–1105.

Hodapp, R.M. (1995). Parenting children with Down syndrome and other types of mental retardation. In M.H. Bornstein (Ed.), *Handbook of parenting: Vol. I. Children and parenting* (pp. 233–253). Mahwah, NJ: Lawrence Erlbaum Associates.

Hodapp, R.M., Dykens, E.M., Evans, D.W., & Merighi, J.R. (1992). Maternal emotional reactions to young children with different types of handicaps. *Developmental and Behavioral Pediatrics, 18,* 118–123.

Hollingshead, A.B. (1958). *Two-Factor Index of Social Status.* Unpublished manuscript, Yale University, New Haven, CT.

Jasnow, M., Crown, C.L., Feldstein, S., Taylor, L., Beebe, B., & Jaffe, J. (1988). Coordinated interpersonal timing of Down syndrome and nondelayed infants with their mothers: Evidence for a buffered mechanism of social interaction. *Biological Bulletin, 175,* 355–360.

Landry, S.H., Garner, P.W., Pirie, D., & Swank, P.R. (1994). Effects of social context and mothers' requesting strategies on Down's syndrome children's social responsiveness. *Developmental Psychology, 30,* 293–302.

Lojkasek, M., Goldberg, S., Marcovitch, S., & MacGregor, D. (1990). Influences on maternal responsiveness to developmentally delayed preschoolers. *Journal of Early Intervention, 14,* 260–273.

Maccoby, E.E., & Martin, J.A. (1983). Socialization in the context of the family: Parent–child interaction. In E.M. Heatherington & P.H. Mussen (Eds.), *Handbook of child psychology: Vol. 4. Socialization, personality, and social development* (pp. 1–101). New York: John Wiley & Sons.

Mahoney, G. (1988). Maternal communication style with mentally retarded children. *American Journal on Mental Retardation, 92,* 352–359.

Mahoney, G., Fors, S., & Wood, S. (1990). Maternal directive behavior revisited. *American Journal on Mental Retardation, 94,* 398–406.

Mahoney, G., & Robenalt, K. (1986). A comparison of conversational patterns between mothers and their Down syndrome and normal infants. *Journal of the Division for Early Childhood, 10,* 172–180.

Marfo, K. (1990). Maternal directiveness in interactions with mentally handicapped children: An analytical commentary. *Journal of Child Psychology and Psychiatry, 31,* 531–549.

Marfo, K. (1991). The maternal directiveness theme in mother–child interaction research: Implications of early intervention. In K. Marfo (Ed.), *Early intervention in transition: Current perspectives on programs for handicapped children* (pp. 177–203). New York: Praeger.

Marfo, K. (1992). Correlates of maternal directiveness with children who are developmentally delayed. *American Journal of Orthopsychiatry, 62,* 219–233.

Marfo, K., & Kysela, G. (1988). Frequency and sequential patterns in mothers' interactions with mentally handicapped and nonhandicapped children. In K. Marfo (Ed.), *Parent–child interaction and developmental disabilities: Theory, research, and intervention* (pp. 64–89). New York: Praeger.

Mash, E.J., & Terdal, L. (1973). Modification of mother–child interactions: Playing with children. *Mental Retardation, 11,* 44–49.

McCathren, R.B., Yoder, P.J., & Warren, S.F. (1995). The role of directives in early language intervention. *Journal of Early Intervention, 19,* 91–101.

McKenry, P.C., Kotch, J.B., & Browne, D.H. (1991). Correlates of dysfunctional parenting attitudes among low-income adolescent mothers. *Journal of Adolescent Research, 6,* 212–234.

Mundy, P., Sigman, M., Kasari, C., & Yirmiya, N. (1988). Nonverbal communication skills in Down syndrome children. *Child Development, 59,* 235–249.

Naglieri, J.A. (1981). Extrapolated developmental indices for the Bayley Scales of Infant Development. *American Journal of Mental Deficiency, 85,* 548–550.

Pellegrini, A.D., Brody, G.H., & Sigel, I.E. (1985). Parents' teaching strategies with their children: The effects of parental and child status variables. *Journal of Psycholinguistic Research, 14,* 509–521.

Petersen, G.A., & Sherrod, K.B. (1982). Relationship of maternal language to language development and language delay of children. *American Journal of Mental Deficiency, 86,* 391–398.

Pine, J.M. (1992). Maternal style at the early one-word stage: Reevaluating the stereotype of the directive mother. *First Language, 12,* 169–186.

Ragozin, A.S., Basham, R.B., Crnic, K.A., Greenberg, M.T., & Robinson, N.M. (1982). Effects of maternal age on parenting role. *Developmental Psychology, 18,* 627–634.

Reis, J.S., & Herz, E.J. (1987). Correlates of adolescent parenting. *Adolescence, 22,* 599–609.

Roach, M.A., Barratt, M.S., Miller, J.F., & Leavitt, L.A. (1998). The structure of mother–child play: Young children with Down syndrome and typically developing children. *Developmental Psychology, 34,* 77–87.

Rodrigue, J.R., Morgan, S.B., & Geffken, G. (1990). Families of autistic children: Psychological functioning of mothers. *Journal of Clinical Child Psychology, 19,* 371–379.

Sackett, G.P. (1979). The lag sequential analysis of contingency and cyclicity in behavioral interaction research. In J.D. Osofsky (Ed.), *Handbook of infant development* (pp. 623–649). New York: John Wiley & Sons.

Schieffelin, B.B., & Ochs, E. (1983). A cultural perspective on the transition from prelinguistic to linguistic communication. In R.M. Golinkoff (Ed.), *The transition from prelinguistic to linguistic communication* (pp. 115–131). Mahwah, NJ: Lawrence Erlbaum Associates.

Schilmoeller, G.L., & Baranowski, M.D. (1985). Childrearing of firstborns by adolescent and older mothers. *Adolescence, 20,* 805–822.

Schneider, P., & Gearhart, M. (1988). The ecocultural niche of families with mentally retarded children: Evidence from mother–child interaction studies. *Journal of Applied Developmental Psychology, 9,* 85–106.

Sloper, P., Turner, S., Knussen, C., & Cunningham, C. (1990). Social life of school children with Down's syndrome. *Child: Care, Health and Development, 16,* 235–251.

Spiker, D., & Hopmann, M.R. (1997). The effectiveness of early intervention for children with Down syndrome. In M.J. Guralnick (Ed.), *The effectiveness of early intervention* (pp. 271–305). Baltimore: Paul H. Brookes Publishing Co.

Stevenson, M.B., Ver Hoeve, J.N., Roach, M.A., & Leavitt, L.A. (1986). The beginning of conversation: Early patterns of mother–infant vocal responsiveness. *Infant Behavior and Development, 9,* 423–440.

Tannock, R. (1988). Mothers' directiveness in their interactions with their children with and without Down syndrome. *American Journal on Mental Retardation, 93,* 154–165.

Tannock, R., Girolametto, L., & Siegel, L.S. (1992). Language intervention with children who have developmental delays: Effects of an interactive approach. *American Journal on Mental Retardation, 97,* 145–160.

Vygotsky, L. (1978). *Mind in society.* Cambridge, MA: Harvard University Press.

Wasserman, G.A., Smilansky, M., & Hahn, H. (1986). A matter of degree: Maternal interaction with infants of varying levels of retardation. *Child Study Journal, 16,* 241–253.

Wickens, T.D. (1989). *Multiway contingency tables analysis for the social sciences.* Mahwah, NJ: Lawrence Erlbaum Associates.

II

Assessment and Intervention

Section II includes chapters on adapting assessment methods to effectively evaluate young children with Down syndrome. Assessing speech, language, and communication skills requires voluntary participation by the child if meaningful information is to be obtained. Developing the child's motivation to develop speech and language skills requires an examiner who is skilled in early assessment as well as experienced with the behavior of young children. The behavior of children with Down syndrome is particularly taxing, requiring testing protocols that can optimize their attention, memory, and speech production skills. Chapter 7 describes the guidelines used to develop an evaluation protocol for speech, language, and communication skills of children with Down syndrome ages 2–10 years. Most of the procedures that the authors used had to be modified to accommodate the abilities of these children. In Chapter 8, Rosin and Swift discuss an intervention program that has proved effective in improving the speech intelligibility of children with Down syndrome. This program is the result of their extensive intervention experience with this population.

In Chapter 9, Murray-Branch and Gamradt discuss the many ways in which assistive technology can be used to improve overall communicative effectiveness. As a result of their clinical experience, they provide numerous examples of how technology can be used to improve classroom instruction, speech and language intervention, and everyday communication. Augmentative and alternative communication systems can help children grasp the symbolic nature of words as well as provide a message delivery system while speech is unintelligible.

In the final chapter in this section, Leddy and Gill describe their success in improving the speech intelligibility of adolescents and adults with Down syndrome. The work described in Chapter 10 is remarkable because it refutes the long-held assumption that speech intelligibility cannot be improved in older children (i.e., children older than age 8 or 9 years) and adults with Down syndrome. They demonstrate that motivation and visual feedback are the keys to continued improvement of speech skills. These chapters make an important contribution to the literature by addressing topics that have been long neglected, providing new data to help parents and professionals select therapeutic techniques.

7

Evaluating Communication to Improve Speech and Language Skills

Jon F. Miller, Mark Leddy, and Lewis A. Leavitt

Since 1986, when the March of Dimes Down Syndrome Project began at The Waisman Center at the University of Wisconsin–Madison, the center has received letters, calls, and e-mail messages from hundreds of parents, speech-language pathologists, teachers, social workers, and other family members or caregivers. These inquiries are often about the best speech-language interventions for individuals with Down syndrome. People's responses are frequently revealing when they are asked to describe a child's language comprehension or when asked "What is this young person's speech production like?" and "What is this person's cognitive and functional status?" It is startling to be told that a child's language comprehension cannot be assessed because the tests on the market are not appropriate for someone with Down syndrome or because the child does not test well. It is equally surprising to be told that the individual's speech production can no longer be tested either because his or her speech has plateaued or because older individuals with Down syndrome cannot improve their speech. The purpose of this chapter is to present contemporary data and assessment guidelines that redirect the communication evaluation process for people with Down syndrome.

UNIQUE FEATURES OF SPEECH, LANGUAGE, AND HEARING ABILITIES OF CHILDREN WITH DOWN SYNDROME

Several research investigators (see Balkany, Downs, Jafek, & Krajicek, 1979; Maurizi, Ottavini, Paludetti, & Lungarotti, 1985; Van Dyke, Popejoy, & Hemenway, 1990) have described the frequency of hearing loss in children with Down syndrome and the effects that such loss can have on their speech and language development. More than 75% of young children with Down syndrome are found to have at least a mild hearing problem sometime during childhood. The hearing problems of young children with Down syndrome fluctuate, but about one third of those children have recurring problems throughout early childhood that can lead to greater language and speech delay. This work informs our recommendation for frequent hearing testing.

Much has been learned (see Chapman, 1997; Fowler, 1995; Miller, 1988; Miller, Leddy, Miolo, & Sedey, 1995) about the verbal language characteristics of people with Down syndrome:

- People with Down syndrome display a specific language impairment relative to cognitive development.
- Communication performance is characterized by better language comprehension than production.
- The vocabulary use of people with Down syndrome is better than their grammar use.
- Progress in speech and language performance are linked to several factors, including hearing status, speech motor function status, nonverbal cognitive level, and chronological age.
- These data demonstrate the possibility of continued progress in communication beyond early childhood.

Many clinicians (see Kumin, 1994, 1996; Leddy & Gill, 1996; Stoel-Gammon, 1997; Swift & Rosin, 1990) have studied the speech intelligibility characteristics of people with Down syndrome and the means of treating the associated speech problems. Their findings, outlined in the following list, affect how clinicians evaluate speech in people with Down syndrome:

- Most family members have some difficulty understanding the speech of their children or siblings with Down syndrome in everyday communication.
- The oral anatomy and motor function of people with Down syndrome affect their speech development and speech intelligibility over time.

- People of all ages with Down syndrome who have reduced speech intelligibility can benefit from intervention protocols to improve effective communication and/or maximize speech production skills.

Buckley (1993, 1995) discovered much about the development of writing and literacy skills in people with Down syndrome, as outlined in the following list:

- Children with Down syndrome as young as age 3 years succeed at reading single words.
- Children participating in early reading and writing experiences that continue through their school years evidence better communication and academic skills than their peers with less literacy experience.

ASSESSMENT PRINCIPLES FOR CHILDREN WITH DOWN SYNDROME

Several basic assessment principles specific to people with Down syndrome should help clinicians at several levels of the assessment process in selecting measures, adjusting how items are presented, and accounting for attention and motivation shifts. These simple practices are based on the combined experiences of the authors of this chapter and those of the clinicians and researchers with whom they have collaborated. If these principles are taken into account in planning and conducting a communication evaluation of a person with Down syndrome, then the reward will be the best data possible for developing a sound intervention plan. Adherence to the following principles, some of which are discussed in greater detail later in this chapter, will lead to optimal assessment practices with people with Down syndrome:

1. Utilize all information sources about current communication abilities across contexts: school, home, child care, and community.
2. Review all data available on motor and cognitive development as well as perceptual (hearing and vision) status to direct the assessment decision-making process.
3. Use flexible communication assessment protocols that can meet the specific attention shifts and motivational challenges of people with Down syndrome.
4. Make sure you account for context in your assessment. Contrast measures conducted within familiar contexts, such as child- or family-centered approaches to assessment, with those taken in the absence of relevant context (i.e., standardized tests).

5. Use criterion-referenced, development-specific milestones, as well as norm-referenced measures.
6. Assess the child's communication environments as well as the child's independent status.
7. Recognize that testing procedures will change across developmental periods as children become more competent and testing content becomes more complex.
8. Adjust testing in light of the knowledge that many people with Down syndrome have a history of failing tests and "escaping" formal assessment procedures.
9. Complete a thorough evaluation that includes assessing cognition, hearing, verbal and printed language comprehension and production, oral nonspeech function, and speech behaviors.
10. Remember that a child's performance in an office or a clinic may represent a very thin slice of the full range of his or her capability.

Communication Development Findings

The discerning clinician who plans to conduct a communication evaluation of a person with Down syndrome and his or her family should be knowledgeable about current assessment approaches, procedures, and tests; the communication characteristics of people with Down syndrome; and the best evaluation practices to employ with this group of people.

A great deal of contemporary information has been disseminated in the 1990s about the communication skills of people with Down syndrome that many families and clinicians are still learning. It is important to synthesize this research about the communication skills of people with Down syndrome to inform practicing clinicians and families. This information is available through various media, including the routine publications of hypermedia sources, videotapes, audiotapes, textbooks, and journals (see Appendixes A–C in this volume). In addition, researchers and clinicians regularly report information about the cognition, hearing, speech, and language of people with Down syndrome to family members and clinicians at international, national, and regional conferences. Reviews of their research are located in chapters in this book, for example, and in Chapman (1997) (for language and communication development) and Stoel-Gammon (1997) (phonological development).

Current Views of Assessment and Their Relevance to Children with Down Syndrome

Discussions of language assessment generally note two basic types of measures: standardized tests and nonstandardized tests. *Standardized tests* have specific administration protocols and normative data for interpreting the performance of an individual using the age or standard score criteria. These tests must be given in the same way each time to ensure that the results reflect consistent administration. These tests are typically required for formal assessments of status, school-based multidisciplinary team evaluations, or other placement decisions. Their principal value lies in their constancy. Each administration is the same; every child is treated the same, regardless of his or her ability. Standardized tests define the performance standard. This "one size fits all" approach rarely meets the needs of children with diverse skills when attempting to document optimum performance. Children's performance continues to be unreliable on standardized tasks beyond age 3 years. This statement is verified whenever the data on any standardized test for children under age 3 years are reviewed because the examiner will find that all measures of variability decrease with the increasing age of the individuals tested. Coggins (1998) identified a number of limitations of standardized tests for children with developmental disabilities:

- Most standardized tests are examiner directed, limiting the child's initiations and spontaneous language.
- Translating standardized test results into clinically useful results is often difficult.
- Rigid test administration guidelines make it difficult to use most measures with atypical children.
- Parents are typically excluded from active participation in the assessment process.

A general rule of thumb is the younger the child, the more variable his or her performance on measures requiring precise administration of items. Young children have little experience with testing and cannot take the examiner's perspective in producing relevant responses to test items. Until the 1990s, there were few standardized measures that could reliably document the language and communication development of young children. The new procedures focus more on the child, improving motivation, and engaging the child to prompt spontaneous responses while providing standardized data sets for interpretation.

Beginning in the 1970s, alternatives to standardized measures began to emerge to provide descriptions of children who were untestable using formal tests. People have referred to these procedures by various names such as *informal tests, criterion reference procedures, play-based assessments, authentic assessments,* or *functional assessments.* All of these procedures had a common goal: to provide a description of the child's language and communication performance based on primarily spontaneous behavior. Many of these procedures have been system-atized so that observations can be recorded in formal ways to aid the clinician in interpretation of the child's behavior. Many of these systems have criterion-referenced data that are derived either from the research literature or from samples of children performing the procedure.

Language Production Samples of language performance can be recorded, transcribed, and analyzed using developmental data aggre-gated in the literature for interpretation (Miller, 1981). Computer pro-grams have been developed to do a variety of analyses of spontaneous language samples at the word, morpheme, utterance, and discourse levels of performance (Miller & Chapman, 1997). The current versions of *SALT: Systematic Analysis of Language Transcripts* not only allow the user to describe the child's language on more than 60 different meas-ures but also each of these measures can be compared with a sample of age-matched peers ages 3–13 years. Data sets for conversational samples and narrative samples exist.

An alternative to recording language samples is the MacArthur Child Development Inventories (CDI) (Fenson et al., 1993). The de-velopment of these procedures was motivated by the limited access to the full range of children's behaviors in laboratory or clinical environ-ments in children younger than age 3 years. Recognizing that parents know the most about their children's development, the researchers who developed the CDI sought a means by which to tap into that knowledge by bypassing retrospective memory or by recalling the ex-act content of their children's speech. The result was the creation of two parent report measures of language: the infant scale for children ages 8–16 months and the toddler scale for children ages 16–30 months. These measures have been found to be equally as reliable for parents of children with Down syndrome as it is for parents of children who are developing typically (Miller, Leddy, Miolo, & Sedey, 1995). They are particularly effective in documenting a child's complete pro-duction vocabulary, at least as complete as it can ever be recorded without creating a diary of every child utterance.

The CDI has also been used to record the words that the child produces using American Sign Language. The measure is efficient, tak-ing about 20 minutes of parents' time; it can be repeated fairly often to document progress; and it can be machine scored, thus reducing data reduction and analysis time. At The Waisman Center, a CDI is scanned, scored, and interpreted and a letter is written to the child's physician by a computer in a few minutes. The CDI infant scale pro-vides data on children's vocabulary comprehension as well as their production of gestures. The CDI gesture scale is particularly important for children with Down syndrome in documenting these children's production attempts using nonstandard means. The CDI gesture scale is an important teaching tool to help parents to recognize all of their children's communicative attempts.

Language Comprehension   Advances in assessing language comprehension have been slower to emerge. Miller and Paul (1995) provided 26 nonstandardized measures of language comprehension taken from the research literature. These measures span children's development from ages 7 months to 10 years for prelinguistic behaviors and lexical, syntactic, and discourse features of language. All of these measures have criterion-referenced data for the features tested as well as scoring forms to reliably score children's performance. All of these measures recognize the child's perspective, and methods are discussed to select and organize stimuli that conform to the child's interests. Focusing on children's interests improves their motivation to respond appropriately. Performance can be documented by using linguistic context or, in cases in which context has been removed, to force the child to respond to only the linguistic stimuli. Documenting the children's ability to use context in understanding language is critical to describing their language comprehension abilities in service of communication.

New and Improved Testing Methods

Two tests of young children's language successfully combine the consistency and comparability of standardized tests with the descriptive power of nonstandardized assessment procedures. These tests are Assessing Prelinguistic and Early Linguistic Behavior in Developmentally Young Children (ALB) (Olswang, Stoel-Gammon, Coggins, & Carpenter, 1987) and Communication and Symbolic Behavior Scale (CSBS) (Wetherby & Prizant, 1993). (For a detailed review of assessment instruments aimed at identifying early language impairment, see McCathren, Warren, & Yoder, 1996). The CSBS also has the distinction of exploring children's emerging communicative development from a social interaction perspective. This advantage provides clinicians with data on the child's everyday use of language based on observations of parent–child interactions. These data can then be used to describe strengths and limitations in children's communication performance.

There are two other procedures that focus on documenting communication strengths and limitations. The first is the Preschool Functional Communication Inventory (PFCI) (Olswang, 1996). Functional assessments focus on overall performance and communication, regardless of the form of the communication or how it is accomplished. These measures are used to document behavior in everyday contexts. A second measure of this type is the Assessment, Evaluation, and Programming System (AEPS) for Infants and Children (Bricker, 1993). AEPS uses elicitation probes to examine six areas: social, fine motor, gross motor, adaptive, cognitive, and social communication. The intent of AEPS is to document baseline performance and to monitor change within classroom-based intervention programs. These procedures organize developmental information to guide the observer in documenting children's communication performance. The observation and elicitation probes provide professionals with appropriate tools to measure performance in child-directed ways. As with all methods, the finer the level of detail of the measurement instrument, the more time that must be invested in the assessment process.

Developing an Assessment Protocol

A speech-language pathologist can help a family design the best communication intervention plan for an individual with Down syndrome when an extensive and complete evaluation has been conducted. This evaluation requires assessing an individual's cognitive status; hearing, verbal, and printed language comprehension and production; oral-motor nonspeech function; speech behaviors; and any communication strengths that the individual possesses or any ancillary areas that the clinician thinks needs to be attended to, such as the person's use of augmentative or alternative communication devices. This thorough evaluation provides a springboard to the development of an effective intervention plan.

Parents' Contribution

Parents have a wealth of information about their children's performance in a variety of contexts. The effective clinician uses parent information liberally to supplement his or her own assessment and observations. When obtaining information from parents, ask concrete rather than abstract questions. Elicit concrete examples. For example, do not ask "Does she respond when you play Pat-a-cake?" Instead, ask "What exactly does she do or say when you play Pat-a-cake?" Parents have such information. It is up to the clinician to ask the right questions to elicit the information as reliably as possible. Eliciting reliable information about past events is difficult because of the fragility of people's memories. Asking about current behavior is much more reliable, as documented (Fenson et al., 1993) in the research on the development of the CDI. For past events, help parents by providing specific dates (e.g., birthdays, holidays). Rather than saying "Tell me what words she used last year," ask "Around the time of the last Super Bowl [*or* At her last birthday], what words was she using?"

Different Assessment Approaches Need to Be Implemented

A number of characteristics associated with Down syndrome make the assessment process challenging. Many of these already have been mentioned in this chapter, but they are reviewed here along with some suggestions that may help the reader develop an effective assessment protocol. Most of the suggestions in this section are not new or even particularly innovative, but they have emerged in the evaluation of several hundred children with Down syndrome at The Waisman Center since the late 1980s.

Consistency of Responding   One of the most frustrating aspects of assessing the communication of children with Down syndrome is their lack of consistency in responding during assessment tasks. This variability is associated with 1) rapid shifts in attention and 2) motivation. Clearly, these constructs are interrelated, and it would be impossible to determine which is causal for any specific behavior. Motivation is central to maintaining consistent response patterns. If a task that is sufficiently motivating can be provided, the children's attention is maintained and their responses are more consistent. Wishart (1988, 1993) suggested that variable performance is simply part of Down syndrome and that there are no behavioral adjustments that can alter their behavior. Rondal (1995), however, documented exceptional performance among people with Down syndrome, which supports the present authors' view. Successful assessments can be conducted with careful preparation and understanding of the interests of each child, what activities they like, and what holds their attention at home and at school. Then the clinician needs to select assessment materials that can be embedded into these activities. One technique found to be helpful is to ask parents to bring their children's favorite toys to the clinic to motivate their children to talk in language-sampling contexts. Clearly, when testing is done in new contexts with new people, children are likely to be distracted by the lack of familiarity and will exhibit increasing inconsistency in responding. Establishing consistency of people and places whenever possible improves the consistency of children's responding. All young children are inconsistent in responding to tasks out of context. This period of inconsistent performance is prolonged—perhaps twice as long—in children with Down syndrome.

Memory   Chapman (1997) and Marcell and Weeks (1988) documented verbal short-term memory impairments in this population. These impairments have significant implications for assessment of language comprehension and production, particularly when standardized procedures are used that require that children process specific stimuli and remember it long enough to provide to appropriate responses. Clearly, memory impairments may also contribute to behaviors that may be labeled as inattention or may result in inconsistent response patterns. Providing visual support enhances children's performance in testing verbal material. Visual support may involve pictures, graphic material, or printed words. Having an instant camera available, for example, is useful in developing practice-testing protocols for comprehension where pictures of family members and clinical staff can be taken and used as stimuli. Modeling correct responses or actions is helpful. In attempting to elicit oral motor movements, the examiner models the appropriate movements by, for example, opening the mouth wide, sticking out the tongue, or pursing the lips. Large mirrors allowing the child and the examiner to sit side by side are also motivating. Considering the influence of memory is important in interpreting children's performance on any elicited task.

Motor Limitations   Although many clinicians report that children with Down syndrome have motor impairments because of hypotonia (Desai, 1997; Frith & Frith, 1974), there is little data to support this claim. The motor impairments of children with Down syndrome are quite variable: Some children perform at age level, and others show significant motor limitations that delay the onset of ambulation and other motor milestones. Testing protocols must take into consideration the motor demands on the child relative to the child's motor abilities. Assessment tasks should require motor responses within the child's capabilities.

Vision   France (1992) provided a detailed account of the visual impairments of children with Down syndrome. He followed a group of 90 children and reported that 49% had visual acuity impairments, with myopia being the most common. He also documented oculomotor imbalance in more than 40% of the children he studied, with convergent strabismus accounting for the majority of these cases. In the majority of the cases France studied, vision correction could be achieved by eyeglasses alone. Thus, clinicians need to be sure the children they are testing can see the testing stimuli. France reported that infants and children with severe disabilities can be tested for acuity with behavioral techniques that use eye gaze as a response. These procedures have proved reliable for those who cannot provide judgment about visual stimuli. Conducting this testing procedure requires a skilled clinician. The results in children's behavior can be dramatic, and the implications for their language and communication skills improvement can be enormous.

Hearing   Hearing remains an issue for children with Down syndrome because of frequent episodes of otitis media. Monitoring hearing should be done every 6 months for the first 10 years of life. Of children whom we studied at The Waisman Center, 33% always had a hearing loss, 33% sometimes had a hearing loss, and only 33% never had a hearing loss. These data were derived after screening out all of those children with significant hearing loss that was due to other causes. In testing oral language, one must know the child's hearing status on that particular day. Audiologists skilled in testing young children can provide relatively efficient assessments of hearing status. Referral to a pediatrician can improve children's hearing through medication if middle-ear infection is present.

CONCLUSIONS

Designing a testing protocol requires attention to the levels of skills and abilities that the child is expected to bring to the task. These skill- and ability-level factors include attentional and motivational differences, memory impairments, hearing and visual impairments, and motor limitations. Each of these can compromise the outcome of the assessment if accommodations are not made. It is also clear that in order to optimize the consistency of children's responding, alternative testing formats must be implemented. Testing formats need to be context based and child centered rather than examiner centered, and flexible in format. Many testing procedures mentioned earlier in this chapter meet these criteria. In addition, a skilled clinician must follow the child's lead to implement these functional, criterion-referenced, play-based assessments. Observational methods also provide important information. Most notable are the recording of speech and language samples that can be transcribed by using the international phonetic alphabet or standard orthography. These transcripts can then be analyzed by using a variety of calculations by computer or by hand. These methods provide clinicians with the opportunity to analyze children's language use in a variety of speaking contexts.

Children with Down syndrome are disadvantaged by standardized tests. These tests assume performance characteristics that are not available to children with Down syndrome: attention to tasks when requested to do so by adults who are strangers, motivation by external stimuli, and sustained effort on tasks for which there is no context relevant to their daily activities. Children's performance levels increase as the rigidity of the testing protocol decreases. Their scores are more reliable because testing can be done over time, data can be collected from other sources such as parents and teachers, and data can be developed by using observational techniques such as language samples in which audiotape and videotape recordings can be used.

Interpretation of children's responses must always be rendered relative to the context in which they occurred. Was the behavior elicited or spontaneous? If elicited, was there a linguistic or an activity-based context present, providing support for the child to generate the appropriate response? If no context was available, as is the case with most standardized procedures, how is a nonresponse treated by the test? As an error? Children who do not respond when expected achieve poor scores on standardized tests. The problem, however, is the poor match of the child to the testing procedure. Information gathered without consideration of the testing context does not reflect the abilities of the individual tested. The interpretation of information gathered by using measures adapted to the child's abilities must be interpreted with caution. The perceptual, motor, and memory impairments of this population require that clinicians always hold open the possibility that data from one testing session may not be reliable. Always expect the data to be wrong, leaving the possibility that the child can do better. Listed at the end of this chapter are some important resources on language assessment that will be useful when developing specific assessment protocols.

Keeping the discussion in this chapter in mind will guide the development of a protocol that will produce reliable data that can be interpreted as a valid index of the speech and language performance of children with Down syndrome. An informed analysis of the assessment procedures and their careful implementation will provide the necessary data for planning intervention programs that will result in improved language and communication skills for people with Down syndrome.

REFERENCES

Balkany, T.J., Downs, M.P., Jafek, B.W., & Krajicek, M.J. (1979). Hearing loss in Down's syndrome: A treatable handicap more common than generally recognized. *Clinical Pediatrics, 18,* 116–118.

Bricker, D. (1993). *Assessment, evaluation, and programming system (AEPS) for infants and children: Vol. 1. AEPS measurement for birth to three years.* Baltimore: Paul H. Brookes Publishing Co.

Buckley, S. (1993). Developing the speech and language skills of teenagers with Down's syndrome. *Down's Syndrome Research and Practice, 1,* 63–71.

Buckley, S. (1995). Teaching children with Down syndrome to read and write. In L. Nadel & D. Rosenthal (Eds.), *Down syndrome: Living and learning in the community* (pp. 158–169). New York: Wiley-Liss.

Chapman, R. (1997). Language development in children and adolescents with Down syndrome. *Mental Retardation and Developmental Disabilities Research Reviews, 3,* 307–312.

Coggins, T.E. (1998). Clinical assessment of emerging language: How to gather evidence and make informed decisions. In A.M. Wetherby, S.F. Warren, & J. Reichle (Eds.), *Communication and language intervention series: Vol. 7. Transitions in prelinguistic communication* (pp. 233–259). Baltimore: Paul H. Brookes Publishing Co.

Desai, S. (1997). Down syndrome: A review of the literature. *Oral Surgery, Oral Medicine, Oral Pathology, Oral Radiology, & Endodontics, 84*(3), 279–285.

Fenson, L., Dale, P.S., Reznick, J.S., Thal, D.J., Bates, E., Hartung, J., Pethick, S., & Reilly, J. (1993). *MacArthur Communicative Development Inventories (CDI)*. San Diego: Singular Publishing Group.

Fowler, A. (1995). Linguistic variability in persons with Down syndrome: Research and implications. In L. Nadel & D. Rosenthal (Eds.), *Down syndrome: Living and learning in the community* (pp. 121–131). New York: Wiley-Liss.

France, T. (1992). Ocular disorders in Down syndrome. In I. Lott & E. McCoy (Eds.), *Down syndrome: Advances in medical care* (pp. 147–156). New York: Wiley-Liss.

Frith, U., & Frith, C. (1974). Specific motor disabilities in Down syndrome. *Journal of Child Psychology and Psychiatry, 15*, 293–301.

Kumin, L. (1994). Intelligibility of speech in children with Down syndrome in natural settings: Parents' perspectives. *Journal of Perceptual and Motor Skills, 78*, 307–313.

Kumin, L. (1996). Speech and language skills in children with Down syndrome. *Mental Retardation and Developmental Disabilities Research Reviews, 2*, 109–115.

Leddy, M., & Gill, G. (1996, July). *Improving communication skills in persons with Down syndrome*. Paper presented at the National Association for Down Syndrome, Miami, FL.

Marcell, M., & Weeks, S. (1988). Short term memory difficulties and Down syndrome. *Journal of Mental Deficiency Research, 32*, 153–162.

Maurizi, M., Ottavini, F., Paludetti, G., & Lungarotti, S. (1985). Audiological findings in Down's syndrome. *International Journal of Pediatric Otorhinolaryngology, 9*, 227–232.

McCathren, R.B., Warren, S.F., & Yoder, P.J. (1996). Prelinguistic predictors of later language development. In K.N. Cole, P.S. Dale, & D.J. Thal (Eds.), *Communication and language intervention series: Vol. 6. Assessment of communication and language* (pp. 57–75). Baltimore: Paul H. Brookes Publishing Co.

Miller, J.F. (1981). *Assessing language production in children: Experimental procedures*. Baltimore: University Park Press.

Miller, J.F. (1988). The developmental asynchrony of language development in children with Down syndrome. In L. Nadel (Ed.), *The psychobiology of Down syndrome* (pp. 167–198). Cambridge, MA: MIT Press.

Miller, J.F., & Chapman, R.S. (1997). *SALT: Systematic Analysis of Language Transcripts* (DOS-Windows version 4.1) [Software program]. Madison: University of Wisconsin–Madison, The Waisman Center, Language Analysis Laboratory.

Miller, J.F., Leddy, M., Miolo, G., & Sedey, A. (1995). The development of early language skills in children with Down syndrome. In L. Nadel & D. Rosenthal (Eds.), *Down syndrome: Living and learning in the community* (pp. 115–120). New York: Wiley-Liss.

Miller, J.F., & Paul, R. (1995). *The clinical assessment of language comprehension*. Baltimore: Paul H. Brookes Publishing Co.

Olswang, L. (1996). *The Preschool Functional Communication Inventory*. Seattle: University of Washington Speech and Hearing Clinic.

Olswang, L., Stoel-Gammon, C., Coggins, T., & Carpenter, R. (1987). *Assessing linguistic behaviors*. Seattle: University of Washington Press.

Rondal, J. (1995). *Exceptional language development in Down syndrome*. New York: Cambridge University Press.

Stoel-Gammon, C. (1997). Phonological development in Down syndrome. *Mental Retardation and Developmental Disabilities Research Reviews, 3,* 300–306.

Swift, E., & Rosin, M.M. (1990). A remediation sequence to improve speech intelligibility for students with Down syndrome. *Language, Speech, and Hearing Services in the Schools, 21,* 140–146.

Van Dyke, D.C., Popejoy, M.E., & Hemenway, W.G. (1990). Ear, nose, and throat problems and hearing abnormalities. In D.C. Van Dyke, D.J. Lang, F. Heide, S. van Duyne, & M.J. Soucek (Eds.), *Clinical perspectives in the management of Down syndrome* (pp. 15–25). New York: Springer-Verlag New York.

Wetherby, C., & Prizant, B. (1993). *Communication and Symbolic Behavior Scales.* Chicago: Riverside.

Wishart, J. (1988). Early learning in infants and young children with Down syndrome. In L. Nadel (Ed.), *The psychobiology of Down syndrome* (pp. 7–50). Cambridge, MA: MIT Press.

Wishart, J. (1993, October). *Cognitive performance of young children with Down syndrome.* Paper presented at the National Research Conference on Down Syndrome, National Down Syndrome Society, Charleston, SC.

ADDITIONAL RESOURCES

Cole, K.N., Dale, P.S., & Thal, D.J. (Eds.). (1996). *Communication and language intervention series: Vol. 6. Assessment of communication and language.* Baltimore: Paul H. Brookes Publishing Co.

Miller, J.F. (1995). Individual differences in vocabulary acquisition in children with Down syndrome. In C. Epstein, T. Hassold, I. Lott, L. Nadel, & D. Patterson (Eds.), *Etiology and pathogenesis of Down syndrome: Proceedings of the International Down Syndrome Research Conference* (pp. 93–103). New York: Wiley-Liss.

Miller, J.F., Sedey, A., & Miolo, G. (1995). Validity of parent report measures of vocabulary acquisition in children with Down syndrome. *Journal of Speech and Hearing Research, 38,* 1037–1044.

Paul, R. (1995). *Language disorders from infancy through adolescence.* St. Louis: C.V. Mosby.

Wetherby, A.M., Warren, S.F., & Reichle, J. (Eds.). (1998). *Communication and language intervention series: Vol. 7. Transitions in prelinguistic communication.* Baltimore: Paul H. Brookes Publishing Co.

8

Communication Interventions

Improving the Speech Intelligibility of Children with Down Syndrome

Peggy Rosin and Edie Swift

When a child is born with Down syndrome, questions arise about when to begin programming to optimize the child's potential. With the advent of early intervention services and the increased awareness of the pervasiveness of communication problems in children with Down syndrome, speech-language pathologists are increasingly being called on to contribute to intervention plans. Previous and ongoing work emphasizes the high incidence of communication problems in children with Down syndrome (Chapman, 1995; Fowler, 1995; Miller, 1987). Whereas remediation has focused primarily on language and cognitive stimulation (Blackbourn & Bankston, 1989; Broadley & MacDonald, 1993; Hanson, 1987; Horstmeier, 1990; Pueschel, 1988; Spiker & Hopmann, 1997), speech intelligibility has been documented as a major contributor to the communication problems of these children (Horstmeier, 1987; Kumin, 1994; Miller & Leddy, 1998). As of 1999, there are no intervention programs or guidelines to assist speech-language pathologists in developing integrated approaches to meet both the speech intelligibility and language communication needs of this population. This chapter provides remediation suggestions for the communication problems of young children with Down syndrome. The remediation approach considers the multiple components of a child's overall communication profile with an emphasis on facilitating the child's speech intelligibility.

The term *intelligibility* encompasses the articulatory and prosodic parameters of speech production as well as the contextual aspects of communication such as listener experience, word predictability, and utterance length (Ansel, McNeil, Hunker, & Bless, 1983). In addition, linguistic accuracy and complexity and nonverbal cues contribute to intelligibility. *Intelligibility* refers to the degree to which a speaker's message can be understood. According to Kent, "there is no more important attribute of speech than its intelligibility" (1991, p. x). Kumin (1994) surveyed 937 parents of children with Down syndrome concerning their perceptions of their children's speech. Ninety-five percent of the children were experiencing some difficulty in being understood by their parents, with a higher percentage of children experiencing difficulty in being understood by people outside their immediate family circles.

Many factors have been suggested as contributors to the reduced speech intelligibility of children with Down syndrome. Table 1 lists the etiological and interactive factors that may influence the speech intelligibility problems of children with Down syndrome. No single factor can explain the complicated communication profiles often observed in children with Down syndrome. A combination of factors that contribute variably to the experiences of any particular individual makes the study of independent areas quite difficult. These interactions may account for the disparate results researchers report when trying to study specific areas of speech intelligibility impairment.

In an effort to disambiguate the factors relating to intelligibility in adolescents with Down syndrome, Rosin, Swift, Bless, and Vetter (1988) looked across communication profiles that included cognition, language production, language comprehension, oral-motor control, and voice. The results were consistent with the idea that intelligibility is affected by an underlying problem with processing sequential verbal information. The interactive relationship between sequencing and the other parameters listed in Table 1 is unknown. Fowler (1995) reported

Table 1. Contributing etiological and interactive factors

Hearing
Overall hypotonicity
Oral structure and function
Voice
Specific cognitive impairment
Specific language impairment
Environmental and input factors

that verbal sequential skills are a specific area of weakness. She reported that the underlying cause may be at a phonological level, "both in perceiving speech and in encoding incoming acoustic information into a representational format that can be accurately and readily retrieved to serve memory, production, and comprehension" (p. 127). Kay-Raining Bird and Chapman (1994) found a specific impairment in auditory memory span in individuals with Down syndrome that they feel overrides sequential difficulties. Conflicting hypotheses leave the clinician with the task of determining how each of these factors contributes to the intelligibility of the specific child with whom intervention is being provided.

Several intervention principles apply regardless of the child receiving speech-language intervention services:

- The child's family and educational contexts must be a consideration in developing therapy targets.
- Assessment and intervention are ongoing and interactive processes.
- Therapeutic goals, objectives, and activities should be functional for the child and relate to the developmental tasks at hand (e.g., play, activities of daily living, school).
- Intervention activities and targets should be structured in a hierarchical manner (i.e., building on what the child knows and can do and then systematically adding complexity to the task while exploring the effects of facilitative techniques).
- Children are highly variable in their abilities, and they must be approached as individuals.

In addition, in working with children with Down syndrome, it is important to realize that many therapeutic techniques are essentially compensatory strategies. Keeping these principles in mind, focus on the communication profiles of three children with Down syndrome presented in the following sections whose stories help to illustrate intervention suggestions.

MARIA'S STORY

Maria is an 18-month-old toddler with Down syndrome. Mrs. Sanchez, her mother, is a single parent who works full time. Maria has been in an early intervention program since age 6 months. She receives services from a physical and occupational therapist as well as the speech-language pathologist who serves as her service coordinator. Services are provided in the child care environment, which is Mrs. Sanchez's preference. Maria is being reevaluated to look at her progress and to set new outcomes for her individualized family service plan (IFSP). Maria has low muscle tone and chronic otitis media. She gestures and uses some vocalizations to communicate. Mrs. Sanchez is concerned about Maria's overall progress, mouth breathing, drooling, and restless sleep. She wonders whether she should be spending more time with Maria at home and what she can do to help with Maria's overall development.

Maria's Communication Profile

Cognition   On the Bayley Scales of Infant Development (Bayley, 1993), Maria had a raw score of 92, a Mental Development Index of 59, and an age equivalency of 13 months. Informal Piagetian cognitive assessment was consistent with sensorimotor Stage V. Maria's play involved the use of toys in a conventional manner, with some occasional mouthing and throwing.

Language Production   Maria uses two or three words with some gestures to indicate her needs.

Language Comprehension   Maria understands single words within the context of routines.

Speech Production   A limited phonetic inventory has been observed with a babbling analysis showing infrequent production of vowels and bilabials.

Feeding   Maria cannot manage chewy foods and has problems tolerating two textures, especially with lumps. She is drinking from a bottle and has difficulty drinking from a cup without a lid.

Oral Motor   She chronically has an open-mouth posture. Drooling has been a problem but is worse now that she is cutting teeth. Maria's tongue appears large in relationship to the cavity with fissures. She also exhibits tactile defensiveness.

Gross and Fine Motor Skills   Maria is scooting and crawling, is using a whole-hand grasp, and is reported to have low tone and some sensory integration difficulties.

Overall Intervention Goals

- Medical referral for chronic otitis media and consultation about open-mouth posture and sleep pattern
- Audiological referral for hearing testing

- Increase frequency and variety of production
- Increase motor and awareness control
- Expand manual sign language and verbal vocabulary

Medical Intervention

Mrs. Sanchez's concerns about Maria's chronic otitis media resulted in an audiological evaluation that showed a mild to moderate bilateral conductive loss. This is consistent with the literature associating hearing loss with Down syndrome (Chapman, 1995; Fowler, 1995; Teele, Klein, Rosner, & The Greater Boston Otitis Media Study Group, 1984). Downs and Balkany (1988) advocated aggressive intervention for hearing loss associated with otitis media and reported that tympanostomy tubes should be placed when serous otitis media produces hearing loss of greater than 15 decibels in both ears for 2 months or longer or when prophylactic antibiotics do not prevent recurrent otitis media. Downs and Balkany also recommended the use of low-gain, low-power hearing aids for children whose anatomy makes tube placement difficult or for whom anesthesia is questionable. Pressure equalization tubes were recommended for Maria. A sleep study showed an atypical polysomnogram. Decisions were made to monitor the growth of her adenoid tissue. Medical staff will balance possible improvement in her sleep pattern against the increased risk for hypernasality following adenoidectomy for children with Down syndrome (Kavanagh, Kahane, & Kordan, 1986; Marcus, Keens, Bautista, Von, & Ward, 1991).

The physician was also questioned about Maria's open mouth and protruding tongue. The doctor discussed a controversial approach, tongue resection, with Mrs. Sanchez. Although some studies of this approach based on parent report have revealed positive results, Maria's doctor did not recommend this radical surgery for Maria. His decision was based on a comparison of controlled studies that showed little or no effectiveness of glossectomy and facial plastic surgery for children with Down syndrome (Katz & Kravitz, 1989). An additional study by Parsons, Iacono, and Rozner (1987) found no significant differences between groups following tongue resection when comparing consonant productions.

Speech-Language Intervention Goals and Methods

Increasing Frequency and Variety of Production A primary goal for Maria is to increase both the frequency and the variety of her speech productions. A number of facilitative techniques

can be employed to increase Maria's limited vocabulary and phonetic inventory:

1. Ask Mrs. Sanchez to identify a) situations in which Maria is
    more verbal and attentive, b) activities that seem to increase
    Maria's vocalizations or talking, c) games or routines that
    Maria knows and enjoys, and d) whether movement or
    music increases Maria's vocalizations. Mrs. Sanchez's insights
    should be used as a starting point for structuring interactions
    with Maria.
2. Describe, discuss, and model the use of general communi-
    cation facilitation techniques such as being responsive to
    Maria's communicative attempts, directing her speech toward
    the ongoing event, using methods for eliciting and main-
    taining Maria's attention while providing input (e.g., in-
    creased inflection), building turn taking and reciprocal ac-
    tions through routine building, and use of modeling and
    expansion techniques to provide the optimal communica-
    tion environment.
3. Explain and demonstrate communication temptations as de-
    scribed by Wetherby and Prizant (1989). For example, begin
    by building an expectation (e.g., roll a ball back and forth a
    number of times) and then violate the expectation (e.g., roll
    Maria a different object such as a baby bottle, block, or doll)
    to see if Maria remarks. Another example is to place an inter-
    esting object into a container and then place it into a trans-
    parent container with a lid and then observe whether Maria
    objects or asks for help.
4. Structure sound play by arranging the environment to in-
    clude objects and actions on the objects that contain the tar-
    geted sounds. This loading of the environment allows a nat-
    ural way to provide auditory bombardment. If, for example,
    bilabial productions are targeted for intervention, toys to be
    made available might include books, Baby Bop, Barney, bub-
    bles, sheep, and musical instruments. The actions on the ob-
    jects can also stress bilabials such as "pop," "blow," or vocal-
    izations producing "ba" as the instrument is struck.
5. Alter the input provided to Maria by exploring variations in
    suprasegmentals (e.g., rate, duration, pitch) and how these
    affect the child's output. A game can be initiated in which
    there is a slow action while vocalizing. A toy animal or doll
    can be moved slowly as the clinician says "hello" slowly in
    greeting, or a toy car can be rolled slowly as a sound is sus-

tained, for example, /ah/. Pitch can be exaggerated from high to low while checking the child's responsiveness.

6. Imitation should be used to gain volitional control of productions. The natural progression of imitation implies that work will begin with gross motor or visible actions within Maria's repertoire to novel behaviors that she cannot see herself make, such as oral motor movements. Sound production is encouraged by imitation of Maria's production, which can be built into verbal routines and imitation of novel stimuli.

7. Pair action with sound. While building a tower with blocks, say "up" for each block. Alternatively, lift Maria up while saying "up." Supersegmentals can be altered and a routine can be built by repeating the action. After lifting Maria a number of times, wait to see whether she indicates a desire to continue the routine by gesture, vocalization, or word.

8. Use any communicative attempt as a bridge to real words. For example, if Maria says "da," say "down."

9. Discuss with Mrs. Sanchez how these facilitative techniques can be incorporated into Maria's daily activities.

Increasing Motor Awareness and Control   Maria's hypotonicity, open-mouth posture, and feeding difficulties make it appropriate to consider direct work on motor awareness and control. It is unclear how nonspeech activities carry over to speech; however, incorporating work on sucking, swallowing, chewing, and oral awareness may assist in preventing future oral awareness problems and improve oral function. Maria's sensory integration problems require special therapeutic attention. Nelson and De Benabib (1991) discussed the importance of sensory preparation of the oral-motor area and presented a rationale for providing sensory input to children with oral motor problems. Table 2 gives their continua of sensory input and the expected related effects.

One important component of Maria's intervention is to facilitate her ability to exert volitional control over the speech production mechanism. Particular concerns about Maria's drooling and open-mouth posture need to be addressed. Table 3 presents a series of observation and elicitation tasks organized by subsystem that are appropriate for Maria. These tasks are expanded in the appendix at the end of this chapter. During each activity, it is important to consider the effects of Maria's posture and position on her motor control. The motor goals of the various team members should be integrated into each activity.

Table 2. Continua of sensory input

Input variables	Continuum of delivery	Continuum of effects
Rhythm	Slow–Fast	Calming–Stimulating
Pressure	Firm–Light	Organizing–Awakening
Repetitions	Consistent–Inconsistent	Sleep inducing–Alerting
Nature of contact	Palm of hand–Finger pads	Quieting–Challenging
Area of control	Proximal–Distal	Stabilizing–Mobilizing
Movement orientation	Midline–Lateral	
Mouth alignment	Closed–Open	

From Nelson, C.A., & De Benabib, R.M. (1991). Sensory preparation of the oral-motor area. In M.B. Langley & J. Lombardino (Eds.), *Neurodevelopmental strategies for managing communication disorders in children with severe motor dysfunction* (p. 146). Austin, TX: PRO-ED; reprinted by permission.

Language

To increase Maria's vocabulary, the consistent use of words paired to actions and objects is emphasized. These overlearned words or phrases are associated with frequently occurring situations and are the foundation for the development of scripts. Constable (1986) discussed the use of scripts in language therapy, provided an excellent rationale for their use, and gave examples of how scripts can be used to free clients to focus on targeted goals. Yoder, Spruytenburg, Edwards, and Davies (1995) found scripts and verbal routines effective in increasing the mean length of utterance in children with developmental delays. Script use can be applied with children of all ages. For infants and toddlers, routines, fingerplays, songs, and nursery rhymes are important early scripts. Children seem to enjoy these immensely.

Table 3. Observation and elicitation tasks

Lips: Imitate a smile or blowing and tactically encourage Maria to get closure around a straw or tube. Build a routine that cues Maria to close her mouth. Use your hands or her toys to give resistance and stimulation. Say "oh" with inflection while knocking over blocks. Say "mm" while she eats.

Tongue: Use mirror play and imitate tongue movements. Using her toothbrush, provide resistance to the tongue by pushing down on the blade. Encourage Maria to swallow by using tactile cues. Use the early developing tongue sounds such as /d/, /t/, and /n/ and come up with a repertoire of simple words that can be used in routines.

Larynx: Model exaggerated inflection during play, singing, and nursery rhymes.

Respiration: Use bubbles, pinwheels, or toy musical instruments while encouraging prolonged respiration.

There has sometimes been a tendency to automatically adopt or reject the use of manual sign based on a philosophical decision rather than on individual communication profiles. In working with Maria, sign language could be used to augment her vocabulary and to express basic semantic notions. The vocabulary selected should be functional, frequently occurring, and agreed on by Mrs. Sanchez, child care staff, and involved professionals.

Maria's Individualized Family Service Plan

Mrs. Sanchez met with the team working with Maria to discuss progress in preparation for the annual review of the IFSP. Mrs. Sanchez is delighted with Maria's first words and acknowledges the many changes she has seen in her play and interpersonal skills. Desired outcomes were discussed. Maria will continue to receive help with feeding from both the speech-language pathologist and the occupational therapist. In addition, because Maria has utterances that may be either jargon or efforts at communication, intelligibility is becoming a concern. Work on relevant speech goals will continue, as will efforts to increase Maria's verbal and signed vocabulary. Mrs. Sanchez is requesting further help with ideas for work at home. Time will be scheduled to model and discuss at Maria's home the integration of therapy goals into Maria's daily routines and into her play.

JAY'S STORY

Jay is a 6-year-old boy with Down syndrome. He has two younger brothers, Andrew and Gary, who are 1 and 3 years of age, respectively. Jay's father works full time, and his mother works part time. Jay communicates by using speech, producing primarily two- to three-word phrases and occasional longer utterances. Most people can understand his single words; however, his intelligibility decreases as he tries to produce longer sentences. At 2 years of age, Jay was taught to use manual signs to augment his communication and reduce his frustration in getting his message across. His parents discontinued using sign language when Jay was about 4 years of age and started to verbalize more. Signs were no longer functional for him. This pattern of sign use has been reported by Sedey, Rosin, and Miller (1991), who interviewed approximately 50 families. Jay has a history of challenging behaviors. He is currently in an early childhood classroom but is ready to make the transition into the kindergarten classroom, where his parents want him fully included in the

school curriculum. They are worried that Jay will not be understood by the teachers and other children and would like to know
how Jay can best be supported in the classroom. They also want
to know how much and which type of speech-language therapy
he should receive. They would like information about what they
can do to help Jay improve his communication skills, particularly
his speech intelligibility.

Jay's Communication Profile

Academic and Cognition Factors   On pre- and early academic measures, Jay showed that he is mastering concepts
typically learned by children 3½–4 years of age. Subtest
scores revealed specific difficulty in auditory memory. Jay is
able to remember two units (digits or words) consistently but
breaks down when he needs to recall three pieces of
information.

Language Production   Based on a language sample and
using Assigning Structural Stage (Miller, 1981), Jay had a
mean length of utterance of 2.3. This factor, in conjunction
with his expressive syntax, placed his abilities in approximately the 2- to 2½-year age range. Specific syntactic impairments included omission of possessives and plurals and
past-tense verbs.

Language Comprehension   Word comprehension based
on the Peabody Picture Vocabulary Test–Revised (PPVT–R)
(Dunn & Dunn, 1981) Form M was equivalent to a standard
score of 67 and an age equivalent of 3 years, 10 months.
Comprehension of syntax was at the 3-1 level on the Test for
Auditory Comprehension of Language–Revised (TACL–R)
(Carrow-Woolfolk, 1985). Using procedures from Miller and
Paul (1995), it appears that Jay does not understand mean-
ing embedded in word order.

Speech Production   Based on a phonological analysis of
the language sample and an articulation test, Jay was found
to use the following processes: stopping, fronting, and final
consonant deletions. Prolonged vowels were noted. Voicing
errors, transpositions, and inconsistency of errors with accom-
panying articulatory groping were also observed. Jay can imitate most phonemes in single syllables with minor distortion
but has difficulty in imitating longer productions.

> ***Oral Motor Structure and Function*** Jay has irregular dentition, and a narrow, high-arched palate was observed. Difficulty with coordinated speech movements occurs more frequently as his speech rate increases.

Overall Intervention Goals

- Improve Jay's intelligibility by using functional phrases with frequently occurring consonants and words
- Improve Jay's articulatory precision
- Systematically explore the effects of input modifications
- Increase the length and complexity of language
- Support transfer of intelligibility strategies to classroom and home

Speech-Language Intervention

Interventions involving the speech intelligibility of children with Down syndrome necessitate a multifaceted approach involving techniques associated with a variety of disorders. The need for this approach is seen clearly in Jay's communication profile. Most appropriate for Jay's intervention are methods taken from apraxia, phonology, and language. A combination of approaches that incorporate structured opportunities for practice in both drill and social contexts are to be employed. The use of drill and an emphasis on functional language are not mutually exclusive (Camarata, 1995). The clinician's challenge is to integrate the procedures from multiple disorders across these two contexts. A further challenge is to motivate Jay while structuring the practice required for motor learning. Principles of motor learning (Strand, 1998) dictate repetitive motor drill; short, frequent practice periods beginning with distributed practice and including a limited number of targets presented with short, clear directions. Immediate knowledge of results is imperative.

    Developmental Apraxia There are aspects of Jay's speech that are consistent with characteristics reported for children with developmental apraxia of speech (DAS) (Swift, McNeil, & Miller, 1991). These aspects include difficulty in sequencing sounds, prolonged vowels, and inconsistency of errors accompanied by groping. Many authors (Blakeley, 1983; Kent & Adams, 1989; Marquardt, Dunn, & Davis, 1985; Marquardt & Sussman, 1991) have associated the inability of the speaker to volitionally coordinate, program, and sequence movements as hallmarks of apraxia of speech. Regardless of whether the diagnosis of developmental apraxia is appropriate for Jay, associated therapy techniques can be applied to his intervention.

Target Selection When selecting targets for intervention, consider the child's overall speech production and specifically where sequencing breaks down. Riley and Riley (1986) gave continua for modifying complexity of syllable structure. Their program modifications included

1. Number of syllables
2. Number of consonants
3. Number of unvoiced consonants
4. Syllable shape

In Jay's case, incorporating their program to improve motor control is reasonable. A target is selected based on its phonetic and linguistic complexity and functional application. Jay's therapy therefore would begin at the phrase level. Here are some general suggestions that should be applied in crafting specific target phrases:

- Consider functional content, including simple whole words or syllables containing early-developing consonants.
- Teach frequently occurring words and consonants (e.g., /t/, /d/, /n/ = 28.7% of all consonants used).
- Introduce sounds that are visibility-articulated.
- Teach vowels early when they present significant interference with intelligibility.
- Select targets that offer maximal articulatory and acoustic contrasts.
- Attend to performance load factors (e.g., increasing sound sequence and its interaction with syntactic complexity).
- Use derivation techniques whereby a sound that can be produced is modified to produce a sound that cannot be produced (e.g., Jay deletes final consonants, including /g/). The target selected is "dog" and "go" and is used with a progressive reduction in intersyllable interval.
- Increase the length of stimuli as the child is successful.

Input Modification The speech-language pathologist varies the input to the child to increase successful production of the selected targets. Explore the following suggestions to determine their effectiveness with each child:

- Associate a tactile cue such as a cotton-tipped swab on the child's tongue or pressure applied well under the child's tongue, upward and toward the base of the tongue, to reinforce back-of-the-tongue speech productions.

- Pair visual symbols with sounds or words or use a mirror for visual feedback.
- Alter input by exaggerating rhythm, stress, and intonation.
- Teach a slowed rate by modifying vowel length.
- Reinforce movement continuity of sounds (i.e., connect syllables) with gestures and intonations (e.g., gross body movements, tapping, swinging an arm, tone and tone changes).
- Increase the length of the time interval between targets and sessions as the child is successful.
- Increase a delay between the clinician's input and the request for imitation.
- Encourage the child to monitor his or her productions during these modifications.

Phonology The influence of the child's phonological system on his or her overall speech intelligibility must be considered in intervention. Techniques borrowed from interventions for phonological disorders can be applied to the speech intelligibility problems of children with Down syndrome. For example, Jay exhibits a number of phonological processes including final consonant deletion. There are a number of techniques that can be applied to Jay's phonological process, including minimal pair contrasts (Fokes, 1982) and the Cycles Remediation Phonological Approach (Hodson, 1982; Hodson & Paden, 1991). If a minimal pair contrast is applied to Jay's process of final consonant deletion, targets can be set up to contrast pairs that differ by the final consonant only (e.g., boo-boot, bye-bite, bee-beet, bow-boat). The task is structured so that the production of the final consonant is essential for the meaning of the word to be clear to the listener.

Hodson and Paden (1991) stressed that even the most unintelligible speech has its own structure and that finding the systematism of the child's speech system opens the door to remediation. The basic procedures used with children with speech intelligibility impairments is to make the child aware of the characteristics of the target sound and elicit a sufficient number of correct productions of the target so that the child is able to use the new skill in spontaneous speech. A multisensory approach facilitates the development of the targeted patterns:

1. Use of auditory bombardment with an auditory trainer for amplification of the target

2. Pairing gesture with sound to enlist the motokinesthetic system
3. A "watch me and do this" approach and incorporating pictures, toys, and hand gestures to increase visual cues
4. Kinesthetic speech production practice

The approach also stresses the use of linguistic cues by developing semantic awareness and contrasts. Some of these suggestions overlap with those proposed previously in this chapter for interventions for apraxia.

One portion of the Hodson and Paden program that is particularly appealing for children with Down syndrome is the auditory bombardment phase, in which the children listen to a set of targeted words using an auditory trainer. Children with Down syndrome have a high incidence of conductive hearing loss and otitis media, and the use of amplification may assist these children to attend to all elements of the word sequence.

Language   Use of scripts are as appropriate for Jay as they are for Maria. Jay's developmental level dictates a more sophisticated content. Because Jay's speech productions consist primarily of two- and three-word phrases, scripts of three and four words are appropriate. Targeted phrases are introduced during the structured intervention sessions and moved to functional context as soon as possible. Classroom themes can be integrated into the therapy sessions to help Jay build relevant event knowledge (Norris & Damico, 1990). Topic boards are another method of assisting Jay to communicate new vocabulary to his teachers, classmates, and parents. The boards can be designed around classroom topics such as dinosaurs or the calendar.

The Multidisciplinary Team Meeting for Jay

Jay will be in a general kindergarten classroom in the fall. School personnel and Jay's parents developed an individualized education program (IEP) that incorporated a number of approaches for addressing his communication needs across contexts. Individual speech and language sessions, work within the classroom, and consultation with teachers will be provided by the speech-language pathologist. The individual sessions will focus on determining the best strategies for improving Jay's speech intelligibility and allowing for targeted and mass practice of those strategies. The strategies will be transferred into the classroom, with the speech-language pathologist joining the class at appropriate times to monitor Jay's use of the strategies and to model effective ways to provide feedback to Jay. The speech-language pathologist will meet with the kindergarten teacher on a weekly basis to find out on which lessons, concepts, and vocabulary to focus in the upcoming week. This information from the teacher will assist in selecting targets for the individual sessions and to develop topic boards that can be used in the classroom. Effective strategies for improving Jay's speech intelligibility will be shared with his parents through the use of notebooks, copies of the topic boards, and regularly scheduled conversations. Jay's parents will be able to provide valuable insights into what they find helpful in working with Jay and messages that he needs to express at home.

MOLLY'S STORY

Molly is an 11-year-old girl who is in a general sixth-grade classroom and receives support from the special education teacher in math and language. Molly loves books and reads at a third-grade level. Molly is socially active and participates in extracurricular activities at school and in her community. She has been swimming and has been involved with Girl Scouts for the past 3 years. Twice weekly, she meets with the speech-language pathologist, who is targeting improved speech intelligibility. The clinician also spends a short period of time each week in Molly's classroom to facilitate the generalization of Molly's skills. Molly will be included in general education classes as she moves into middle school. This reevaluation of her communication abilities will help in developing her upcoming IEP.

Molly's Communication Profile

Academic and Cognition Factors   Achievement testing and classroom performance revealed that Molly's math, writing, and spelling skills are as expected for a first-grade child, whereas her reading is at a third-grade level. Her short-term auditory memory as tested by the Token Test for Children (DiSimoni, 1978) showed a particular problem in that area.

Comprehension of Language   Molly's responses to the Peabody Picture Vocabulary Test–Revised and The Clinical Assessment of Language Comprehension (Miller & Paul, 1995) indicated that her understanding of single words was at an

(continued)

Molly's Communication Profile (*continued*)

age equivalency of 7 years, 6 months, and that her understanding of syntax and semantics was consistent with her cognitive abilities.

Language Production   Mean length of utterance was 4.4 morphemes, with structures being consistent with Brown's Post–Stage V. Molly's spontaneous speech is marked by multiple disfluencies involving repetitions of initial sounds and syllables as well as frequent reformulation.

Speech Intelligibility   In addition to reformulation, Molly had a number of other speech characteristics consistent with cluttering. Her rate was rapid and tended to increase toward the end of her utterances. Her final consonants were not well marked and were often imprecise. Using the Assessment of Intelligibility of Dysarthric Speech (Yorkston & Beukelman, 1981), Molly's speech was intelligible in 65% of her sentences. She continued to have difficulty in producing fricatives in blends.

Oral Motor Structure and Function   Tongue fissures and large tonsils were observed. Acceleration during single-syllable diadochokinetic tasks and difficulty in sequencing multiple syllable tasks were noted. Imprecision was particularly evident on lingual-alveolar phonemes.

Voice was evaluated by using perceptual judgments as well as *C-Speech* (Milenkovic, 1997), a software program, to determine fundamental frequency and pitch range. Her conversational speech was judged to be monopitch. Her fundamental frequency was lower than for children of Molly's age who were typically developing. Her pitch range was limited, but her vocal intensity was as expected. Her larynx was visualized using a 70-degree rigid endoscope, and diffuse edema was observed. Her nasal resonance was measured by using the nasometer, a computer-based tool that gives a ratio of nasal acoustic energy to oral–nasal energy, and she was found to be hypernasal.

Overall Intervention Goals

- Improve language formulation.
- Use repair strategies to assist Molly when her listener does not understand her intended message.

- Target rate reduction.
- Improve resonance balance to decrease negative attention to Molly's voice.
- Increase vocal inflection through the use of visual cues.

Speech-Language Intervention

Improving Speech Intelligibility Children with Down syndrome have a higher incidence of fluency problems (Miller & Leddy, 1998). Disfluency can be manifested as frank stuttering behaviors as well as difficulty with language formulation. In addition, children with Down syndrome have motor control difficulties, which, as Dworking (1991) noted, co-occur with prosodic insufficiency. Molly's complex of symptoms, which include disfluency, voice, and prosodic difficulties, affects both her speech and her language and underlie her reduced intelligibility. For Molly, techniques borrowed from fluency, voice, and language form the core of her intervention. All of Molly's goals can be worked on simultaneously. The following are some examples of remediation techniques:

- Using Molly's own language sample or narrative as the content for the session (Hogan and Strong, 1994, provided useful strategies for narrative teaching that are organized by story presentation stage, language skill focus, and grade level.)
- Using key words from the narrative to generate sentences to be used for the rate program
  a. Rate reduction sequence:
      1. Model slow rate with controlled stimuli.
      2. Prolong consonants and vowels.
      3. Exaggerate mouth movements.
      4. Stress each syllable.
      5. Stress the final consonants.
      6. Work on appropriate phrasing and pausing.
      7. Try unison speaking and fade the clinician's input.
- Visual learning is frequently a strength for many children with Down syndrome (Buckley, 1995; Buckley & Bird, 1993; Fowler, Doherty, & Boynton, 1995). Written input that incorporates Molly's schoolwork forms a reasonable basis for work on language formulation (Oelwein, 1995).
- Using word retrieval strategies:
  a. Visualization (e.g., "loci," or picturing location of event and recalling objects and actions that occurred in order to recall desired word)

  b. Semantic mapping processes to build event knowledge
  c. Classification activities (e.g., categorize by function, object, synonyms, antonyms)
- Using repair strategies:
  a. Teach Molly to watch for nonverbal indicators and listen for verbal indicators that her message has not been understood.
  b. When confronted with communication failure, teach Molly to think about her strategies (e.g., rate reduction) and apply them in real communicative exchanges.
- Improving resonance balance:
  a. Model exaggerated forward articulatory movement.
  b. Use tactile and/or visual feedback (e.g., nasometer).
  c. Use a tape recorder to provide auditory feedback.

Differences in prosody and sequenced movements have been described in both people with Down syndrome and those with apraxia of speech (AOS) (Schumacher, McNeil, & Yoder, 1984). Melodic intonation therapy (MIT) has been found to be effective for people with AOS (Doszak, McNeil, & Jancosek, 1981). It might therefore be appropriate for children with Down syndrome. MIT was described by Sparks and Holland (1976) as a technique that focused on the formulation of expressive language through the use of intoned sequences. More specifically, MIT consists of hierarchial levels of difficulty. Each level has a series of steps that increase the length of the intoned segments, decrease the person's dependence on the clinician, and reduce the reliance on intonation. MIT is another technique that could be used to work toward Molly's goals. Our clinical experience has indicated that modification in the MIT protocol is necessary. For example, it has been useful to include visual feedback for pitch variation. It is useful to employ functional phrases whenever possible.

The Reevaluation of Progress for Molly

After the reevaluation of Molly's academic and communication abilities, Molly and her parents met with the general and special education teachers and the speech-language pathologist to complete the IEP for Molly's move to the middle school program in the fall. Molly continues to show progress in all areas, with strengths in reading and social skills. Molly will continue to receive the support of a speech-language pathologist, both for direct therapy to improve her intelligibility and for consultation with her teachers to assist in generalizing techniques to classroom contexts.

CONCLUSIONS

This book tries to specify the effects of Down syndrome on people's communication development. Although there is great variability, people with Down syndrome seem to share characteristics, and to anticipate them is to be a more efficient clinician. At the same time, there is a trap in assuming that because a child has Down syndrome, there is a predictable course of intervention. In each case, it is imperative that diagnosis of skills be an ongoing process that leads to a communication profile from which therapeutic decisions are made. In addition, the clinician is faced with extracting therapeutic techniques from across the literatures presented for specific disorders. The human system can present patterns that are arrived at in a number of ways, and only so many behavioral avenues are available from which to draw therapies. Thinking creatively across disorders is one of the satisfying parts of clinical work. If this is not complicated enough, it is necessary to consider that not only the child but also his or her environment is constantly changing.

REFERENCES

Ansel, B., McNeil, M., Hunker, C., & Bless, D. (1983). The frequency of verbal acoustic adjustments used by cerebral palsied-dysarthric adults when faced with communicative failure. In W. Berry (Ed.), *Clinical dysarthria* (pp. 85–108). San Diego: College-Hill Press.

Bayley, N. (1993). *Bayley Scales of Infant Development* (2nd ed.). San Antonio, TX: The Psychological Corporation.

Blackbourn, J.M., & Bankston, D.W. (1989). Development of functional use of oral language in a child with Down syndrome. *Perceptual and Motor Skills, 68,* 1137–1138.

Blakeley, R. (1983). Treatment of developmental apraxia of speech. In W. Perkins (Ed.), *Dysarthria and apraxia* (pp. 23–33). New York: Thieme-Stratton.

Broadley, I., & MacDonald, J. (1993). Teaching short term memory skills to children with Down syndrome. *Down Syndrome: Research and Practice, 1*(2), 56–62.

Buckley, S. (1995). Teaching children with Down syndrome to read and write. In L. Nadel & D. Rosenthal (Eds.), *Down syndrome: Living and learning in the community* (pp. 158–169). New York: Wiley-Liss.

Buckley, S., & Bird, G. (1993). Teaching children with Down's syndrome to read. *Down's Syndrome: Research and Practice, 1,* 34–39.

Camarata, S. (1995). A rationale for naturalistic speech intelligibility intervention. In M.E. Fey, J. Windsor, & S.F. Warren (Eds.), *Communication and lan-*

guage intervention series: Vol. 5. Language intervention: Preschool through the elementary years (pp. 63–84). Baltimore: Paul H. Brookes Publishing Co.

Carrow-Woolfolk, E. (1985). Test for Auditory Comprehension of Language–Revised (TACL–R). Allen, TX: DLM Teaching Resources.

Chapman, R.S. (1995). Language development in children and adolescents with Down syndrome. In P. Fletcher & B. MacWhinney (Eds.), Handbook of child language (pp. 641–663). Oxford, England: Blackwell Publishers.

Constable, C. (1986). The application of scripts in the organization of language intervention contexts. In K.E. Nelson (Ed.), Event knowledge: Structure and function in development (pp. 205–230). Mahwah, NJ: Lawrence Erlbaum Associates.

DiSimoni, F. (1978). Token Test for Children. Hingham, MA: Teaching Resources Corp.

Doszak, A., McNeil, M., & Jancosek, E. (1981). Efficacy of melodic intonation therapy with developmental apraxia of speech. Paper presented at the annual meeting of the American Speech-Language-Hearing Association, Los Angeles.

Downs, M.P., & Balkany, T.J. (1988). Otologic problems and hearing impairment in Down syndrome. In V. Dmitriev & P.L. Oelwein (Eds.), Advances in Down syndrome (pp. 19–34). Seattle, WA: Special Child Publications.

Dunn, L.M., & Dunn, L.M. (1981). Peabody Picture Vocabulary Test–Revised (PPVT–R). Circle Pines, MN: American Guidance Service.

Dworking, J.P. (1991). Motor speech disorders: A treatment guide. St. Louis: Mosby–Year Book.

Fokes, J. (1982). Problems confronting the theorist and practitioner in child phonology. In M. Crary (Ed.), Phonological acquisition (pp. 13–34). San Diego: College-Hill Press.

Fowler, A. (1995). Linguistic variability in persons with Down syndrome: Research and implications. In L. Nadel & D. Rosenthal (Eds.), Down syndrome: Living and learning in the community (pp. 121–131). New York: Wiley-Liss.

Fowler, A., Doherty, B., & Boynton, L. (1995). The basis of reading skill in young adults with Down syndrome. In L. Nadel & D. Rosenthal (Eds.), Down syndrome: Living and learning in the community (pp. 182–196). New York: Wiley-Liss.

Hanson, M. (1987). Teaching the infant with Down syndrome: A guide for parents and professionals. Austin, TX: PRO-ED.

Hodson, B.W. (1982). Remediation of speech patterns associated with low levels of phonological performance. In M. Crary (Ed.), Phonological intervention (pp. 97–115). San Diego: College-Hill Press.

Hodson, B.W., & Paden, E.E. (1991). Targeting intelligible speech: A phonological approach to remediation (2nd ed.). Austin, TX: PRO-ED.

Hogan, K., & Strong, C. (1994). The magic of "Once upon a time": Narrative teaching strategies. Language, Speech, and Hearing Services in the Schools, 25, 76–89.

Horstmeier, D. (1987). Communication intervention. In S.M. Pueschel, C. Tingey, J.E. Rynders, A.C. Crocker, & D.M. Crutcher (Eds.), New perspectives on Down syndrome (pp. 263–268). Baltimore: Paul H. Brookes Publishing Co.

Horstmeier, D. (1990). Communication. In S.M. Pueschel, A parent's guide to Down syndrome: Toward a brighter future (pp. 233–257). Baltimore: Paul H. Brookes Publishing Co.

Katz, S., & Kravitz, S. (1989). Facial plastic surgery for persons with Down syndrome: Research findings and their professional and social implications. American Journal on Mental Retardation, 94(2), 101–110.

Kavanagh, K.T., Kahane, J.C., & Kordan, B. (1986). Risks and benefits of adenotonsillectomy for children with Down syndrome. *American Journal of Mental Deficiency, 91*(1), 22–29.

Kay-Raining Bird, E., & Chapman, R.S. (1994). Sequential recall in individuals with Down syndrome. *Journal of Speech and Hearing Research, 37,* 1369–1380.

Kent, R. (1991). Foreword. In B.W. Hodson & E.E. Paden, *Targeting intelligible speech: A phonological approach to remediation* (2nd ed.). Austin, TX: PRO-ED.

Kent, R., & Adams, S. (1989). The concept and measurement of coordination in speech disorders. In S. Wallace (Ed.), *Perspectives on the coordination of movement* (pp. 415–450). Amsterdam: Elsevier/North Holland.

Kumin, L. (1994). Intelligibility of speech in children with Down syndrome in natural settings: Parents' perspectives. *Perceptual and Motor Skills, 78,* 307–313.

Marcus, C., Keens, T., Bautista, D., Von, P., & Ward, S. (1991). Obstructive sleep apnea in children with Down syndrome. *Pediatrics, 88,* 132–139.

Marquardt, T., Dunn, C., & Davis, B. (1985). Developmental apraxia of speech. In J. Darby (Ed.), *Speech and language evaluation in neurology: Childhood disorders* (pp. 113–129). New York: Grune & Stratton.

Marquardt, T., & Sussman, H. (1991). Developmental apraxia of speech. In D. Vogel & M. Cannito (Eds.), *Treating disordered speech motor control: For clinicians by clinicians* (pp. 341–390). Austin, TX: PRO-ED.

Milenkovic, P. (1997). *CSPEECH* [Computer program]. Madison: University of Wisconsin–Madison.

Miller, J.F. (1981). *Assessing language production in children.* Baltimore: University Park Press.

Miller, J.F. (1987). Language and communication characteristics of children with Down syndrome. In S.M. Pueschel, C. Tingey, J.E. Rynders, A.C. Crocker, & D.M. Crutcher (Eds.), *New perspectives on Down syndrome* (pp. 233–262). Baltimore: Paul H. Brookes Publishing Co.

Miller, J.F., & Leddy, M. (1998). Down syndrome: The impact of speech production on language development. In R. Paul (Ed.), *Communication and language intervention series: Vol. 8. Exploring the speech–language connection* (pp. 163–177). Baltimore: Paul H. Brookes Publishing Co.

Miller, J.F., & Paul, R. (1995). *The clinical assessment of language comprehension.* Baltimore: Paul H. Brookes Publishing Co.

Nelson, C.A., & De Benabib, R.M. (1991). Sensory preparation of the oral-motor area. In M.B. Langley & J. Lombardino (Eds.), *Neurodevelopmental strategies for managing communication disorders in children with severe motor dysfunction* (pp. 131–158). Austin, TX: PRO-ED.

Norris, J., & Damico, J. (1990). Whole language in theory and practice: Implications for language intervention. *Language, Speech, and Hearing Services in the Schools, 21,* 212–220.

Oelwein, P.L. (1995). *Teaching reading to children with Down syndrome: A guide for parents and teachers.* Bethesda, MD: Woodbine House.

Parsons, C.L., Iacono, T.A., & Rozner, L. (1987). Effect of tongue reduction on articulation in children with Down syndrome. *American Journal of Mental Deficiency, 91,* 328–332.

Pueschel, S.M. (1988). *The young person with Down syndrome: Transition from adolescence to adulthood.* Baltimore: Paul H. Brookes Publishing Co.

Riley, G., & Riley, J. (1986). Oral motor discoordination among children who stutter. *Journal of Fluency Disorders, 11,* 335–344.

Rosin, M., Swift, E., Bless, D., & Vetter, D. (1988). Communication profiles of children with Down syndrome. *Journal of Communication Disorders, 12,* 49–64.

Schumacher, J., McNeil, M., & Yoder, D. (1984, November). *Efficacy of treatment: Melodic intonation therapy with developmentally apraxic children.* Paper presented at the annual meeting of the American Speech-Language-Hearing Association, San Francisco.

Sedey, A., Rosin, M., & Miller, J.F. (1991, November). *A survey of sign use among children with Down syndrome.* Poster presented at the annual convention of the American Speech-Language-Hearing Association, Atlanta, GA.

Sparks, R., & Holland, A. (1976). Melodic intonation therapy for aphasia. *Journal of Speech and Hearing Disorders, 41,* 287–297.

Spiker, D., & Hopmann, M. (1997). The effectiveness of early intervention for children with Down syndrome. In M.J. Guralnick (Ed.), *The effectiveness of early intervention* (pp. 271–305). Baltimore: Paul H. Brookes Publishing Co.

Strand, E. (1998, March). *Treatment of developmental apraxia of speech.* Workshop presented in Madison, WI.

Swift, E., McNeil, M., & Miller, J.F. (1991, March). *A second look at the apraxia of speech and linguistic profiles of treated glactosemic children.* Paper presented at the Annual Gatlinburg Conference, Key Biscayne, FL.

Teele, D., Klein, J., Rosner, B., & The Greater Boston Otitis Media Study Group. (1984). Otitis media with effusion during the first years of life and development of speech and language. *Pediatrics, 74*(2), 282–287.

Wetherby, A.M., & Prizant, B. (1989). The expression of communicative intent: Assessment guidelines. *Seminars in Speech and Language, 10,* 77–91.

Yoder, P., Spruytenburg, H., Edwards, A., & Davies, B. (1995). Effect of verbal routine contexts and expansions on gains in the mean length of utterance in children with developmental delays. *Language, Speech, and Hearing Services in the Schools, 26,* 21–32.

Yorkston, B., & Beukelman, D. (1981). *Assessment of intelligibility of dysarthric speech.* Tigard, OR: C.C. Publications.

Appendix: Observation and Elicitation Tasks for the Oral-Motor System

LIPS

1. Nonspeech tasks
   a. Smile (tickle child).
   b. Kiss baby, kiss mommy.
   c. Blow a kiss.
   d. Close lip around a straw or tube.
   e. Use of lips to clean away food placed on lips.
2. Speech tasks
   a. "O, oh" (knock toy over).
   b. "Mm" (while eating).
   c. Set out toys that can be acted upon with bilabial (include p, b, or m).
   d. Say, "Where's mama? Call mama."
   e. Ask names of toys.
   f. Use bubbles and imitate pop as bubbles disappear.
   g. Use xylophone and sing bilabial sound or word up and down scale.
   h. Ask the child to imitate the words, baby, mama, puppy, etc.

TONGUE

To determine what movements the child is capable of making, observe the child's tongue's function by

1. Listing all vowels and consonants to determine the tongue's function in production of the sounds:

     a. t, d, n (tongue tip)
     b. g, k (tongue dorsum)
     c. Vowel production (consider using the cardinal vowel chart)
     d. "ba," "ga," "da," or words such as buttercup, pat-a-cake
2.   Observing use of jaw movement for tongue sounds
3.   Observing spontaneous tongue movements:
     a. Tongue thrust in swallowing
     b. Tongue protrusion in play
     c. Licking lips
     d. Tongue movement while eating

Nonspeech Tasks

1.   Allow the child a taste of a sucker, then hold the sucker in front of the lips to elicit tongue protrusion. Next, hold in the corners of the mouth to elicit tongue lateralization. It may be necessary to hold the child's head gently in midline.
2.   Place peanut butter on a tongue depressor (same procedure as the sucker).
3.   Give the "raspberries"/lingual interlabial bilabial trill.
4.   Use a model (e.g., clinician, puppet, doll) to demonstrate tongue protrusion and lateralization.
5.   Use mirror play.
6.   Pretend to put the baby to sleep by making the /sh/ sound.
7.   Make a "Freddie the Frog tongue"; protrude it rapidly to catch a fly.
8.   Use the tongue to pretend to sweep out the house.
9.   Play "Simon Says" and use mouth movements.

Speech Tasks

1.   If the child will repeat or imitate sounds, syllables, or words, ask the child to imitate words that stress use of the tongue in the following ways:
     a. Tongue tip sounds t, d, n; "no"; "daddy"; "dog"—start with sounds or words not within the child's repertoire
     b. Dorsum of tongue k, g, "go," "cake," "key"
     c. Range of vowel sounds, such as "pi," "pe," "pa," "pu"
2.   Use bite block to determine jaw independence.
3.   Slowly increase diadochokinetic rates.
     a. Model performance.
     b. Use visual markers.
     c. Count number of times p, t, k are produced per second.
     d. Have child produce words as rapidly as possible (e.g., buttercup, pat-a-cake).

JAW

Observe the function of the jaw in the following ways:

1. Mobility of jaw
    a. During speech
    b. Nonspeech movements
    c. Eating
2. Is jaw thrust present?
3. Grading of jaw
    a. Smooth movement while chewing
    b. Smooth movement from consonant-vowel (CV) (B to CV)
4. Stability of jaw
    a. Sustained vowel
    b. Single-word production

To help determine the child's dependence of jaw movement for production of bilabial and lingual sounds, a bite block can be used to sta-
bilize the jaw and eliminate its contribution to sound production. For
children whose cognitive abilities are under 2 or 3 years of mental age,
the use of a bite block is difficult. For use with any child, make certain
that the bite block can be retrieved easily by holding on to it or at-
taching a string to it.

Nonspeech Tasks

1. Chatter your teeth and say "B-r-r-r cold." How many times can
   the upper and lower incisors be clinched together?
2. Make monster faces with various mouth openings.
3. Pretend to yawn.

VELOPHARYNX AND HARD PALATE

Speech Tasks

1. Ask the child to imitate syllable strings or words that contain nasal
   and nonnasal contrasts (e.g., mama, puppy, baby).
2. While looking in the mirror, open your mouth and say "ah"
   sharply and watch the palate move.
3. Vary the context and amount of effort of the production.

LARYNX

Speech Tasks

1. Choose sounds or words within the child's repertoire that contain
   a voiced–voiceless contrast.

2. Elicit variation in pitch by the following means:
   a. Model the sound "ah" on a sliding scale.
   b. Use visual cues (e.g., hands, paper cues) to demonstrate rising and falling pitch contours.
   c. Imitate a fire siren (e.g., Fisher-Price Village).
   d. Use a xylophone to sing a musical scale.
   e. Sing simple songs or nursery rhymes. Ask the child's parents which songs the child may know.
   f. Role-play with Fisher-Price people or puppets and use a low "daddy's voice" and a high "baby's voice."
3. Demonstrate phonation of a vowel (count number of seconds sustained for respiration also). Listen for voice onset and phonation time a) if child imitates, have child repeat the contrasting sounds or words (e.g., Sue–zoo, do–to); b) if child will not imitate, arrange environment to encourage the labeling of toys with voiced–voiceless contrast; and c) if child does not produce words, have toys available that the clinician can act upon and produce sounds to stimulate production.
4. Ask the child to talk softly because the baby is sleeping (e.g., "Sh, baby is sleeping" modeling the quiet voice) or ask the child to whisper a secret.

RESPIRATION

The minimum cognitive age at which to expect success with respiration elicitation task is at minimum 2 years.

1. Hold airplane in front of child. Get child to phonate "ah" as the plane attempts to get to the airport. If child stops phonating, the plane crashes.
2. Present child with bubbles, balloons, and whistles; encourage child to blow as long as he or she can.
3. If the child can count, attempt to have the child count to 10 in one breath.
4. Use water manometers.
   a. U-tube manometers can be used with food coloring so that the water displacement is more visible to the child.
   b. Hold a toy animal at the level (5 centimeters) to which you want the child to displace the water. Tell the child that by blowing through the tube, he or she can feed the animal.
   c. Use a beaker manometer with the straw immersed by 5 centimeters. Encourage the child to blow into the straw for 5 seconds.

5. Use bubbles, candles, or pinwheels to encourage the child to blow as you vary the distance of the object from his or her mouth.
6. Visual displays are beneficial in encouraging the child to sustain phonation.
    a. Let the child watch the stopwatch's hands move on the dial.
    b. Start the child phonating and lift his or her hands from his or her lap above the head.
    c. Use your hands and show the child that you want him or her to stretch the sound out as you move your hands apart.
    d. Use your fingers as counters; as the child phonates, drop one finger at a time and encourage the child to phonate until all 10 fingers are down.
7. To determine whether the child can make rapid changes in air volume,
    a. Ask the child to attempt sighs through the nose
    b. Have the child sniff or pant
8. Variations in loudness
    a. Give child the model of how to vary vocal loudness by producing sounds or a word or by singing a simple song.
    b. Whisper a secret.
    c. Tell the child, "Sh, quiet. The baby is sleeping."
    d. Demonstrate calling mama loudly and say, "Let's call to mom in the next room."
    e. Use a xylophone or drum; hit the instrument softly and produce a quiet sound/word, and hit the instrument hard and produce a loud sound/word.

9

Assistive Technology

Strategies and Tools for Enhancing the Communication Skills of Children with Down Syndrome

Jamie E. Murray-Branch and Julie E. Gamradt

The increasing options available to individuals with Down syndrome present a new challenge to those who provide them with services. Family members, teachers, habilitation and rehabilitation therapists, doctors, and nurses are continually looking for new teaching strategies and tools that will help those with Down syndrome realize their maximum potential. Computers and communication aids represent one new group of tools and strategies to help meet this need.

Children with Down syndrome work to gain effective communication skills so that they can lead full and active lives. Effective communication enables these children to meet their basic needs; develop independence; form social relationships; and gain access to educational, recreational, and vocational opportunities (Blackstone, 1992). This chapter focuses on the use of computers and communication aids as assistive technology (AT) tools that help those with Down syndrome achieve their maximum communication potential. Specifically, these AT tools can help children with Down syndrome develop skills and perform communication behaviors that are particularly challenging to them. This chapter focuses on AT as it supports the following communication behaviors:

1. Enhancing thinking skills related to communication development
2. Learning to use symbols (i.e., words) for communicating
3. Using alternate methods to express ideas when speech is difficult to understand
4. Learning to use words in combination to create longer sentences
5. Learning to understand sentences of greater length
6. Establishing social relationships with peers

Children with Down syndrome who master these skills are able to be more independent and successful. Skills 1, 2, and 4 in the preceding list allow children with Down syndrome to talk about their interests and experiences (past, present, and future) by using symbols (i.e., words) that others understand. When problems arise that are secondary to speech that is difficult to understand, children can continue to communicate successfully in conversations by using Skill 3. With Skills 4 and 5, AT can help children with Down syndrome communicate in ways that may otherwise not be possible. Skill 6 supports the development of positive relationships with friends and expands a child's social circle.

ROLE OF COMPUTERS AND COMMUNICATION AIDS WITH CHILDREN WITH DOWN SYNDROME

Computers and communication aids can serve two roles for children with Down syndrome: an educational role involving instructional activities and an assistant role in which the technology itself serves as an AT device to help children express themselves (Vanderheiden & Cress, 1992). As instructional instruments, computers and communication aids are not meant to replace more commonly used teaching tools or experiences. Instead, they provide a positive addition to a menu of teaching options. The computer and communication aids can be part of a full set of teaching activities, including discussion groups, role-play, and hands-on learning experiences. This chapter's emphasis is on the contributions of AT to communication instruction. In addition, there is a large body of information regarding AT as it applies to general academic instruction in special education for those readers who are interested in this topic (Budoff & Hutton, 1982; Friedman & Hofmeister, 1984; Kolich, 1985; Lehrer, Harckham, Archer, & Pruzek, 1986).

Used for assistive purposes in communication programs, computers and communication aids function to "enhance or extend skills that an individual already has" (Vanderheiden & Cress, 1992, p. 1). An individual may use AT devices and services temporarily or permanently to adjust to a lifelong communication need. For example, older children with Down syndrome who have limited speaking abilities can use a microcomputer with speech output capabilities to speak on the telephone (see Table 1). In such a case, the computer is supporting the child's communication over the telephone, a task that the child could not do without the use of that AT device (see Figure 1).

Helpful Features of Computers for Teaching Children with Down Syndrome

Those who have not used computers for instructional purposes may ask "How does a computer support the development of speech and language skills in children with Down syndrome?" Experienced educators identify motivation as one of the computer's most positive contributions to learning (Lasky, 1984; Meyers, 1984; Schery & O'Connor, 1992). Pictures, animation, and sound features stimulate children's interests in exploration and discovery (Blackstone, 1992; Chapman & Miller, 1980; Male, 1988; Vanderheiden, 1981). Beyond motivation, Tanenhaus (1991) outlined other important characteristics of the computer that specifically support children with language or learning problems. She identified the following features as significant:

1. The computer helps children understand that they can have an effect on their surroundings, which in turn builds self-confidence.
2. The computer allows for repeated success by providing responses (i.e., feedback on accuracy, instructions) based on the child's actions.
3. The computer is never impatient and is always forgiving.
4. The computer allows children to learn at their own rates.

When considering computers for teaching communication skills, intervention teams must investigate software options. (See the appendix at the end of this chapter for a list of software resources and guides.) The intervention team's aim is to select the software programs that most effectively address a particular communication goal and support the learning style of the child. Software programs such as *SpeechViewer* (IBM, 1992) and *PepTalk* (Shriberg, Kwiatkowski, & Snyder, 1989) are designed specifically to support developing speech skills. These programs provide children with information on several aspects of speech that researchers have identified as difficult for children with Down syndrome: pronunciation, speed of talking, and volume (Rosin, Swift, Bless, & Vetter, 1988). Language skills involve learning how to use words to express ideas. Language can be supported through computer-based software programs such as *Living Books* (Broderbund Software, 1993). These types of software-based story experiences often do not re-

Table 1.   Key terms used in the discussion of assistive technology

Term	Definition
Adaptive input	Alternative inputs to the computer that accommodate physical, motor, or intellectual needs of the computer user; types of adaptive input include the touch window, single switches, and alternative keyboards. (See Figure 2 for an alternative keyboard being used as an adaptive input to the computer.)
Aided methods of communication	Communication aids separate from the body such as communication books and speech output devices.
Assistive technology devices	Any piece of equipment or product system, whether acquired commercially off the shelf, modified, or customized, that is used to increase or improve functional capabilities of individuals with disabilities. (See Figures 1, 4, 5, and 6.)
Assistive technology services	Any service that directly assists an individual with a disability in the selection, acquisition, or use of an assistive technology device.
Augmentative and alternative communication devices	All communication that supplements or augments speech (or writing) or sometimes replaces speech (or writing) when speech is not a viable means of communication.
Communication aids	A physical object or device that helps people conduct conversations, make their basic needs known, and write. Typical aids include communication books, communication boards, and mechanical devices. (See Figures 1, 4, 5, and 6.)
High-technology communication aids	Communication aids with electronic parts that have spoken and/or printed output. (See Figures 1, 5, and 6.)
Input	The way in which the computer user controls the computer. Standard input devices include the standard keyboard, joystick, mouse, and trackball.
Light-technology communication skills	Communication aids without any electronic or moving parts such as communication books, communication boards, and wallets. (See Figure 4.)
Output	The way in which the computer user obtains information from the computer, such as by seeing information presented on the computer screen or by hearing auditory feedback.
Software	A program (i.e., application) that the computer runs.
Speech output	Speech that the computer or a communication aid produces; enables spoken messages to be programmed into communication aids by using digitized or synthesized output. *Synthesized output* uses a speech synthesizer to produce an electronic voice. *Digitized output* allows messages to be programmed much like talking into a tape recorder.
Symbols	Ways to represent thoughts and ideas. Words are spoken symbols. Symbols commonly used on communication aids include real objects, photographs, and line drawings. (See Figure 8.)
Unaided methods of communication	Methods of communication involving only the body, such as gestures, sign language, and facial expressions.

Sources: Brandenburg and Vanderheiden (1986); Individuals with Disabilities Education Act (IDEA) of 1990 [20 U.S.C. ch. 33 § 140]; Smith, Vanderheiden, and Fox (1990); Vanderheiden and Yoder (1986).

Figure 1.   Jenny uses a voice output communication aid and a speaker phone to help when making telephone calls. (Voice output communication aid courtesy of Zygo Industries, Inc.)

quire reading skills and present high-interest stories with music and sound effects. The software provides children with choices and allows them to create a new story or move through a preprogrammed story. There are multiple opportunities for using words to request items, ask questions, and comment on what is being seen. As with all software programs, their effectiveness is dependent on creative instruction provided by parents, teachers, and therapists (Tanenhaus, 1991).

Software programs can have particular features that promote communication skills learning and development in children with Down syndrome. Cress and Goltz (1989) noted the following features as being important in these areas:

1. Immediate feedback to the user
2. Presentation of one idea per display
3. Realistic pictures that help accomplish the task
4. Animation or movement
5. Highlighting to call attention to new or more important information on the screen

In addition, speech output is an important software feature for children with cognitive impairments. Speech output often contains preprogrammed messages that focus children's attention and give them clear information about what they are doing with the computer. Speech output can also describe and label actions and objects as they appear on the screen. This information supports the child's early understanding of words and their meanings (i.e., language). The case study involving Erica presented further along in this chapter gives an example of using the computer to increase a child's early vocabulary development (see Figure 2).

Helpful Features of Communication Aids for Teaching Children with Down Syndrome

Communication aids or augmentative and alternative communication (AAC) systems include unaided methods (e.g., pantomime, gestures, American Sign Language [ASL]) and aided methods of communication. This chapter's focus is on aided methods of communication. However, multiple investigations have supported the use of unaided methods for instruction and communication in populations with cognitive disabilities, including Down syndrome (Abrahamsen, Cavallo, & McCluer, 1985; Fristoe & Lloyd, 1978; Kouri, 1989; Musselwhite & St. Louis, 1982; Oliver & Halle, 1982; Romski & Ruder, 1984; Sedey, Rosin, & Miller, 1991).

Low-technology communication aids consist primarily of communication books, communication boards, and wallets (see Figures 3 and 4). The child with Down syndrome points to symbols on the com-

Figure 2.   Sean is using the computer with an alternative keyboard to complete his homework. (Intellikeys keyboard courtesy of IntelliTools.)

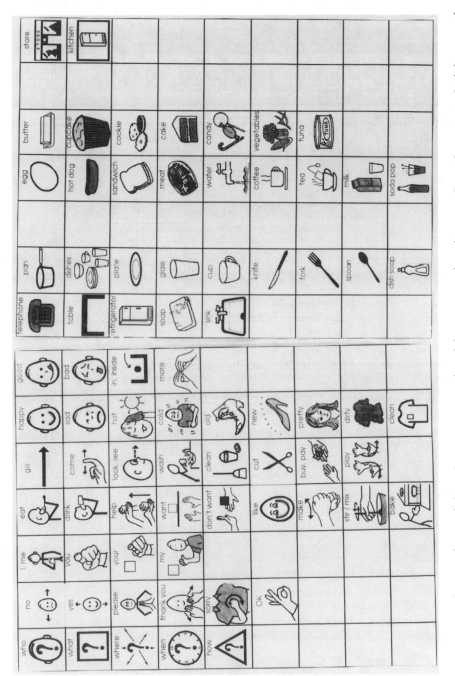

Figure 3. Line drawings referring to feelings, objects, actions, time, physical characteristics, and social amenities. (Picture Communication Symbols courtesy of Mayer-Johnson Co. Copyright © 1981–1998 by Mayer-Johnson Co., Post Office Box 1579, Solana Beach, California 92075 USA; [619] 550-0084 [telephone], [619] 550-0449 [fax]; www.mayer-johnson.com)

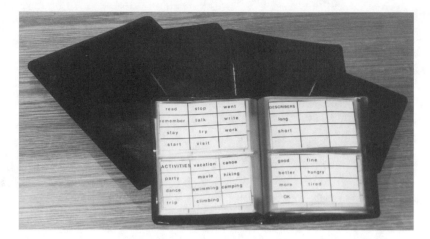

Figure 4. Photograph of several wallet-size communication books containing vinyl pockets with vocabulary inserts. (Courtesy of Mayer-Johnson Co. Copyright © 1981–1998 by Mayer-Johnson Co., Post Office Box 1579, Solana Beach, California 92075 USA; [619] 550-0084 [telephone], [619] 550-0449 [fax]; www.mayer-johnson.com)

munication aid to express ideas. The person talking with the communication aid user must look at what the child is pointing to and decide what the child is saying with the symbols. This requires that the person receiving the information be physically near the child during the conversation in order to see the communication aid.

High-technology aids typically have speech or voice output using computer technology. These aids are portable and are either carried by the person or attached to the person's wheelchair. The child selects a symbol on the communication aid, and preprogrammed messages are spoken. The person receiving the message can be a distance away from the communication aid user because voice output is available. Symbols are placed on both low-technology communication aids and high-technology communication aids to represent thoughts and ideas that individuals wish to convey.

Understanding and using speech remains a primary focus of communication programs for children with Down syndrome (see Figure 5). Since the late 1970s, however, intervention teams have begun to incorporate AAC aids into their instruction. The question frequently asked by those new to these systems is, "Why are communication aids beneficial to children with Down syndrome?" The following list summarizes the communication aid and symbol features that support language learning and use by children with Down syndrome:

1. *Symbols are visual:* Symbols used on communication aids are visual and concrete. As presented in Table 1, commonly used symbols

Figure 5. A portable digitized electronic communication aid that is simple to program and use. (Courtesy of Zygo Industries, Inc.)

include real objects, photographs, and line drawings. Researchers have identified children with Down syndrome as having visual learning abilities that are sometimes stronger than their listening abilities (Pueschel, Gallagher, Zartler, & Pezzulo, 1987). Thus, looking at symbols and hearing words simultaneously may be a helpful way for these children to learn language (Light & Lindsay, 1991). Given the frequency of middle-ear infections and associated hearing losses in children with Down syndrome, the addition of visual information seems even more important. Teachers and parents can supplement their speech with visual symbols by simply pointing to pertinent symbols on a communication aid as they give directions to or ask questions of these individuals.

2. *Symbols are permanent:* Symbols used on communication aids are generally static, meaning that they do not move or change. Unlike speech and ASL, which take place in time and are dynamic (i.e., fade after being presented), symbols used on communication aids are constant. This characteristic is helpful from several perspectives. First, the static nature of symbols gives children more time to think about the symbols themselves and their associated meanings; thus, the symbols help children as they attempt to learn the meanings of words. Second, when attempting to express an idea, children who use communication aids do not have to recall which symbol they wish to use; they only have to recognize the symbol on the communication display. Recognition of symbols requires less thinking and memory skills than does recall (Light & Lindsay, 1991). Therefore, expression of ideas by using communication aids can be less taxing than expression using other com-

munication methods such as speech and ASL, which rely on the children's ability to recall the speech sounds or the signs associated with particular words.

3. *Symbols are easy to recognize:* Symbols used on most communication aids involving children with Down syndrome look similar to the objects, actions, and people they represent. This close physical resemblance, called *iconicity,* can reduce the time that children need to learn symbols and readies them to begin using symbols to express ideas (Mirenda & Locke, 1989). Because the symbols are iconic, people interacting with children who are using these symbols can often easily understand or guess the meaning, which enhances the success of interactions between children and others. If speech output is part of a communication aid, there is even less of a barrier to these children's successful communication with unfamiliar people. As education of children with Down syndrome moves toward teaching in natural, least restrictive environments, the iconic nature of symbols becomes an even greater asset. For a child like Bill, described in a case study further on in this chapter, both low- and high-technology aids supported his participation in school activities. His low-technology system was helpful in his conversations with friends during face-to-face interactions. Speech output on his high-technology aid served an important communication role in that it allowed him to successfully participate in group activities such as show and tell.

4. *Communication aids require limited motor skills:* Low- and high-technology communication aids require that the child select a desired symbol on a communication aid. For most children with Down syndrome, this behavior involves pointing to a symbol. Symbol sizes can be adjusted to match the motor capabilities of the child. For example, symbols can be 1″ × 1″ or 4″ × 4″, depending on the child's needs. No significant motor coordination or strength is required. Children with Down syndrome may be able to perform only simple motor tasks, given their difficulties with fine motor movements (Tingey, 1988); therefore, this option for expression is highly desirable.

5. *Communication aids are easy to construct:* In the past, the construction of picture displays and the programming of communication aids was a highly time-consuming and arduous task. New technologies and software programs are making it easier and quicker for communication board displays to be constructed. The software program *BoardMaker* (Mayer-Johnson Co., 1991), for example, has reduced the time needed for building picture-based communication displays by more than 50%. Once created, displays

can be saved and stored on disks. In the event that a communication aid is lost, the communication boards can be retrieved and printed easily. These advances allow teachers to incorporate communication aids into their instruction programs efficiently and quickly.

6. *Communication aids support early reading skills:* Symbols on displays typically include the printed word above the symbol itself. High-technology aids provide children with the visual symbol, the printed word, and a clear pronunciation of the word. The pairing of the printed word with a symbol that children understand can facilitate early reading skills. Many reports from parents and instructors indicate the positive effect of communication aids on children's ability to recognize words by sight and understand the relationship between letters and their sounds. Research under way in the late 1990s is exploring this issue further.

In summary, communication aids and symbols have many important features that support the communication development and performance of children with Down syndrome. The next two sections of the chapter highlight the specific ways in which AT can be used to address common communication needs of children with Down syndrome.

COMMUNICATION INTERVENTION: HOW ASSISTIVE TECHNOLOGY SUPPORTS THE COMMON COMMUNICATION NEEDS OF CHILDREN WITH DOWN SYNDROME

Several aspects of communication, including producing speech, learning words, and producing and understanding sentences, are difficult for children with Down syndrome to master (Chapman, Kay-Raining Bird, & Schwartz, 1990; Fowler, 1990; Rosin et al., 1988). Through a careful assessment, intervention teams can identify primary areas of communication development to target for a given child. The following subsection describes areas of common difficulty for children with Down syndrome and the ways in which AT and appropriate teaching strategies have been used to address those needs.

Supporting Thinking Skills Through Computer Technology

Because of cognitive impairments, some children with Down syndrome have difficulty in understanding basic ideas related to language learning (i.e., cause-and-effect relationships, sequencing skills, basic classification, categorization skills) (Miller, 1987). A child who is struggling with cause-and-effect relationships, for example, appears to interact arbitrarily with objects and people; these children do not seem to understand that their particular actions cause specific outcomes. Without knowledge of cause-and-effect relationships, children have difficulty in understanding how words will help them in obtaining what they want and need.

Intervention teams may attempt to stimulate a child's understanding of cause-and-effect relationships through play and activities of daily living. In addition, there are software programs specifically designed to promote children's understanding that their actions result in certain outcomes. One example of this is the *Build a Scene* software program (Cooper & Koeff, 1991). In this program, children add a part to a picture each time they touch the computer input device. The software "says" encouraging messages to the child, such as "Make some more," to help keep the child's motivation high. The team may choose an alternative to the standard input devices on the computer (e.g., keyboard) to help highlight the direct relationship between touching the computer and having something happen. Adaptive input devices are often needed to support children who have thinking or motor impairments. With the appropriate input device, children are better able to concentrate on learning the content of the lesson that the computer presents. The following are examples of appropriate adaptive inputs for individuals with cognitive impairments:

1. A touch window, which is a window placed on the computer screen that the child touches to activate the computer
2. A touch pad, which is a larger surface area; pictures can be placed on the touch pad, and the user can activate the computer by touching them on the pad
3. Alternative keyboards, which are keyboards of various sizes that can be customized by changing the size of the keys and changing the labels placed on the keys
4. Single switches, which the user touches to operate simple software programs (Cress & French, 1993; Cress, French, & Tew, 1991; Cress & Goltz, 1989)

A touch screen works well for clearly establishing cause-and-effect relationships. Instructors can support children's understanding by providing praise and emphasizing what has happened on the screen and why.

Prompt-free instruction strategies are helpful when attempting to support certain thinking skills. Within a prompt-free framework, no verbal instructions, prompts, or cues are given (Mirenda & Santagrossi, 1985). The intervention team member sets up the instruction materials so that the child's actions, whether purposeful or accidental, highlight the idea being taught. For example, to support the understanding of cause-and-effect relationships by using software, instructors may begin by using an alternative input such as a large touch window and place it near the child's hand. Because of its nearness to the child's hand, the touch window will likely be touched and the software will change the picture on the computer screen. After multiple experiences within this prompt-free condition, intervention teams may set up the equipment so that a more purposeful and intentional action is required in order for the child to activate the program. In this instance, the instructors can change the input method from a large touch window to a particular key on the keyboard. The child must aim for this target, showing an understanding that a specific action affects the picture being presented on the screen. Throughout these learning experiences, the instructors refrain from giving any verbal instruction or prompting. Consequently, the children are directing their own learning and functioning independently. In the case study of Erica, presented later in this chapter, Erica responded positively to this prompt-free approach and began to initiate more both in speech and in play activities. This suggested that she developed a better understanding of her behavior and its impact on what happened in her classroom and at home.

Learning to Use Symbols

Often children with Down syndrome are slow in using spoken words, despite having made gains in their thinking skills (Miller, Sedey, Miolo, Rosin, & Murray-Branch, 1991). Teams may observe that the child has acquired few spoken words when compared with other children with comparable levels of cognitive functioning. Both unaided and aided methods of AAC are options for fostering the child's communication. During this critical period of early language development, symbols presented on low- and high-technology aids provide a simple way to begin to enhance children's symbolic communication skills. The visual nature of the picture symbol significantly reduces challenges to memory and to the child's motor system. Both are critical factors to consider for the child with Down syndrome who has known impairments in these areas (Kay-Raining Bird & Chapman, 1994). Children simply need to recognize the symbol and touch it at appropriate times to make a comment or a request (Reichle & Yoder, 1985). Children can also physically hand a symbol to someone as part of the conversation. Instructors can model and teach this behavior to emphasize how the symbol can be used to talk. In the early stages of teaching Erica, she was taught to hand a symbol representing bubbles directly to the teacher during playtime. Later, after showing clear understanding of the picture–symbol relationship, she learned that touching the symbol on a communication board was sufficient for expressing a request.

Several training approaches are helpful in introducing children to using symbols with augmentative communication systems, including the modeling techniques presented by Leonard (1975). Using these techniques, the child with Down syndrome has the opportunity to observe others, including peers and adults, use their symbols for communicating within activities. Peers are often the most effective teachers in that children frequently imitate other children. As with Bill, whose case study is also presented later in this chapter, teachers allowed peers to use his symbols during snacktime. No direct instruction was given to Bill to use the symbols. However, shortly after seeing other children pointing to his symbols while talking about the pictured items, Bill began to use the symbols himself.

Goossens', Crain, and Elder (1994) referred to modeling by using communication aids and symbols as *aided language stimulation*. With this technique, key words associated with a language-learning activity are presented as symbols on a communication aid. For many children, the symbols used are simple line drawings with the words they represent printed above them. While speaking, the instructor points to the related symbols as part of the learning experience. Goossens' and colleagues suggested that aided language stimulation techniques can easily be combined with strategies that promote children's early language development. They suggested using short, grammatically complete phrases to talk about ongoing activities. Instructors are encouraged to speak slowly, avoid direct questions (e.g., What is that?) and directives (e.g., "Point to _____"), and use activities that are highly familiar and playful for the children when teaching children who are cognitively young. This type of instruction technique is helpful for children with Down syndrome and others who experience difficulty in listening to and/or comprehending spoken words alone. Children with fluctuating hearing losses, attention problems, or slower thinking skills benefit from having this additional avenue for gathering information.

Besides modeling, instructors can offer choices and present materials in such a way as to promote children's early symbol use (Ellis Weismer, Murray-Branch, & Miller, 1993). For example, children can be offered several opportunities to make choices (e.g., "Do you want _____ or _____?"), or comments can be carefully framed to encourage a specific response (e.g., Comment: "You look thirsty. I have some juice." Desired response: "I want juice."). Intervention teams may also set up situations to promote the child's need to use symbols (i.e., words) to request or to comment. This technique is called *environmental engineering* (Schuler & Goetz, 1983). Objects can be put out of reach or can have missing components as a means by which to encourage children's symbol use for requesting help or to comment. The team can provide natural and positive feedback to the child, such as "Here is the _____ you asked for. You let me know you wanted it by pointing to the picture." In response to an incorrect behavior, the intervention team member can inform the child to be more specific when making a request or comment, such as "I don't understand what you want. Here are your choices," while pointing to the picture symbols representing choices.

Using Alternative Methods to Express Ideas When Speech Is Difficult to Understand

Children with Down syndrome may have adequate speech capabilities for most situations. There may be occasions, however, when their speech is not understood when they are talking with certain people or in specific situations. These experiences can be frustrating and discouraging for both the children and the people to whom they are speaking. Both low- and high-technology communication aids can be helpful as a backup for children when these types of situations occur (see Figure 6).

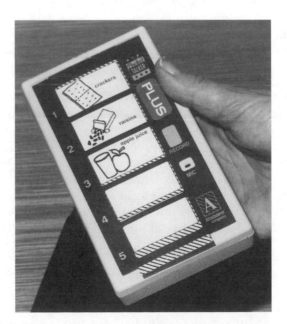

Figure 6.   A small, handheld, high-technology communication aid. This system adds a voice to a basic picture communication display. (Courtesy of Attainment Company, Inc.)

When investigating aided communication techniques for this purpose, the intervention team must assess the child's ability to communicate in many real-life situations. Sometimes family members, teachers, and friends can report which words the child with Down syndrome is consistently having difficulty saying. In other instances, the difficult-to-produce words and what the child is trying to say may not be so obvious. Direct observation of the child in multiple situations is helpful in identifying this information. During this type of observation, the team identifies situations in which the child is actively speaking. The observer notes the types of things that the child must communicate within these situations, what the child is attempting to say, and the child's degree of success in attempts at expressing this information (Brown, Shiraga, York, Zanella, & Rogan, 1984; Carlson, 1981). In instances in which the child has difficulty in communicating through speech, words and phrases that are appropriate for the situation are noted. Later, the intervention team and the child select symbols to represent these intended messages. The type of communication aid (high or low technology) is determined based on many factors such as the need for a voice, portability, and the number of required messages. In the case study of Neil described later in this chapter, Neil used his low-technology system as a backup primarily in the community. The described process was used to identify key messages that the team needed to include in his system. Figure 7 presents an observational tool for recording the information used to address this communication problem.

Using Words in Combination to Create Longer Sentences

Children with Down syndrome may begin to use words for communication, but many have difficulty in combining words to create longer, more complex messages (Fowler, 1990; Miller, Murray-Branch, Sedey, Miolo, & Rosin, 1991; Rondal, 1978). The reasons for the problem with expressions using longer sentences continue to be studied. Meanwhile, children often show nonverbally that they are trying to create more complex messages. They often use pantomime to reenact events, or they say single words that relate to each other (e.g., "Mom Dad," "McDonald's French fries") as a means of expressing more complex ideas.

Displays on communication aids can help children present complex thoughts by using a logical sequence of symbols. Symbols related to particular topics or activities are grouped together on a display called a *topic board* or *miniboard*. Within these displays, words are organized by their meaning or function in a sentence. As such, all symbols referring to people, action words, location words, feeling words, and so

COMMUNICATION INVENTORY

Time Length	Setting	Area	Communication Requirements and Associated Vocabulary	Performance (note mode of communication)	Participatory Activities, Possible Vocabulary, and Strategies	Observed Activities and Possible Vocabulary

Figure 7. Observation form for documenting communication performance and needed vocabulary in real-life situations. (Adapted from Carlson, 1981; reprinted by permission from the American Speech-Language-Hearing Association.)

forth are grouped into subcategories on the display. These subcategories of words are arranged from left to right using the organizational sequence of a basic sentence (i.e., "who," "doing," "what," "where," "why"). This arrangement helps children construct sentences (Brandenburg & Vanderheiden, 1986; Mirenda, 1985). Examples of symbol combinations to create longer sentences are "Tammy ate pizza and coke" or "I want the red sunglasses." Symbols on the display depict the major components of the sentences. In the sentence "Tammy ate pizza and coke," symbols on the display depict the words "Tammy," "eat," "pizza," and "coke."

As was the case in the early stages of using words, modeling using aided language stimulation is a helpful teaching technique (see Figure 8). To meet the goal of longer sentences, teams focus on modeling combinations of symbols to create a message. Instructors can also set up conversations that require the child to use complete messages. When asking about where materials should be placed, instructors can phrase the question so that the child says both the name of the object and its general location (e.g., Question: "Where does the bowl go?" Desired response: "bowl + sink"). If a complete message is not given, the instructor can pretend to misunderstand the child's intent (e.g., Confused teacher response: "The book goes in the sink?" Desired child response: "no, bowl, + sink"). These carefully constructed cues and prompts can be used to guide the child toward complete responses (Bennett, Gast, Wolery, & Schuster, 1986; McDonnell, 1987). The organization of displays on aids supports children with Down syndrome in their expression of ideas using more than one word.

Understanding Sentences of Greater Length

Studies (Chapman et al., 1990; Hartley, 1982) have shown that children with Down syndrome have a greater-than-expected level of difficulty in understanding long and complex sentences. These children's inability to remember information produced through speech and their slower rates of processing new information may be partially responsible for this difficulty (Marcell & Weeks, 1988). Intervention team members may observe that when information is presented through speech at typical speaking rates, children with Down syndrome may not follow directions correctly or may answer questions inappropriately. Sometimes more abstract words referring to location (e.g., under, between, behind) and time (e.g., before, after) are also misunderstood. In these instances, additional information provided with both speech and visual symbols on communication aids helps the child understand.

When giving directions, key terms related to location, size, and color can be depicted through a visual symbol (e.g., photograph, line

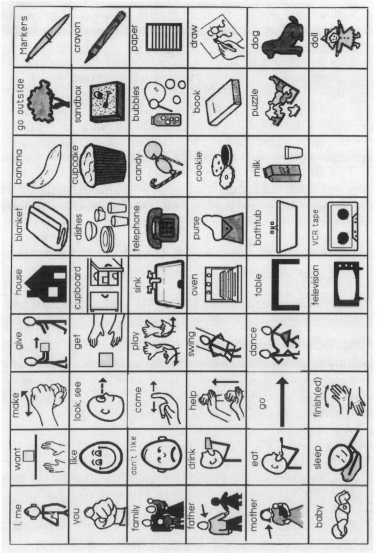

Figure 8.   A display of line drawings for constructing short phrases to make choices. (Picture Communication Symbols courtesy of Mayer-Johnson Co. Copyright © 1981–1998 by Mayer-Johnson Co., Post Office Box 1579, Solana Beach, California 92075 USA; [619] 550-0084 [telephone], [619] 550-0449 [fax]; www.mayer-johnson.com)

drawing). The instructor simultaneously points to the symbol while presenting the direction. To help a child understand questions, instructors can use a symbol to represent the type of question being asked when stating the question. For example, a stick figure can be used to represent a "who" question, and a building can be used to represent a "where" question. With some children, the addition of such visual support has resulted in greater accuracy in the children's first responses to questions.

Symbols placed on schedules or calendars help children in understanding future and past events. Instruction involves intervention team members' reviewing the child's schedule verbally while placing a picture symbol representing that event on a schedule. A printed message placed next to the picture symbol in the schedule may also support the use and potential development of reading skills. For many children, organizing information from left to right and removing completed items can assist them in comprehending the passage of time and sequences of events. When speech output is available, children with Down syndrome can review their schedules by looking at and listening to prerecorded messages. They can replay the message as often as needed to help increase their understanding and memory of the information. In the case study of Jenny, described later in this chapter, symbols used in conversation and on a calendar decreased her confusion and frustration with new information and unfamiliar routines. Jenny was much more cooperative once these supports were available to help her understand.

Establishing Social Relationships with Peers

The literature describes children with Down syndrome as being interested in socializing with others and sensitive to instances when their friends do not understand them (Coggins & Stoel-Gammon, 1982; Coggins, Carpenter, & Owings, 1983). In the early stages of social development and peer interaction, children's delays in speech and language skills may not have a significant effect on their social relationships. This is due in part to the way in which children develop these relationships. Play is often the basis for establishing friendships. Often language skills are not critical to these early interactions. Children play next to each other, sharing experiences without a significant amount of talking. As children age, social interactions are more dependent on turn taking, sharing objects and information, and discussing events (Tanenhaus, 1991). Differences in thinking, motor, and language skills in children with Down syndrome can create barriers to the development of social relationships (Prutting, 1982). If a child's speech is highly difficult to understand and/or if vocabulary and sentence abilities are limited, social relationships may be difficult to develop with increasing age.

The computer provides opportunities for children with Down syndrome and those without disabilities to come together to play. Team members can customize software so that children with varying levels of skill can fully participate in the computer program. In addition, with the aid of the computer, children with Down syndrome can take a leadership role in social interactions. An example is with the software program *I Can Play Too* (Mervine & Ziegler, 1992). In this software package, high-interest games for children are presented by way of line drawings on the computer screen. Speech output is also included. Comments and questions used by children playing these games are programmed into the software. The game *Go Fish* is one such program option. With this software, the child with Down syndrome who has limited speaking skills can fully participate in the card game by using understandable speech and joking comments such as "I'll get you next time." Peers have the opportunity to form relationships with the child in a play activity that is age appropriate and enjoyable for all. Tanenhaus (1991) reported that both parents and siblings of children with Down syndrome consider computer-centered recreation activities as significant contributions to their family social time. It is important to note, however, that teams often must provide basic guidance and customize the software for it to be successful in social activities.

Communication aids provide another contribution to social interaction by helping the child participate in conversations that are critical to developing friendships. Especially in the teen years, calling friends on the telephone, discussing interests, and using slang are extremely important. Communication aids with appropriate vocabulary and speech output can assist a child in social-verbal interactions. To develop such systems, intervention team members identify language used in social interactions that is popular and highly predictable. For example, when seeing a teenage peer in the hallway, typical comments and questions may include "Hey man, how's it going?" "Did you see any good movies lately?" "Awesome," or "No way." Intervention teams can record conversations involving children of the appropriate age group.

To teach communication skills, intervention team members can develop scripts for children with Down syndrome. A script is a prepared conversation for a particular situation that two or more people can rehearse. While practicing these scripts, children have the opportunity to rehearse making appropriate comments and answering commonly presented questions by using the communication aid. Scripts and role-play activities involving peers can give children experience with the natural pace of conversations (Constable, 1983; Culatta & Horn, 1992). These activities prepare the child with Down syndrome for real-life conversations that will ultimately provide skills needed for future relationships.

CASE STUDIES: EFFECTIVE USE OF ASSISTIVE TECHNOLOGY IN MEETING THE NEEDS OF CHILDREN WITH DOWN SYNDROME

The following case studies highlight the ways in which AT helped improve the communication skills of four individuals with Down syndrome. The types of communication problems that each individual with Down syndrome faced and the associated teaching tools, goals, and strategies used are described in each case.

ERICA

At the beginning of her AAC intervention, Erica was age 4 years, 8 months. Testing indicated that she had mental retardation requiring intermittent supports. Erica was able to identify familiar objects by their use. She understands a variety of simple line drawings. With regard to language comprehension, Erica understands single words and has limited understanding of sentences. Her understanding of language seems equal to her thinking skills. Erica uses a few spoken words and some single signs (used infrequently); but there is a large gap between her ability to understand and her ability to express herself. Erica imitates more words than she uses on her own. Her productions of words and signs are unclear, and she sometimes presents strings of speech that appear to be meaningful but are not understood. Erica's hearing status is normal. Erica's daily living skills include independence in eating and dressing (except for small buttons or fasteners). At times, Erica appears frozen in place and unable or unwilling to move or to join in activities; periodically she refuses choices and opportunities to interact with people and materials around her.

Development of Expressive Vocabulary

Erica's intervention team expressed concern that her thinking skills and understanding of spoken language are much higher than her ability to express herself by using speech. She does not often spontaneously use words to express herself.

Case History/Intervention Program

Erica was completing her last semester in an early childhood program when her intervention team began considering a low-technology communication aid for her (see Figure 9). She was receiving a number of therapies within her school day, including speech-language services. Erica generally spoke using single words. The number of words she used was smaller than expected because her understanding of words was a strength. Erica's family wanted her to attend kindergarten at her neighborhood school the following school year. Her skill development in all areas, including communication, was viewed as critical to achieving this goal.

The intervention team introduced low-technology communication aids to Erica. The communication aids, called *miniboards,* consisted of one or two pictures relating to a particular game or activity (e.g., house, bubbles). On the bubble board, Erica used the pictures to request the bubbles or to ask to blow. The pictures were 1″ × 1″ line drawings that were colored to look realistic. The therapist introduced the miniboards within fun play activities.

Figure 9.   Erica talks to her kindergarten classmate using a low-technology communication aid during free play. (Picture Communication Symbols courtesy of Mayer-Johnson Co. Copyright © 1981–1998 by Mayer-Johnson Co., Post Office Box 1579, Solana Beach, California 92075 USA; [619] 550-0084 [telephone], [619] 550-0449 [fax]; www.mayer-johnson.com)

The miniboards were used to make comments and requests during play. It was important for Erica to see others using the miniboard to communicate (e.g., modeling, aided language stimulation) so that she could learn how to use it herself. Miniboards were used in school and at home. Staff and family received materials and training to allow this to happen.

A prompt-free strategy (Mirenda & Santagrossi, 1985) was also used as a teaching method. This technique involved teaching Erica how to use symbols for communication through natural consequences (e.g., she touched a symbol for bubbles, and that activity was quickly initiated) without presentation of cues from others.

The team also used a computer with adaptations and specialized and general software with Erica. A touch window or a single switch were used instead of the keyboard during some activities. This simplified the task of operating the computer. The teacher's aim was to use this tool to help increase Erica's willingness to initiate communication and to participate in activities with others. In some cases, the activities also provided instruction on academic skills (e.g., letter identification).

Outcomes/Future Considerations

The use of miniboards and the related teaching strategies (e.g., modeling, prompt-free strategy) were viewed as having a positive impact on Erica's communication. Erica's willingness to communicate with others increased while she used the communication aids. Her speech was also noted to increase during the period of time in which the communication aids were used. Erica's team ultimately discontinued use of the communication aids following a sharp increase in her speaking abilities. Erica's mother was delighted that Erica was speaking more and reported that she was grateful that the communication aids were available to Erica when she needed them.

NEIL

At the beginning of his AAC intervention, Neil was 17 years old. No specific information on cognitive status was provided by his team. Neil recognizes some printed words, learns best when he is directly doing activities, and knows some basic time and number concepts. Neil's language comprehension depends on his previous experience within similar situations to help him understand what others are saying. Neil's average sentence length was one to three words. He used poor grammar, and his single-word vocabulary was approximately 300–400 words. Neil speaks rapidly, and he is understood primarily by people who are familiar with his speech pattern. He has a mild to moderate mixed hearing loss (i.e., sensorineural and conductive hearing loss) in both ears. Neil's daily living skills are that he independently uses buses, has basic housekeeping skills, and prepares and assembles cold foods. Neil is highly social and athletic and participates in many competitive athletic events.

Development of Early Sentences

Neil's mother expressed that she was "really concerned that when Neil gets into situations where people don't know him that he won't get the whole message out. When he just says 'no' and 'yeah,' it is hard to really understand what he means."

History/Intervention Program

Neil participated in a public school program for students with moderate to severe cognitive disabilities (see Figure 10). The school program focused primarily on developing Neil's skills for living and working in the community. Neil received speech-language services throughout his public school education. A primary focus of services in the elementary school period was on

Figure 10.   Neil uses speech and his communication wallet to tell his mom about his day.

development of his speech skills. It was not until Neil was 11 years of age that a significant hearing loss was identified. Following the fitting of hearing aids, some people noted a slight improvement in Neil's speaking and comprehension skills. Neil continued to experience difficulty in expressing himself using more than one word at a time, however. In response to concern about this difficulty, the intervention team identified instances in which Neil was having problems expressing his thoughts. They completed an inventory of his communication requirements at home and at school. This inventory helped identify vocabulary items that could be included in a communication book. Key vocabulary that depicted ideas, objects, people, places, feelings, and questions were listed. Neil's sight-word reading skills made it possible to present some words and phrases in printed form in the communication book. Other vocabulary items were represented by simple 1″ × 1″ line drawings with the word printed above it. The vocabulary was organized by event or by topic in a small wallet with vinyl pockets. Neil easily carried the wallet from place to place in his pants pocket or fanny pack. Tabs were placed on the pages to help Neil quickly locate the word or picture he wanted to express. The words and pictures were organized to make it easy to combine words and pictures to create sentences. Several complete messages that Neil frequently needed were also included in the book. Examples included the following:

People	Actions	Places	Feelings	Phrases
Tom	bowl	Union	excited	Let's go bowling.
Mom	eat	school	great	What's for lunch?

The speech-language pathologist provided instruction to Neil within daily situations in which he needed to communicate. The therapist primarily taught Neil by using the pictures to express herself (e.g., modeling) and emphasized combining pictures to make short sentences. Part of therapy also included pretending to be in real situations (e.g., role playing with scripts) to allow rehearsal of key skills related to talking to people. Neil was encouraged to use his speech, gestures, and the wallet with picture symbols. Neil's team worked cooperatively on the goal of combining pictures to create short sentences when he was talking to others.

Outcomes and Future Considerations

Neil is meeting his communication needs with a combination of speech, gestures, and his communication wallet. In the future, his family will consider having Neil move into his own apartment with regular support from staff. When that time comes, Neil may need a communication aid with speech output primarily for speaking on the telephone. Neil could use the aid similarly to his communication book emphasizing complete and clear messages.

JENNY

Jenny's house parent expressed concern that "I have been frustrated by the limitations that I encounter trying to communicate effectively with Jenny. She is an alert young woman who . . . would benefit greatly, as I and the rest of the household would, from [her having] increased communications skills."

Accommodating Language Comprehension Problems

At the beginning of AAC intervention, Jenny was 26 years old. She was able to match and copy printed words, and she understood simple line drawings and the idea of past and future events. Assessment of language comprehension indicated that Jenny often failed to respond to people and experienced significant difficulty in understanding others. Expressively, Jenny used a combination of speech (generally single words and short phrases) and gestures and had previous exposure to ASL and use of a picture communication book, with the latter having been discontinued. Jenny spoke rapidly, used speech infrequently, and was difficult to understand. Her hearing status involved an initial report of a mild hearing loss; later testing revealed moderate to severe hearing loss involving both ears because of frequent middle-ear problems. Jenny lived in a foster home in which a house parent was present at all times. She had limited independence in the community (e.g., did not cross streets or ride the city bus). Jenny loved to be with people and became upset if her routine was changed.

History/Intervention Program

Jenny was living in a foster home when she was first referred for AAC services (see Figure 11). Limited information was available about her previous educational programming. Friends and staff said they were frustrated with their attempts to talk with Jenny.

Figure 11. Jenny prepares for talking to people in the community. Her low- and high-technology communication systems help her understand what she may need to say to others.

They viewed Jenny as someone who was bright and had a great interest in and potential for communicating. Jenny's poor communication skills confused them. Jenny rarely initiated interactions with others. Some intervention team members thought she intentionally ignored them when they talked to her. Jenny started a new job when her AAC support began.

The intervention team evaluated Jenny's communication skills and abilities in everyday activities. Based on the evaluation, a communication book was designed to help her understand others as well as to help her express her thoughts and needs. The intervention team identified pictures and signs that helped Jenny understand others. In addition, they identified words and phrases that were important for Jenny to say.

The book consisted of 1" × 1" black-and-white line drawings of important vocabulary and phrases. To help with understanding instructions at her new jobsite, a display of symbols representing each of her job tasks was arranged in a left-to-right sequence. Jenny moved a dot from symbol to symbol as she completed her tasks. If the sequence of tasks needed to be changed, her supervisor pointed to the pictures to help explain the new order.

A small calendar was taped in the back of the communication book. Friends and staff recorded important events in the calendar using printed words and hand-drawn pictures. The purpose of the calendar was twofold: It helped Jenny understand and remember upcoming events and assisted Jenny when she talked to others about important events.

Outcomes and Future Considerations

Jenny's increased ability to respond to questions when pictures were present helped the intervention team recognize that she had a potentially significant hearing loss. Subsequent testing revealed this to be true. Jenny's ability to understand others has improved since the intervention team developed her communication book and calendar and she obtained hearing aids. People who talk to Jenny also use signs and gestures that help her understand. Jenny more regularly starts conversations and is successful in getting her message across by using a combination of speech, gestures, her communication book, and her calendar. Jenny is beginning to use a high-technology communication aid. The addition of speech to her communication aid has made it possible for Jenny to talk in more places (e.g., restaurants, stores) and on the telephone. Her house parent of 3 years wrote to the therapist, "I am amazed when I think back to our initial hopes for Jenny and see how outgoing and communicative she has become!"

BILL

Bill's parents expressed concern that Bill uses sign language and that "it is difficult for people who do not sign to understand him. We would like a system to enable Bill to communicate with a variety of people."

Enhancement of Social Relationships
within General Education Classrooms

At the beginning of the AAC intervention program, Bill was 8 years old. He understood the idea of past and future events; categorized things; and understood simple line drawings representing objects, actions, locations, and feelings. Bill comprehended simple sentences related to familiar present and past events, had difficulty in understanding less familiar sentences, and depended strongly on routine to support his understanding. His language production consisted of the use of signs to make requests and choices and the use of words and signs to say major ideas in a message (e.g., "Grandma house eat soup please"). Bill's parents reported that Bill used 99 different ASL signs (his signs were approximations because he had some problems making the signs with his hands). Bill's speech was limited to one or two words, and his words were difficult to understand. Most of his speech involved word approximations consisting of the vowel sound "uh" as in "cup." His hearing status was normal. In terms of daily living skills, Bill dressed himself with help, made his bed, helped clean up the house, and ate independently. Bill was social and played games with his siblings.

History/Intervention Program

Bill was a student in a general education kindergarten classroom who primarily used signs to communicate (see Figure 12). He re-

Figure 12.   Bill uses his high-technology communication aid to converse. (Voice output system courtesy of Zygo Industries, Inc.)

ceived special education support within his general classroom. Bill's social circle expanded in his kindergarten classroom. The other children did not know ASL, however. Bill's intervention team was interested in strategies and tools to help Bill talk with peers and to more fully participate verbally in his school program.

Bill's intervention team developed miniboards for him to use at school and at home. Miniboards were placed in Bill's classroom (e.g., environmental engineering) so that they were available to all of the children in the class. This enabled other children to use the miniboards while talking to Bill and encouraged Bill to talk, too. The speech-language therapist and general classroom teacher provided instruction on using the miniboards in the classroom during typical teaching activities. Within a short period, children were talking more to Bill, and Bill was communicating with his low-technology communication system. A lightweight, digitized speech output communication aid was recommended for Bill. The display had thirty-two 1-inch locations. Several pages of vocabulary were programmed into the system so that Bill could talk about a variety of topics (e.g., McDonald's, games, cooking). Initially, activities were set up in the classroom (e.g., environmental engineering) so that Bill used his speech output aid. Bill directed other children during games like Simon Says and taught a friend how to make an art project that he had constructed during therapy. Bill quickly learned the symbols and their related meanings. The intervention team highlighted full messages that helped Bill talk like other children (e.g., "That's cool," "You want to play?" "Cowabunga, dude").

Bill's entire team was supportive of the inclusion of AT into his programming. They consistently had materials ready to go and established routines throughout the day in which the low- and high-technology aids were incorporated. In addition, they were willing to have necessary communication materials available in the classroom for developing spontaneous conversation and social interaction between peers.

Outcomes and Future Considerations

Bill showed competency in using his AAC systems across a variety of places and partners. Bill's parents said that Bill especially liked symbols expressing humorous thoughts or comments. Bill began making gains in his speech around the time of the introduction of his communication aids. Because of the gains Bill has made in speech, more of his classroom communication is through speech only. Bill's low- and high-technology AAC devices will continue to play an important role in places where he talks with unfamiliar people.

SUMMARY OF CASE STUDIES

Critical to the effectiveness of AT in each of these cases was a well-organized intervention team that was willing to consider new ideas and to share their expertise. Only when teams work effectively do those with Down syndrome experience the benefits of AT. Working well as a team begins with a unifying purpose or mission and a basic sense of trust and respect among team members (York et al., 1985). All team members must view AT as valid teaching aids or valid AT devices and be willing to include them in the communication program. The case studies illustrate how a team approach that includes the following characteristics often results in the best outcomes for the child:

1. Joint team activities (team jointly performs various activities including regular team meetings, assessment, development of materials, and instruction of the child)
2. Staff development (team members accept, support, and expand each other's knowledge and expertise, which in turn benefits the child and the team)
3. Role release (team members share teaching activities and responsibilities across areas of knowledge or expertise) (Lyon & Lyon, 1980)

Sometimes it is necessary to contact outside resources (e.g., experts in using a particular type of AT) for support. These individuals provide technical support to the team when the team is in the process of selecting and using unfamiliar AT. Often these sources have equipment that a child can try. They may also have personnel with expertise in how to help teach children to use these tools successfully. (See the appendix at the end of this chapter for a list of technical support resources.) The primary goal of these team efforts is to have the necessary AT available and complete when children with Down syndrome need it. Unfortunately, all too often, a child with Down syndrome may never experience the benefits of a particular type of AT. This is frequently due in part to the team's difficulties in coordination, development of materials, and use of teaching strategies.

CONCLUSIONS

This chapter describes AT (computers and communication aids) and the way in which it can be used within communication intervention programs involving children and adolescents with Down syndrome. Although AT alone cannot meet every child's needs, it can be one of several approaches used to improve communication skills. Both computers and AAC systems (low-technology and high-technology aids) provide innovative additions to traditional approaches to communication intervention.

Since the late 1970s, the vision for children with Down syndrome has broadened in part because of the passage of federal legislation such as the Education for All Handicapped Children Act of 1975 (PL 94-142), the Americans with Disabilities Act of 1990 (PL 101-336), and the Individuals with Disabilities Education Act (IDEA) of 1990 (PL 101-476). These legislative landmarks have resulted in a wider variety of opportunities being presented to children with Down syndrome than previously. Societal opinions of those with disabilities are also slowly changing and adding to the new vision for children with Down syndrome. New images of ability and competency are replacing previous societal presumptions of inability. Individuals with Down syndrome consequently have many more opportunities to learn, work, and recreate in society.

REFERENCES

Abrahamsen, A., Cavallo, M., & McCluer, J. (1985). Is the sign advantage a robust phenomenon? From gesture to language in two modalities. *Merrill-Palmer Quarterly, 31,* 177–209.

Americans with Disabilities Act (ADA) of 1990, PL 101-336, 42 U.S.C. §§ 12101 *et seq.*

Bennett, D.L., Gast, D.L., Wolery, W., & Schuster, J. (1986). Time delay and the system of least prompts: A comparison in teaching manual sign production. *Education and Treatment of Children, 5,* 117–129.

Blackstone, S. (1992). For consumers: Changing times for people with Down syndrome. *Augmentative Communication News, 5*(2), 1–3.

Brandenburg, S., & Vanderheiden, S. (1986). *Communication board design and vocabulary selection.* Madison: University of Wisconsin–Madison, TRACE Research and Development Center of Communication Control and Computer Access for Handicapped Individuals.

Broderbund Software. (1993). *Living books* [Computer program]. San Rafael, CA: Author.

Brown, L., Shiraga, B., York, J., Zanella, K., & Rogan, P. (1984). The discrepancy analysis technique in programs for students with severe handicaps. In L. Brown, M. Sweet, B. Shiraga, J. York, K. Zanella, P. Rogan, & R. Loomis (Eds.), *Educational programs for students with severe handicaps* (Vol. XIV, pp. 1–50). Madison, WI: Madison Metropolitan School District.

Budoff, M., & Hutton, L. (1982). Microcomputers in special education. Promises and pitfalls. *Exceptional Children, 49,* 123–128.

Carlson, F. (1981). A format for selecting vocabulary for the nonspeaking child. *Language, Speech, and Hearing Services in the Schools, 12,* 240–245.

Chapman, R.S., Kay-Raining Bird, E., & Schwartz, S.E. (1990). Fast mapping of words in event contexts by children with Down syndrome. *Journal of Speech and Hearing Disorders, 55,* 761–770.

Chapman, R.S., & Miller, J.F. (1980). Analyzing language and speech communication in the child. In R.L. Schiefelbusch (Ed.), *Nonspeech language and communication: Analysis and intervention* (pp. 159–196). Baltimore: University Park Press.

Coggins, T.E., Carpenter, R.L., & Owings, N.O. (1983). Examining early intentional communication in Down's syndrome and nonretarded children. *British Journal of Disorders of Communication, 18,* 98–106.

Coggins, T.E., & Stoel-Gammon, C. (1982). Clarification strategies used by four Down's syndrome children for maintaining normal conversational interaction. *Education and Training of the Mentally Retarded, 17,* 65–67.

Constable, C. (1983). Creating communicative context. In H. Winitz (Ed.), *Treating language disorders: For clinicians by clinicians* (pp. 97–120). Baltimore: University Park Press.

Cooper, R.J., & Koeff, B. (1991). *Build a scene* [Computer program]. Dana Point, CA: R.J. Cooper and Associates.

Cress, C., & French, G. (1993, June). *Predictions of computer interface skills for children with mental retardation.* Poster presented at the Rehabilitation Engineering Society of North America 16th Annual Convention, Las Vegas, NV.

Cress, C., French, G., & Tew, J. (1991, June). *Age-related differences in normally developing children.* Paper presented at the annual conference of the Rehabilitation Engineering Society of North America, Kansas City, MO.

Cress, C., & Goltz, C. (1989, October). *Tips for selecting and evaluating software.* Paper presented at the annual Closing the Gap Conference, Minneapolis, MN.

Culatta, B., & Horn, D. (1992, November). *Scripted play and story enactments to facilitate language and literacy.* Miniseminar presented at the national convention of the American Speech-Language-Hearing Association, San Antonio, TX.

Education for All Handicapped Children Act of 1975, PL 94-142, 20 U.S.C. §§ 1400 *et seq.*

Ellis Weismer, S., Murray-Branch, J., & Miller, J.F. (1993). Comparison of two methods for promoting productive vocabulary in late talkers. *Journal of Speech and Hearing Research, 36,* 1037–1050.

Fowler, A. (1990). Language abilities in children with Down syndrome: Evidence for a specific syntactic delay. In D. Cicchetti & M. Beeghly (Eds.), *Children with Down syndrome: A developmental perspective* (pp. 302–328). New York: Cambridge University Press.

Friedman, S., & Hofmeister, A. (1984). Matching technology to content and learners: A case study. *Exceptional Children, 51,* 130–134.

Fristoe, M., & Lloyd, L.L. (1978). A survey of the use of non-speech communication systems with the severely communication impaired. *Mental Retardation, 16,* 99–103.

Goossens', C., Crain, S., & Elder, P. (1994). *Engineering the preschool environment for interactive symbolic communication.* Solana Beach, CA: Mayer-Johnson Co.

Hartley, X.Y. (1982). Receptive language processing by Down's syndrome children. *Journal of Mental Deficiency, 87,* 344–347.

IBM. (1992). *Speechviewer II* [Computer program]. Boca Raton, FL: IBM Special Needs System.

Individuals with Disabilities Education Act (IDEA) of 1990, PL 101-476, 20 U.S.C. §§ 1400 *et seq.*

Kay-Raining Bird, E., & Chapman, R.S. (1994). Sequential recall in individuals with Down syndrome. *Journal of Speech and Hearing Research, 37,* 1369–1380.

Kolich, E. (1985). Microcomputer technology with the learning disabled: A review of the literature. *Journal of Learning Disabilities, 18,* 428–431.

Kouri, T. (1989). How manual sign acquisition relates to the development of spoken language: A case study. *Language, Speech, and Hearing Services in the Schools, 20,* 50–61.

Lasky, E.Z. (1984). Introduction to microcomputers for specialists in communicative disorders. In A.H. Schwartz (Ed.), *Handbook of microcomputer applications in communicative disorders* (pp. 1–15). San Diego: College-Hill Press.

Lehrer, R., Harckham, L., Archer, P., & Pruzek, R. (1986). Microcomputer-based instruction in special education. *Journal of Educational Computing Research, 2,* 337–355.

Leonard, L. (1975). Modeling as a clinical procedure in language training. *Language, Speech, and Hearing Services in the Schools, 6,* 72–85.

Light, J., & Lindsay, P. (1991). Cognitive science and augmentative and alternative communication. *Augmentative and Alternative Communication, 7,* 186–203.

Lyon, S., & Lyon, G. (1980). Team functioning and staff development: A role release approach to providing integrated educational services for severely handicapped students. *Journal of The Association for the Severely Handicapped, 5*(3), 250–263.

Male, M. (1988). *Special magic: Computers, classroom strategies and exceptional students.* Mountain View, CA: Mayfield Publishing Co.

Marcell, M.M., & Weeks, S.L. (1988). Short-term memory difficulties in Down's syndrome. *Journal of Mental Deficiency Research, 32,* 153–162.

Mayer-Johnson Co. (1991). *BoardMaker* [Computer program] Solana Beach, CA: Author.

McDonnell, J. (1987). The effects of time delay and increasing prompt hierarchy strategies on the acquisition of purchasing skills by students with severe handicaps. *Journal of The Association for Persons with Severe Handicaps, 12*(3), 227–236.

Mervine, P., & Ziegler, B. (1992). *I can play too* [Computer program]. Solana Beach, CA: Mayer-Johnson Co.

Meyers, L.F. (1984). Unique contributions of microcomputers to language intervention with handicapped children. *Seminars in Speech and Language, 5,* 23–34.

Miller, J.F. (1987). Language and communication characteristics of children with Down syndrome. In S.M. Pueschel, C. Tingey, J.E. Rynders, A.C. Crocker, & D.M. Crutcher (Eds.), *New perspectives on Down syndrome* (pp. 233–262). Baltimore: Paul H. Brookes Publishing Co.

Miller, J.F., Murray-Branch, J.E., Sedey, A.L., Miolo, G., & Rosin, M. (1991, March). *The transition from single words to multi-word utterances with Down syndrome.* Paper presented at the Gatlinburg Conference on Research and Theory in Mental Retardation and Developmental Disabilities, Key Biscayne, FL.

Miller, J.F., Sedey, A.L., Miolo, G., Rosin, M., & Murray-Branch, J.E. (1991, November). *Spoken and sign vocabulary acquisition in children with Down syndrome.* Poster presented at the National Convention of the American Speech-Language-Hearing Association Convention, Atlanta, GA.

Mirenda, P. (1985). Designing pictorial communication systems for physically able-bodied students with severe handicaps. *Augmentative and Alternative Communication, 1*(2), 58–64.

Mirenda, P., & Locke, P. (1989). A comparison of symbol transparency in non-speaking persons with intellectual disabilities. *Journal of Speech and Hearing Disorders, 54,* 131–140.

Mirenda, P., & Santagrossi, J. (1985). A prompt-free strategy to teach pictorial communication system use. *Augmentative and Alternative Communication, 1,* 143–150.

Musselwhite, C.R., & St. Louis, K.W. (1982). *Communication programming for the severely handicapped: Vocal and non-vocal strategies.* San Diego: College-Hill Press.

Oliver, C., & Halle, J. (1982). Language training in the everyday environment: Teaching functional sign use to a retarded child. *Journal of The Association for the Severely Handicapped, 8,* 50–62.

Prutting, C. (1982). Pragmatic as social competence. *Journal of Speech and Hearing Disorders, 47,* 123–133.

Pueschel, S.M., Gallagher, P., Zartler, A., & Pezzulo, J. (1987). Cognitive and learning processes in children with Down syndrome. *Research in Developmental Disabilities, 8,* 21–37.

Reichle, J., & Yoder, D. (1985). Communication board use in severely handicapped learners. *Language, Speech, and Hearing Services in the Schools, 16,* 1–11.

Romski, M.A., & Ruder, K.F. (1984). Effects of speech and sign instruction on oral language learning and generalization of action and object combinations by Down syndrome children. *Journal of Speech and Hearing Disorders, 49,* 293–302.

Rondal, J.A. (1978). Developmental sentence scoring procedure and the delay-difference question in language development of Down's syndrome children. *Mental Retardation, 16,* 169–171.

Rosin, M., Swift, E., Bless, D., & Vetter, D. (1988). Communication profiles of adolescents with Down syndrome. *Journal of Childhood Communication Disorders, 12,* 49–64.

Schery, T.K., & O'Connor, L.C. (1992). The effectiveness of school-based computer language intervention with severely handicapped children. *Language, Speech, and Hearing Services in the Schools, 23,* 43–47.

Schuler, A.L., & Goetz, L. (1983). Toward communicative competence: Matters of method, content and mode of instruction. In B.M. Prizant (Ed.), *Seminars in Speech and Language, 4,* 79–91.

Sedey, A., Rosin, M.G., & Miller, J.F. (1991, November). *The use of signs among children with Down syndrome.* Poster presented at the National Convention of the American Speech-Language-Hearing Association Convention, Atlanta, GA.

Shriberg, L.D., Kwiatkowski, J., & Snyder, T. (1989). *Peptalk* [Computer program]. Tucson, AZ: Communication Skill Builders.

Smith, R.O., Vanderheiden, G., & Fox, L. (1990). *Specialization in technology service delivery: What is an interface specialist?* Paper presented at the annual conference of Rehabilitation Engineering Society of North America, Washington, DC.

Tanenhaus, J. (1991). *Home-based computer programs for children with Down syndrome.* New York: National Down Syndrome Society.

Tingey, C. (1988). *Down syndrome: A resource handbook.* San Diego: College-Hill Press.

Vanderheiden, G. (1981). *Practical application of microcomputers to aid the handicapped.* Madison: University of Wisconsin, TRACE Research and Development Center on Communication, Control, and Computer Access for Handicapped Individuals.

Vanderheiden, G., & Cress, C. (1992, June). *Application of artificial intelligence to the needs of persons with cognitive impairments: The companion aid.* Paper presented at the International Rehabilitation Engineering Society of North America Conference, Toronto, Ontario, Canada.

Vanderheiden, G.C., & Yoder, D. (1986). Overview. In S. Blackstone (Ed.), *Augmentative communication: An introduction* (pp. 1–28). Rockville, MD: American Speech-Language-Hearing Association.

York, J., Long, E., Caldwell, N., Brown, L., Zanella-Albright, K., Rogan, P., Shiraga, B., & Marks, J. (1985). Teamwork strategies for school and community instruction. In L. Brown, B. Shiraga, J. York, A. Udvari-Solner, K. Zanella-Albright, F. Rogan, E. McCarthy, & R. Loomis (Eds.), *Education programs for students with severe intellectual disabilities* (Vol. 15, pp. 229–276). Madison: University of Wisconsin and the Madison Metropolitan School District.

Appendix: Resource List

This appendix list provides information on software resources, conferences, periodicals, networks, and databases related to technology and people with disabilities. No recommendations or endorsements are implied by the inclusion of any organization in this appendix on this list. Contact each resource provider for more specific and up-to-date information.

SOFTWARE RESOURCES

Closing the Gap, Inc.
Post Office Box 68
Henderson, Minnesota 56044
(507) 248-3294
World wide web site: http://www.closingthegap.com/

Publishes *Closing the Gap*, a bimonthly magazine that provides information on the use of computers in special education and rehabilitation. The magazine includes a "Software Previews" column, user comments, articles, and suggestions. The company also publishes an annual product directory.

National Down Syndrome Society (NDSS)
666 Broadway
New York, New York 10012
(800) 221-4602

Provides a series of booklets on software and computer use with children with Down syndrome. Information in the booklets was collected by Joan Tanenhaus as part of a computer education program.

CONFERENCES

California State University–Northridge
18111 Nordhoff Street–DVSS
Northridge, California 91330
(818) 677-1200

Closing the Gap, Inc.
Post Office Box 68
Henderson, Minnesota 56044
(507) 248-3294
World wide web site: http://www.closingthegap.com/

International Society for Augmentative and Alternative Communication (ISAAC)
49 The Donway West, Suite 308
Toronto, Ontario M3C 3M9
CANADA
(416) 385-0351
World wide web site: http://www.isaac-online.org/
Internet email address: secretariat@isaac-online.org

United States Society for Augmentative and Alternative Communication (USAAC)
c/o James F. Neils
Post Office Box 5271
Evanston, Illinois 60201-5271
(847) 869-2122

NEWSLETTERS AND JOURNALS

Augmentative Communication News
Augmentative Communication, Inc.
One Surf Way, Suite 237
Monterey, California 93940
(831) 649-3050

A bimonthly newsletter covering topics in augmentative communication. Each issue contains sections on consumer issues, equipment, clinical news, governmental affairs, and research.

ConnSENSE (Connecticut's Special Education Network for Software Evaluation)
University of Connecticut
Box U-64
249 Glenbrook Road
Storrs, Connecticut 06269-2064
(860) 486-5076
(860) 486-0172

Concerned with evaluating courseware for students with disabilities. ConnSENSE has a telecommunications system for special education administrators and a telecommunications project for students with disabilities. It publishes the *ConnSENSE Bulletin,* which contains reviews of software as they apply to students with special needs. Lists upcoming events and technological breakthroughs for people with disabilities as well as resource and reference information.

Exceptional Parent Magazine
555 Kinderkamack Road
Oradell, New Jersey 07649
(201) 634-6550

This publication is published 10 times per year and is designed for parents of children with disabilities. Much of the material is written by parents, and information on technology is included. One issue per year is devoted strictly to technology.

BOOKS

Assistive Technology Sourcebook
Enders, A., & Hall, M. (1990). *Assistive technology sourcebook.* Washington, DC: RESNA Press; available from Rehabilitation Engineering Society of North America, 1700 North Moore Street, Suite 1540, Arlington, Virginia 22209; (703) 524-6686 (telephone), (703) 524-6639 (TTY).

Enders and Hall provide an exhaustive listing of resources for individuals with disabilities and the professionals working with them. Their book also contains helpful, brief articles explaining major concepts and philosophies of and technical information on all major areas of assistive technology.

Teaching Reading to Children with Down Syndrome
Oelwein, P. (1995). *Teaching reading to children with Down syndrome.* Bethesda, MD: Woodbine House.

This guide provides reading instruction guidelines to help meet the needs of children with Down syndrome. The suggestions are directed specifically to parents.

Trace ResourceBook
Borden, P., Fatherly, S., Ford, K., & Vanderheiden, G. (1998). *Trace ResourceBook.* Madison: University of Wisconsin–Madison, The Waisman Center, Trace Research and Development Center; available from Trace Research and Development Center, 5901 Research Park Boulevard, Madison, Wisconsin 53719-1252; (608) 262-6966, (608) 263-5408 (TDD).

This approximately 900-page directory lists about 1,500 assistive technology products for communication, control, and computer access for people with disabilities. Each product entry includes a description, price, and photograph (when available). Products are cross-referenced by functions and features. Additional information resources are also listed.

SELF-HELP AND ADVOCACY GROUPS

Alliance for Technology Access
2175 East Francisco Boulevard, Suite L
San Rafael, California 94901
(415) 455-4575
(415) 455-0491 (TTY)

This organization, formerly called the National Special Education Alliance, comprises a national network of local self-help groups concerned with computers and people with disabilities. Each group is locally self-operated and self-funded. Contact the national office to ask about the group nearest you.

Closing the Gap, Inc.
Post Office Box 68
Henderson, Minnesota 56044
(507) 248-3294
World wide web site: http://www.closingthegap.com/

Closing the Gap organizes a national conference, workshops, and training. It also publishes a newspaper dedicated to the latest in technology for people with disabilities.

Macomb Projects
Western Illinois University
27 Horrabin Hall
One University Circle
Macomb, Illinois 61455
(309) 298-1072

Trains special education teachers in computer applications.

National Down Syndrome Congress (NDSC)
1605 Chantilly Drive, Suite 250
Atlanta, Georgia 30324
(404) 633-1555
(800) 232-6372

NDSC is an organization of parents and professionals that provides information on services for people with Down syndrome.

National Rehabilitation Information Center (NARIC)
8455 Colesville Road, Suite 935
Silver Spring, Maryland 20910
(301) 588-9284
(800) 34-NARIC

NARIC is a rehabilitation information service research library funded by the National Institute on Disability and Rehabilitation Research of the U.S. Department of Education. It provides access to NIDRR-funded reports and information on assistive devices and disseminates other rehabilitation-related information resources. NARIC also offers a computer bulletin board system called *ABLE INFORM.*

Rehabilitation Engineering
Society of North America (RESNA)
National Office
Technical Assistance Project
1700 North Moore Street, Suite 1540
Arlington, Virginia 22209-1903
(703) 524-6686
(703) 524-6639 (TTY)
World wide web site: http://www.resna.org/hometa1.htm

RESNA is a national association that provides information and technical assistance to state assistive technology programs. Contact the association to obtain the contact information for the program in your area.

The Arc
500 East Border Street, Suite 300
Arlington, Texas 76010
(817) 261-6003

The Arc provides information and makes referrals regarding assistive technology and mental retardation. It publishes information, including position statements on a variety of issues affecting people with mental retardation and their families.

Trace Research and Development Center
University of Wisconsin–Madison
5901 Research Park Boulevard
Madison, Wisconsin 53719-1252
(608) 262-6966 (voice)
(608) 263-5408 (TDD)

The Trace Research and Development Center is a research and resource center on technology and disability. The center's chief area of specialty is providing access to computers and other electronic devices. Its activities include research, product development, creating and distributing information materials, and answering questions from consumers and service providers concerning computer access. The center operates a publication service; ask for a publications and media brochure.

NETWORKS, BULLETIN BOARDS, AND DATABASES

ABLEDATA
Macro International
8455 Colesville Road, Suite 935
Silver Spring, Maryland 20910
(800) 227-0216
World wide web site: http://www.abledata.com/

ABLEDATA is a computerized listing of all commercially available products for rehabilitation and independent living. There are three ways to access the database: calling the ABLEDATA office, conducting a search of the World Wide Web by computer modem, and running the database on an individual computer. To run the database on your computer, you will need to obtain it in CD-ROM or floppy disk format. The third option is available through Macro International (on CD-ROM) and through the Trace Center (on CD-ROM or floppy disks) at http://trace.wisc.edu/.

Cooperative Database Distribution
Network for Assistive Technology (Co-Net)
Trace Research and Development Center
University of Wisconsin–Madison
5901 Research Park Boulevard
Madison, Wisconsin 53719-1252
(608) 262-6966 (voice)
(608) 263-5408 (TDD)
World wide web site: http://trace.wisc.edu/publications/

Co-Net contains the "Trace Cooperative Electronic Library," which is an integrated collection of information resources on disability. A single CD-ROM disk allows one to look up products, services, and documents pertaining to disability.

INTERNET SITES WITH FOCUS ON DOWN SYNDROME

webmaster@downsnet.org

Interested people can subscribe to an Internet e-mail address focused on issues regarding Down syndrome. Internet users can subscribe by sending an e-mail message to <webmaster@downsnet.org>. Your message should read: <(SUBSCRIBE down-syn <first name> <last name>).

http://www.familyvillage.wisc.edu/

The Family Village provides key information regarding research, services, and resources for individuals with disabilities.

10

Enhancing the Speech and Language Skills of Adults with Down Syndrome

Mark Leddy and Gary Gill

In the late 1960s and early 1970s, many states and the federal government enacted legislation mandating services for people with disabilities. By the 1970s, school systems were providing special services for students with cognitive disabilities. Near the end of the 1970s and well into the 1980s, early childhood programs and birth-to-3 programs emerged to capitalize on and enhance early childhood development. Intensive therapy at such an early age was designed to facilitate development in many areas, including communication. Children with Down syndrome who were enrolled in these programs are now adolescents and adults. They are likely to have experienced thousands of hours of intervention and developed some degree of successful communication skills. Nonetheless, many of these adults and their family members are looking for continued opportunities to improve communication.

From 1994 to 1997, we provided communication assessments to more than 40 men and women with Down syndrome. These individuals ranged in age from the late teens to the late 50s. We noticed a striking difference between the younger and older adult groups. These adults reflected the different cultures and educational environments in which they had lived. Many of the younger adults had experienced early intervention and were excited about and interested in working with speech-language pathologists. The older adults, however, were reluctant to engage in formal testing procedures and were leery of the clinicians with whom they worked in our clinics.

Although adults with Down syndrome are products of their education, so are adults who are typically developing. Many of the speech-language pathologists who have provided services to children with Down syndrome in early intervention programs have been biased by the principles that founded those programs. Professionals have been pessimistic about what could be accomplished with adults who have cognitive disabilities because these individuals have aged beyond the developmental years, beyond the time when traditional treatment was thought to be effective.

Like so many of our peers, we were skeptical, too. We initially doubted that adults with developmental disabilities could successfully modify their communication patterns or improve their basic speech and language skills. We were wrong! We quickly overcame our skepticism when we encountered many adults with Down syndrome, along with their families or caregivers, who expressed a strong desire to improve communication skills. After conducting a series of extensive evaluations, we began to speculate that the interesting communication challenges that these adults face might be treatable, given that these individuals had so many communication strengths and such a high motivation level for therapy. One young woman with Down syndrome and her caregiver were insistent about receiving therapy services. Within weeks of initiating a treatment program with this woman, we learned that speech and language skills could be improved and that this improvement could also be seen during communication at home and outside the clinical setting. As a result of this experience, we soon began enrolling more adults with cognitive disabilities in treatment, and by the summer of 1997, we had enrolled 12 adults with cognitive disabilities in therapy, 5 of whom had Down syndrome.

The communication assessments that we conducted taught us that most adults with Down syndrome evidenced strengths in the following areas: visual memory, vocabulary and semantics, the use of reading and writing, the use of hand signs and gestures to communicate, and the motivation to communicate. We hypothesized that we could emphasize these strengths as tools in treatment to help adults with Down syndrome address their communication challenges and improve communication. Typical challenges included reduced speech intelligibility, difficulties with auditory memory and comprehension, and poor grammatical construction skills.

In addition to playing off of the strengths of individuals, we found that several key principles were essential to effective intervention. These included emphasizing the use of the speech and language skills in very specific communication contexts. Although treatment was initiated in a clinical setting, the new skills were practiced during small-group social interactions at the clinic and during visits to the individual's community. In addition, treatment was aimed at achieving a series of small skill goals that would lead to greater success when these gains were combined to achieve larger communication goals.

There are multiple treatment approaches and specific interventions that we found helpful when working with adults who have Down syndrome. We believe that if speech-language pathologists employed these treatment procedures, then they will successfully assist some adults with Down syndrome to communicate more effectively. The following are a few examples of specific clinicial methods that we employed when working with adults with Down syndrome:

- Because many adults with Down syndrome have strong visual-perceptual skills, it is generally wise to emphasize these skills, incorporating reading material into intervention planning as a means of improving verbal communication skills. Examples of how this can be accomplished include the use of oral and silent reading practices to improve speech intelligibility, spoken vocabulary and grammar, the use of writing to stimulate spoken grammar, and encouraging writing as an alternative means of communicating.
- Adults with Down syndrome need to learn skills to prevent communication failure and strategies to repair their communication when it breaks down. They need to learn to recognize when their communicative partners do not understand them. These adults need to be taught to watch others' facial expressions and body movements for signs of confusion and misunderstanding and to ask their communicative partners key questions about the discussion content to check their partners' levels of understanding.
- Keep family members and other communicative partners of adults with Down syndrome involved in the treatment program. A few primary communicative partners must learn the strategies that a given adult with Down syndrome effectively uses for repairing communication failures. When failures occur, these communicative partners can assist with the repairs. Adults with Down syndrome thus get daily communication practice in meaningful contexts and real-life situations using the skills that they learn in their intervention sessions.
- If one of the goals of intervention is to improve speech intelligibility so that an adult's speech can be more easily understood, intervention will involve following the lead of the adult with the speech problem to identify the person's difficulty and using the person's words to cue him or her to speak more clearly. Instruction examples include the following: "Change your talking," "Speak clearly,"

"Use all your words," and "Say it so I can understand you." In addition, teach skills to reduce the person's speaking rate or rate bursts, and, if articulation is a focus of the intervention, use a general approach that is not speech sound specific. For example, instruct the person to open his or her mouth more when he or she is speaking.

- If a goal of intervention is to increase the individual's spoken message content, then work primarily on improving syntactic constructions to improve the length and content of the individual's messages. The emphasis on message length and syntax generally improves the individual's message content by including greater communicative detail and elaboration. More specifically, work on grammatical constructions that match what the person with Down syndrome wants to functionally communicate and that are the easiest for that person to learn. In practice, this will be a small set of simple sentence patterns. These patterns will encourage the use of whole-sentence statements and questions instead of single-word utterances and facilitate the use of "wh-" words, pronouns, and descriptive words.

- It is common for clinicians to focus on the adult's successful exchange of messages with a secondary focus on speech skills. For individuals who have extremely poor speech intelligibility or who are completely nonverbal, the use of hand signs or signing, a printed or picture communication book or board, and written messages can be used to facilitate their message exchanges. When working on this skill, the adult with Down syndrome needs to learn to recognize when messages have been conveyed successfully and when to take turns communicating with his or her partners.

SUCCESSFUL INTERVENTIONS

Keeping in mind the general communication principles and several specific techniques outlined in the previous section, we present the following communication profiles. These reports illustrate the types of intervention goals and treatment techniques we use and reflect composite summaries of our experiences with various adults with Down syndrome.

Nicholas Learns to Increase His Sentence Meaning and Length

Nicholas was a 43-year-old male with Down syndrome who was healthy and living with two other adult males in a community-supported private home. He was employed part time in a county government office, where he filed and sorted documents, delivered mail, and ran intradepartmental errands for the staff. Nich-

olas primarily communicated by verbalizing his thoughts in two-
to four-word phrases such as "Go eat" and "Mail go Sue office."
His comprehension of spoken language was much better, and he
understood multistep directions and several complex syntactic
constructions. Nicholas could read single words and short sentences easily. His speech was intelligible to the majority of listeners, with only an occasional complaint that someone could not
understand his speech. Nicholas in turn complained that people
did not always understand what he said to them, saying, "People
don't know."

Nicholas's intervention goals centered on increasing message
content as a means of preventing communication failure. Achieving this goal required using printed text and helping Nicholas
recognize ways that he could elaborate or increase the length and
complexity of his messages. An intensive 6-week period of individual and group interventions was scheduled for Nicholas. He
was seen two times per week for individual language therapy
and once per week for a group intervention. The group session
was scheduled immediately following the final individual session
of the week. Individual sessions allowed Nicholas to work on
specific strategies to improve the content of his messages to prevent communication failure. The group session allowed Nicholas
the opportunity to practice these strategies in more natural communication exchanges that emphasized successful communication to achieve a group process, such as working together in the
kitchen cooking or completing an art project. Nicholas and the
other members of the group generally selected the projects from
a menu of choices. The clinicians accompanied members so that
they could cue them to use their new strategies, and the clinicians created scenarios that would require them to use these new
communication skills (e.g., materials or utensils were missing,
which required participants to request items or to share them).

At the beginning of individual interventions, Nicholas and
one of his two clinicians would engage in a brief conversation
with only two or three exchanges such as

Clinician: Nicholas, what did you do at work today?
Nicholas: I work mail.
Clinician: And what else did you do at work?
Nicholas: I eat.

The clinicians would teach Nicholas about varied grammatical markers, such as past-tense markers ("-ed"), past-tense irreg-
ular verbs, and prepositions, writing most of this information on
a marker board. They would then write the conversational ques-

tions and statements on the marker board, and Nicholas would identify the length of each statement. He would then be instructed to "use a full sentence," "make it longer," or "say it with more words" and would restate each sentence, such that "I work mail" would become "I worked on mail." The revision would replace the previous statement on the marker board. After creating a grammatically improved utterance, Nicholas would be instructed to elaborate on his statement to recount additional information about his work in the mailroom that day. He would describe the other events that took place in the mailroom while the clinicians wrote the events down on the marker board. The clinicians would take time to teach Nicholas about articles, adjectives, and the use of conjunctions. One of the clinicians and Nicholas would then repeat the conversation, first using the written sentences on the marker board as a script and then removing the marker board so that the script was completed from memory. Using this process resulted in Nicholas's creating longer utterances that conveyed greater meaning, such as "I worked in the mailroom with Lew" or "I delivered the mail, and I helped Jon copy."

These changes were immediate in individual sessions and quickly began to carry over into group intervention sessions. During the first few weeks of group therapy, the clinicians occasionally had to remind Nicholas to "use full sentences"; but by the end of the intervention period, Nicholas was spontaneously producing longer and more complete utterances and occasionally a longer one, usually when he used a conjunction to combine two sentences. This increase in Nicholas's message length was coupled with greater message content and more complex syntactic constructions. Subsequent reports from co-workers and community support providers indicated that there was a dramatic reduction in Nicholas's communication failure and that they understood what Nicholas was talking about more often than they had in the past. Nicholas is just one example of how interventions can be used to increase message content, primarily by focusing on increasing the adult's utterance length and teaching him or her to use more complex sentence structures as well as articles, adjectives, and verb constructions.

Alexander Learns to Improve His Speech Intelligibility

Alexander was a 23-year-old male with Down syndrome who lived with his parents. His health was generally good, but he was being treated for esophageal reflux and thyroid dysfunction. He worked full time in a restaurant cleaning tables. He rarely spoke to people, because they could not understand him. Alexander spoke lengthy utterances that were generally completely unintelligible to most listeners. Only Alexander's parents understood what he said to them, and they only understood about 75% of what he said. When he spoke to others, the result was generally communication failure. His hearing was within typical limits, and there was nothing remarkable about his speech structures other than that the esophageal reflux appeared to have created irritation to his vocal folds. Clinicians also discovered that Alexander frequently watched sporting events and wrestling on television, yelling throughout the programs. The clinicians suspected that this behavior, coupled with his esophageal reflux, was contributing to his severely hoarse voice production, which may have reduced his speech intelligibility. Clearly, however, Alexander's speech contained frequent vowel distortions and consonant deletions, substitutions, and distortions.

Alexander began receiving interventions in individual sessions twice per week. Because Alexander had good reading and writing skills, these skills were used as building blocks for successful communication skills development. During evaluation, Alexander's speech intelligibility during oral reading of phrases and sentences was 68% as compared with his intelligibility during conversational speech, which was only 43%. Reading aloud slowed Alexander's speed, controlled his tendency to rush through phrases, and gave the clinicians an opportunity to point out various sounds that he was leaving out of words. Alexander was instructed to read aloud at home, at work, and in intervention sessions so that he had frequent daily practice in speaking at a slower rate. In addition, he was taught to ask his parents and his clinicians if they understood what he said when he read a phrase aloud. The clinicians specifically used a phonics approach to relate the written text to Alexander's sound production. Alexander began writing stories for his parents and clinicians and then read them aloud to practice his speech production. This simple practice, paired with gamelike tasks in which if he omitted a speech sound from a word he lost a point and in which he earned a point if he correctly produced the word, led to dramatic improvements after 18 months of intervention. At the end of the treatment period, his speech intelligibility in conversation had nearly doubled to 78% and his intelligibility during oral reading increased to 92%. Alexander had begun to speak more with his co-workers and with family members other than his parents. In addition to the interventions just described, the clinicians taught Alexander not to yell during live sporting events or while watching them on television so that he would earn a monthly "family reward" for using his "soft voice." They also consulted with his gastroenterologist, who modified his antireflux medication. The results of these interventions were not as dramatic; but his voice quality did improve, which may have contributed to his increased intelligibility.

CONCLUSIONS

In general, we found that the young adults who participated in evaluations, including the subset who enrolled in treatment, were very different from the older adults. These young adults were characterized by several striking features: They had some functional reading skills, they knew how to play the communication game from a pragmatic perspective, and they exhibited a certain communication self-confidence. We believe that these features are the result of these young adults' educational experiences. For these young adults, their communication development was fostered by years of special education classroom instruction by talented educators and special services from social workers, psychologists, occupational therapists, physical therapists, and speech-language pathologists.

The older adults who participated in assessments and in therapy did not exhibit the same skills that the younger adults evidenced. These older adults did not have functional reading skills. They often would defer to their caregivers and family members to communicate for them rather than speak for themselves. In addition, these older adults were passive communicators who did not appear to know how to play the communication game. It is interesting to note that these adults showed no signs of the deteriorating cognitive or communication function that is thought to describe the majority of adults with Down syndrome.

Traditional developmental theory suggests that by adolescence, people with Down syndrome experience a plateau in learning. This perspective is frequently used to justify limiting speech-language services to adolescents and adults with Down syndrome. Adults with Down syndrome and their families or caregivers frequently report that speech-language services are discontinued when they reach adolescence or early adulthood and that they are informed that their progress has plateaued and that they have no prospects for improvement. When the learning curves of people with Down syndrome are examined, however, tremendous variability in their communication skills learning is found. Although some individuals plateau in adolescence, others continue to learn well into adulthood. This was evident to us when we provided communication treatment to adults with Down syndrome. The treatment that we provided to adults with Down syndrome lasted for many months. It may have taken 24 months of weekly therapy to help one individual reach a goal, whereas it may have taken another individual 30 months of twice-per-week intervention to reach a similar goal. Our sample was small, but each individual was able to achieve a measure of success.

The future for adults with Down syndrome is promising. We have seen that some adults with Down syndrome can improve their communication skills. Large-scale investigations are needed to identify which interventions are most effective for improving speech and language skills in adults. University faculty in the field of communication disorders and speech-language pathologists across the United States need to teach beginning clinicians, educators, health care providers, and community service support personnel that speech and language interventions can make a difference in the lives of adults with Down syndrome. Parents and families of people with Down syndrome need to know this as well. Local speech-language pathologists should be encouraged to provide these much-needed services. In addition, the state and federal governments as well as private and public organizations need to be encouraged to fund needed research to investigate the effectiveness of interventions.

III

Thinking About the Future

Section III includes two chapters and is followed by three appendixes. Chapter 11, by Seltzer and Krauss, describes their longitudinal studies of families with aging children with developmental disabilities. These studies include almost 100 families with middle-age children with Down syndrome. This chapter is included in this book to provide a vista of familial considerations and of possible futures for children with Down syndrome as they age and as a way of underlining the importance of communication on family functioning, home, community, and employment. Chapter 11 describes the extensive and effective adaptations that families use to accommodate the unique abilities of a person with Down syndrome throughout the life span.

Chapter 12, by Miller, Leddy, and Leavitt, reflects on the present state of knowledge and the challenges of an increasingly technological future that will require greater demands for communication and literacy skills. Changes are needed in public policy regarding the provision of services for children in light of advancing scientific knowledge. The editors of this book also recognize the need for parents and professionals to update their knowledge from reliable sources.

Appendix A provides a selected reading list of books, newsletters, and magazines that can be of help in understanding Down syndrome and general child development and in providing language and communication activities throughout the child's development. In Appendix B, Helen Hartman, the parent of a child with Down syndrome, provides a list of web sites that she has found helpful in keeping abreast of new research findings and professional activities related to Down syndrome. Readers will find these resources helpful in keeping up with advances in research, educational activities, and clinical practice. Appendix C discusses the medical care of children with Down syndrome and provides in tabular form the recommended evaluations of these children proposed by the American Academy of Pediatrics.

11

Families of Adults
with Down Syndrome

Marsha Mailick Seltzer
and Marty Wyngaarden Krauss

This chapter focuses on adults with Down syndrome and their families with whom they have lived throughout their lives. Lifelong family-based care for such individuals is typical in the United States (Fujiura & Braddock, 1992). Indeed, only about 15% of people with mental retardation live in licensed residential environments. The others live with or under the supervision of their families. On the basis of this prevalence alone, information about the contexts and consequences of family-based care is sorely needed.

We have conducted research on more than 400 older families of adults with mental retardation who lived at home when the study began in 1988. More than one third of these families have an adult member with Down syndrome. The other two thirds have a son or a

This chapter supported by Grant R01 AG08768 from the National Institute on Aging and by the Joseph P. Kennedy, Jr., Foundation, the March of Dimes Birth Defects Foundation, the Retirement Research Foundation, the Starr Center for Mental Retardation at Brandeis University, and The Waisman Center at the University of Wisconsin–Madison.

The authors are grateful to Gordon Gurney for permission to publish his poem at the end of this chapter.

The terms *mild, moderate, severe,* and *profound* are used to describe the degrees of mental retardation experienced by individuals in the research sample discussed in this chapter because the data were collected prior to the publication of the 1992 American Association on Mental Retardation (AAMR) classification system.

daughter with a different etiology of mental retardation. All of these families gave birth to and reared their children with mental retardation in an era when community services were not as rich or as available as they are in the late 1990s. There were few, if any, early intervention programs for infants and toddlers; there was no federally established right to education; there were only scattered adult day programs; there were limited supports available to families; and the public's attitude toward people with disabilities was generally scornful. Professional guidance for parents included the warning that their children with mental retardation would have a shortened life span, that their children's capacity for learning was extremely limited, that their children's effect on other family members was likely to be deleterious, and that the only source of care for their children was in an institutional environment. The dismal early prognoses that are so frequently recounted by older parents of adults with mental retardation prompted some to relinquish care of their young children to state-run institutions; for most, however, their decision was to do the best they could and raise their children with mental retardation along with their other children.

The research discussed in this chapter has focused on these families with an adult member with mental retardation, specifically on the current functioning and circumstances of the adult family member with mental retardation and his or her plans for the future. The findings from this research, by and large, are that the families have demonstrated remarkable resilience and fortitude; express appreciation for their development of tolerance and patience, which they attribute to their experiences as parents of a person with mental retardation; and have weathered a sea change in public attitudes and support for people with mental retardation that serves to reinforce the decisions they made decades ago to raise their children at home (Seltzer & Krauss, 1989, 1994).

This chapter summarizes a series of analyses that support these conclusions, focusing particularly on adults with Down syndrome and their families. Whereas the other chapters in this book focus on young children, the average adult with Down syndrome discussed in this chapter was about 31 years of age at the time the research was conducted. This chapter departs from the other chapters in this book in three ways. First, there is the obvious difference of the age of the people with Down syndrome. Second, this chapter focuses simultaneously on two units of analysis: the adult with Down syndrome and his or her aging parents. Third, whereas other chapters in this book focus on communication abilities, the research discussed in this chapter examines the physical, psychological, and social well-being of adults with

Down syndrome and their parents. The conceptualization of well-being discussed in this chapter is thus quite broad. The overarching importance of communication abilities for the issues examined in this chapter are recognized, however. Communication is critical to the relationship between an adult with Down syndrome and his or her parents as well as the extent to which the adult is able to be integrated into the larger community and establish personal relationships. Thus, though this chapter does not explicitly focus on communication, it is an underlying theme of the research it discusses.

This chapter is based on a life-course perspective (Clausen, 1986), a perspective that investigates both the continuities and the changes that characterize an individual's development and family relationships from one stage of life to another. This perspective has been particularly lacking in research on people with mental retardation, which instead has disproportionately emphasized early childhood. Because adults with Down syndrome (as well as adults with other types of mental retardation) enjoy a longer life span and greater social visibility (Zigman, Seltzer, & Silverman, 1994) than in the past, however, interest in their adult stage of life has quickened. In the past, the long stretch of adulthood received remarkably little attention in the scientific literature, reflecting the assumption that this is a quiescent or even stagnant period of life for individuals with mental retardation. Yet there is ample evidence from the general literature that development is a lifelong process for both individuals (Hetheringon, Lerner, & Perlmutter, 1988) and families (Carter & McGoldrick, 1989; Seltzer & Ryff, 1994). Therefore, widening the focus of the research on Down syndrome has the potential to enrich as well as expand understanding of developmental trajectories among this group.

In parallel with the need to focus attention on the adulthood of people with Down syndrome, there is a need to learn more about their parents. In the past, parents of people with Down syndrome could expect to outlive their sons or daughters; in the late 1990s, however, this expectation is not borne out because of the longer life spans of these individuals. The period of family care has extended to 50 or even 60 years, and the impact of a family member with mental retardation on the family is therefore considerably more pronounced. For these reasons, there is much to be gained by applying the life-course perspective to parents of adults with Down syndrome as well as to their adult children.

Four issues are addressed in this chapter. First, the study's major findings regarding the well-being of older families caring for a son or daughter with mental retardation at home are described. This discussion, which includes but is not limited to the subsample of individuals with Down syndrome, provides the context in which specific findings about families of adults with Down syndrome should be placed. Given the dearth of research on the consequences to families of providing lifelong care to family members with mental retardation, the results of the quantitative and qualitative analyses yield an instructive overview of the challenges and triumphs of an unheralded cohort of families. Second, the well-being of the families of adults with Down syndrome is compared with the well-being of other families in the research whose children's mental retardation is due to other causes. This comparison was prompted by other research that demonstrates that families of young children with Down syndrome tend to fare better than other families, at least with respect to the degree of social support received and the effects on parents' well-being. Third, differences between the adults with Down syndrome in the study and the other sample members with respect to their health and functional and behavioral characteristics are examined. Finally, results based on analyses regarding the future care plans developed by families of adults with Down syndrome are presented.

Before these four issues are addressed, however, a brief description of the research methods employed and sample characteristics, as well as a profile of the daily lives of adults with Down syndrome, is presented. This discussion yields information about the types of programs in which the individuals with Down syndrome participate, the range of therapeutic and support services that they receive, their social activities, and their relationships with family members.

The overall goal of the study is to describe the well-being of older families with an adult child with mental retardation and to investigate the factors that account for variation in familial well-being. Furthermore, attempts are made to account for patterns of stability and change in families' well-being during the years when the end of parental caregiving may be approaching and to describe the transition to post-parental care.

STUDY DESCRIPTION

The research discussed here, which began in 1988, is based on an ongoing longitudinal study of 461 families. At the time the study was initiated, all families met two criteria: 1) The mother was age 55 or older, and 2) the mother had a son or a daughter with mental retardation who lived at home with her. More than one third (37%; $n = 170$) of the adults in the study have Down syndrome; the others have a diagnosis of cerebral palsy (14%), epilepsy (10%), autism (3%), or other or unknown disabilities (36%). All families volunteered to participate in the study.

Data are collected from families every 18 months. At each point of data collection, the mother is interviewed in her home and completes a set of self-administered measures. In families in which the father is living, he provides data as well. In addition, at various points during the study, data have been obtained from adult siblings and from the adult family member with mental retardation. Qualitative and quantitative data are collected from each member of the family.

Table 1 shows that at the first point of data collection, the mothers in the study ranged in age from 55 to 85 years (mean = 66 years). Two thirds (66%) of the mothers were married; of the remaining mothers, most were widows (28%), with only a few being separated or divorced

Table 1.   Characteristics of the sample of families of adults with mental retardation

Characteristics of the mothers	
Mean age	66 years
Age range	55–85 years
Marital status	
Married	66%
Widowed	28%
Separated/Divorced	6%
Mean number of children	4.0
Level of education	
Less than high school education	19%
High school graduate	41%
Post–high school education	40%
Employment status	
Employed full or part time	25%
Not employed	75%
Race	
Caucasian	98%
Other	2%
Characteristics of the adults with mental retardation	
Mean age	34 years
Age range	15–66 years
Gender	
Male	54%
Female	46%
Level of mental retardation	
Mild	38%
Moderate	41%
Severe	15%
Profound	6%
Health status	
Excellent	47%
Good	41%
Fair	10%
Poor	3%

(6%). On average, these mothers had four children, including the son or daughter with mental retardation. Nearly two thirds of the mothers (60%) had no education beyond high school, but one fourth (25%) were employed outside the home. Virtually all mothers (98%) were Caucasians.

The sons (54%) and daughters (46%) with mental retardation ranged in age from 15 to 66 years (mean = 34 years) when the study began. Most have mild (38%) or moderate (41%) mental retardation; fewer have severe (15%) or profound (6%) mental retardation. Nearly all (more than 90%) had left home on a daily basis for a job or a day program, such as a sheltered workshop or supported employment. When the study began, the majority were in excellent (47%) or good (41%) health as described by their mothers.

As described further along in this chapter, a series of comparisons of the well-being of the families of adults with Down syndrome and the other families in the sample were conducted using data collected between 1988 and 1990. Prior to investigating differences in well-being, however, it was necessary to compare these two groups with respect to background characteristics. Identification of factors that might differentiate the two groups of families, apart from the diagnosis of the adult child with Down syndrome, was important in order to rule out any potentially confounding variables as alternative explanations for between-group differences. To this end, the two groups were examined for differences with respect to the mother's age, marital status, level of education, employment status, and number of children and with respect to the age, gender, and level of mental retardation of the adult child with Down syndrome.

As shown in Table 2, the two groups of mothers were more similar to each other than they were different. The mothers of the adults with Down syndrome were similar to the other mothers in the study in terms of marital status (about two thirds of both groups were married), level of education (about 40% had some post–high school education), and employment status (one quarter were employed). The two groups were different in only two respects: The mothers of adult children with Down syndrome were significantly older (about 67 years versus 65 years) and had larger families (averaging 4.3 children among mothers with children with mental retardation versus 3.8 children among mothers of adult children without Down syndrome). The adults with Down syndrome did not differ from the other adults with regard to level of mental retardation (about 80% had mild or moderate mental retardation), but they were different with respect to gender (more males than females with Down syndrome) and age (the adults with Down syndrome were younger by 3 years). These four differ-

Table 2. Diagnostic differences in background characteristics

	Children with Down syndrome (n = 170)	Other children (n = 291)	F
Mother			
Age	66.78	65.07	2.73 p = .007
Marital status (% married)	67%	66%	0.37
Level of education (% college graduates)	16%	14%	0.71
Employment status (% employed)	25%	26%	0.31
Family income	$23,800	$24,020	0.16
Number of children in family	4.33	3.76	3.04 p = .003
Adult with mental retardation			
Age	31.34	35.29	5.50 p < .001
Gender (1 = female; 0 = male)	0.39	0.51	2.42 p = .016
Level of retardation (3 = mild; 0 = profound)	2.04	2.16	1.46

n, subsample population; F, result of analysis of variance.

ences in background characteristics (age of mother, age of adult with mental retardation, number of children in family, and gender of the adult with Down syndrome) were controlled in comparative analyses presented further along in this chapter.

The measures used in this analysis include characteristics of the mother and her son or daughter with mental retardation, indices of maternal well-being and mothers' feelings about parenting, and assessments of family functioning. These are detailed in Table 3. (For more detailed descriptions of study methods and findings, see Krauss & Seltzer, 1993; Krauss, Seltzer, & Goodman, 1992; Seltzer, Begun, Seltzer, & Krauss, 1991; Seltzer, Greenberg, & Krauss, 1995; Seltzer & Krauss, 1994; and Seltzer, Krauss, & Tsunematsu, 1993.)

CONTEMPORARY LIFE CIRCUMSTANCES OF ADULTS WITH DOWN SYNDROME

Prior to discussing the study findings, a brief description of the life circumstances of adults with Down syndrome who live with their families is presented in this section. The available literature about the lives of adults with mental retardation has disproportionately focused on those who live in community residences (Lakin, Hill, & Bruininks,

Table 3.   Measures and variable definitions

Measures of maternal well-being	
Depression	CES-D (Radloff, 1977) self-administered 20-item scale (range of scores, 0–60)
Life satisfaction	Philadelphia Geriatric Center (PGC) Morale Scale (Lawton, 1972) self-administered 17-item scale (range of scores, 0–17)
Caregiving burden	Zarit Burden Scale (Zarit, Reever, & Bach-Peterson, 1980) self-administered 29-item scale (range of scores, 0–58)
Caregiving stress	Questionnaire on Resources and Stress–Friedrich version (Friedrich, Greenberg, & Crnic, 1983) self-administered 52-item scale (range of scores, 0–52)

Family social climate
  Cohesiveness
  Expressiveness
  Conflict
	Family Environment Scale (Moos, 1974) three self-administered nine-item scales (range of scores on each, 0–9)

Informal support
  Size of network
  Satisfaction
	Social Networks in Adult Life (Antonucci, 1986); size = number of network members; satisfaction = rating scale (0–3)

Measures of the well-being of adults	
Functional abilities	Barthel (Mahoney & Barthel, 1965) and IADL Index (modified) 16-item scale (range of scores, 0–64)
Behavior problems	Inventory for Client and Agency Planning (Bruininks, Hill, Weatherman, & Woodcock, 1986) (range of scores, 0–8)
Health status	0 = poor; 1 = fair; 2 = good; 3 = excellent
Hearing impairment	0 = no; 1 = yes
Vision impairment	0 = no; 1 = yes
Clarity of speech	0 = not understandable; 1 = some words understandable; 2 = most words understandable; 3 = most speech understandable

1988) or other out-of-home placements. Much less is known about those adults who continue to live at home.

The adults with Down syndrome in this study span a 40-year age range. The youngest was 20 years of age at the time of our research, and the oldest was 60 years of age. For those on the younger end of the age continuum, adulthood had just begun; those at the other end of the continuum faced the challenges of declining health and retirement. Three fourths of the adults with Down syndrome in the sample were between 30 and 45 years of age at the time of the research, however. These are the years of middle adulthood for those with Down syndrome, given their shorter average life span.

One dominant feature of the life circumstances of the adults with Down syndrome in the sample is that, although they lived at home with their parents, virtually all (93%) received formal services. The average adult in the sample received 4.3 services, most commonly employment services or supports, social work or service coordination, transportation, and social and recreation activities. Three fourths of the adults with Down syndrome in the sample received all of these services.

Nearly all of the adults (91%) in the sample engaged in some type of work. Fully 23% held a job in the community (either in competitive employment or with the assistance of supported employment), and another 59% participated in sheltered workshops. The remaining adults attended day activity centers or some other type of day program. On average, the adults worked or attended these day programs for an average of 29 hours each week. For some, work was an opportunity to be with friends. Nearly half of the adults (47%) got together with their co-workers in their free time during 1 year of the study, and about one third (30%) did so at least monthly. One adult with Down syndrome explained, "I work hard at the center, and then there are socials, dances, polkas, and other things for rest and relaxation there."

In addition to time spent with co-workers, most of the adults with Down syndrome in the sample spent their free time with relatives other than those with whom they lived. For 82%, there was at least monthly contact with relatives. The relatives with whom the adults had the most contact, other than their parents, were their brothers and sisters. Indeed, more than 50% of the adults with Down syndrome had engaged in each of the following activities with a sibling during the year preceding this round of data collection: visiting in one another's homes, staying overnight, going out for a meal, running errands or going shopping, participating in a recreation activity together, or visiting another relative together. One man reflected on a particularly pleasurable time with his brother: "My brother came down for my mother's birthday, and we went out for ice cream. Then we took a ride and went sightseeing. We went to a flea market. I am happy when I can spend time with him and do things with him. I enjoy doing that."

It was also common for the adults with Down syndrome to participate in organized group recreation activities, with nearly two thirds (60%) reporting monthly or more frequent participation. About one third spent time at least monthly with friends other than those at work (34%) or got together with neighbors (28%). One woman enthusiastically described her favorite activities: "I go horseback riding, to the movies, out to eat, shopping with Mom, visiting Debbie, going dancing." Finally, nearly half (46%) of the adults participated in church-sponsored social activities.

The fullness of the lives of the adults with Down syndrome in the sample was noteworthy with respect to family relationships, service utilization, employment, and social activities. Yet, parents' single greatest concern regarding the services and supports that their sons or daughters received was the inadequacy of the social or recreation activities available to them. Furthermore, as discussed in a subsequent section of this chapter, parents of adults with Down syndrome are also concerned about how to maintain the current life circumstances of their adult children beyond the period of parental care.

STUDY FINDINGS

With the profile of the life circumstances of the adults with Down syndrome that was discussed in the previous section as a context, the discussion in this section of the chapter presents the study findings.

Impact of Lifelong Caregiving

The first set of analyses described in this section concerns the impact on parents of providing care to their child with Down syndrome over a period of decades. These aging parents face a unique dual challenge: They must provide continuing care and support to their child because of their child's disabilities while coping with emerging manifestations and consequences of their own aging. At first blush, this dual challenge suggests negative outcomes for those who experience it. However, unexpectedly positive well-being has been found in older parents in our research (Seltzer & Krauss, 1989). Specifically, as shown in Table 4, the well-being of these mothers of adults with mental retardation is comparable to that of their age-peers who have not provided lifelong care and superior to that of caregivers for elderly family members for whom the period of caregiving has been much shorter (Krauss & Seltzer, 1993). Specifically, they have better self-rated health than family caregivers, lower levels of depressive symptoms, and higher levels of life satisfaction. Rather than manifesting signs of burnout or depletion, these mothers have no greater caregiving burden or stress than family caregivers whose period of family care has been considerably shorter in duration. As one parent in the study expressed, "This child has taught me an appreciation for the little things in life that we all take for granted. My other children learned about love and caring from Cindy. I don't ask, 'Why me?' I ask, 'Why not me?'"

In accounting for this favorable level of well-being in older mothers whose adult children continue to live at home, three explanations are advanced here. First, there are selection factors regarding which families elect to have their children live at home into adulthood. Parents in poor health and those who cannot adapt to the disability of their child may place their child out of the home prematurely. Because

Table 4.   Comparison of well-being with normative samples

Indicators	Mothers in present study	Family caregivers	Older noncaregivers
Health (% in good or excellent health)	71%	67%[a]	60%[b]
Depression (mean Center for Epidemiological Studies Depression Scale score)	10	16–17[c]	10[d]
Life satisfaction (mean Philadelphia Geriatric Center [PGC] Morale Scale score)	12	8[e]	13[e]
Caregiving burden (mean Zarit Burden score)	30	31[f]	N/A
Caregiving stress (mean Questionnaire on Resources and Stress scale)	16	19[g]	N/A

[a] Stone, Cafferata, and Sangl (1987).
[b] Bumpass and Sweet (1987).
[c] Pruchno, Michaels, and Potashnik (1990); Pruchno and Resch (1989).
[d] Gatz and Hurwicz (1990).
[e] Gallagher et al. (1985).
[f] Zarit, Reever, and Bach-Peterson (1980).
[g] Friedrich, Greenberg, and Crnic (1983).

the majority of people with mental retardation in the United States live at home, however, other explanations are needed to account for the pattern of salutary outcomes observed in their parents.

A second explanation for the favorable well-being in the mothers in the sample is that it is possible that the stresses associated with having a child with a disability are greatest during the early childhood period, when the diagnosis is new and the child's abilities and special needs are not yet fully understood. As the child grows into adulthood, parents tend to accommodate to the son's or daughter's limitations and develop an appreciation for his or her strengths. A parent's comments illustrate this point:

> In the beginning, it was very hard to take. As soon as it starts, you would like it to be ended. But then, you just learn to take it. I'm blessed the way it is now. She's a great help. It's become positive. I know in the beginning that I was thinking that this was the worst thing that could happen to anybody. But now I would love to tell other ones that it happened to that it isn't the worst thing.

A third factor accounting for positive well-being in the mothers in the study is that they enjoy unexpected benefits from their later-life parenting experiences. Many report a sense of feeling needed, of having a continued purpose in life, and the development of a different set of personal and family values. One mother in the study explained that

> There have been benefits to the whole family. She has kept me busy and increased my tolerance for differences in the world. I've learned to accept

things we can't change. I'm grateful for the help we've received. She's broadened my life.

The critical point to emphasize here is that aging parents of adults with mental retardation experience a range of emotions regarding their continued active parenting responsibilities, including feelings of gratification and frustration. The net effect of these feelings, however, does not translate into poorer mental health or poorer well-being for this group of parents as compared with other older parents who do not have a child with a disability. There is a difference in the family, as Featherstone (1980) testified, but that difference does not necessarily imply an impairment.

Comparisons of Families of Adults with Down Syndrome and Other Families

The next set of findings concerns differences between families of adults with Down syndrome and those of families whose adult child's mental retardation is due to other factors. This comparison grows out of past research on families of young children with Down syndrome, which has shown that these families have an "advantage" as compared with families of young children with other types of mental retardation. Specifically, parents of children with Down syndrome do not report the same degree of personal or familial distress as parents of children whose mental retardation is due to other factors (see, e.g., Gallagher, Beckman, & Cross, 1983; Kazak, 1987). Reasons for this superior adaptation by parents of children with Down syndrome include the high prevalence of Down syndrome as compared with other types of mental retardation, which may result in greater public knowledge about and social support for this disability. Also, some children with Down syndrome may have a more easygoing temperament than other children with mental retardation, making caring for them less stressful.

There has been no research that has examined whether the salutary outcomes reported in parents of young children with Down syndrome are also observed in the later years of the family's life course. Discontinuities in parents' well-being could result from the age-related health, cognitive, and functional problems experienced by older adults with Down syndrome (Zigman et al., 1994). During the long stretch of early and middle adulthood before such problems become prominent, however, patterns of individuals' and families' well-being manifested earlier in the life course may become evident.

It was hypothesized that the older mothers in the study whose sons or daughters had Down syndrome would differ from the mothers of adults with other types of mental retardation in three ways:

1. They would perceive their family environments to be more cohe-
    sive, more expressive, and less conflicted (as found for young fam-
    ilies by Mink, Nihira, & Meyers, 1983).
2. They would have more social support (as reported among young
    families by Erickson & Upshur, 1989; Goldberg, Marcovitch, Mac-
    Gregor, & Lojkasek, 1986).
3. They would feel less stressed and less burdened by parenting (as
    reported with regard to parents of young children by Goldberg et
    al., 1986; Holroyd & McArthur, 1976; Minnes, 1988; Noh, Dumas,
    Wolf, & Fisman, 1989).

Thus, the study's conceptualization of well-being in these analyses
included three components:

1. The cohesiveness, expressiveness, and level of conflict in the fam-
    ily environment
2. The level of social support available to the mother and her feelings
    of satisfaction with support
3. Maternal level of stress and burden associated with caregiving

Support was found for these hypotheses (see Table 5). Specifically, regarding the family environment, the mothers of adults with Down
syndrome perceived their families to have significantly less conflict

Table 5. Comparison of families' well-being

Factor measured	Families of adults with Down syndrome	Families of other adults	F
Famlies' social climate			
Cohesiveness	7.92	7.53	6.16 $p = .013$
Expressiveness	5.68	5.50	1.46
Conflict	1.24	1.73	9.74 $p = .002$
Mothers' informal support			
Size of network	7.94	7.04	4.08 $p = .004$
Satisfaction with support	2.73	2.60	2.18
Maternal reactions to caregiving			
Stress	15.13	19.09	13.70 $p < .001$
Burden	27.28	30.52	12.60 $p < .001$

Data are expressed in terms of analysis of covariance (F) adjusted for the mothers' ages and number
of children in the family, and for the age and gender of the adults with mental retardation.

than did the other mothers, although the two groups did not differ in their levels of cohesion or expressiveness. Regarding the mothers' level of social support, although satisfaction with social support did not differ between the two groups, mothers of adults with Down syndrome had significantly larger social support networks than mothers of adults with other types of mental retardation. Finally, they reported significantly less stress and burden associated with caregiving than did mothers of adults with other types of mental retardation.

One family in the study that exemplifies this profile consists of the parents, who are in their 60s; their daughter with Down syndrome who is age 28; and four other grown children. The daughter with Down syndrome lives at home and has a cleaning job in a movie theater in town. She enjoys a close relationship with her siblings; has dinner every Wednesday evening with one brother and his family; works out with her sister every Saturday morning at the health club; and visits the other two siblings, who live out of state, for vacations each year. The family members get along well, enjoy each other's company, and experience little conflict. The parents are proud of the accomplishments of their daughter with Down syndrome and do not feel that she is a source of stress in their lives. The mother said, "You are never the same after having a [child with a disability]. You are probably more responsible and protective of that child. You are concerned about the family being strong. You look at the basics."

The findings from this comparison of mothers of adults with Down syndrome and mothers of adults with other types of mental retardation suggest that differences in maternal psychological and social well-being, which past research identified in parents of young children, were durable across the life course. Although the children with Down syndrome in the study have become adults and their parents are either approaching or in their old age, the relative advantage enjoyed by these families in comparison with parents of adults whose mental retardation is due to other factors remains similar to patterns reported in families whose child is 3 decades younger.

Comparisons of Adults with Down Syndrome and Other Adults

This subsection examines differences between the adults with Down syndrome and their counterparts with other types of mental retardation. It is possible that the more favorable well-being of the mothers of adults with Down syndrome, as reported in the previous section, was the result of the functional and behavioral characteristics of their sons and daughters with Down syndrome rather than being based on etiology per se. To this end, the adults with Down syndrome and the other adults in the sample were compared with respect to their functional abilities, health status, behavior problems, sensory impairments, and communication abilities. These all are factors that might affect a parent's experience of providing lifelong care to a son or a daughter with mental retardation.

Past research suggested that adults with Down syndrome have better functional abilities (Greenspan & Delaney, 1983; Johnson & Abelson, 1969; Loveland & Kelley, 1988; Silverstein et al., 1985; Zigman, Schupf, Lubin, & Silverman, 1987) and fewer behavior problems (Greenspan & Delaney, 1983; Hodapp & Dykens, 1994) than adults with mental retardation caused by other factors. Although this profile of superior functional abilities and fewer behavior problems was derived from research conducted primarily on adults with Down syndrome who lived in out-of-home placements, a similar profile in adults who continued to live with their parents was expected.

As noted previously, there is ample evidence in the literature that older adults with Down syndrome are at risk for accelerated aging (Eyman & Borthwick-Duffy, 1994; Zigman et al., 1994). Based on this research, it was hypothesized that the adults with Down syndrome would have poorer health and more sensory impairments than adults with mental retardation caused by other factors. Based on research reported in this book that documents the specific communication impairments of children with Down syndrome, it was hypothesized that the adults with Down syndrome in the sample would have poorer expressive language than the other adults with other types of mental retardation.

As shown in Table 6, consistent with the hypothesis, the adults with Down syndrome in the sample had superior functional abilities

Table 6.   Comparison of adults with Down syndrome and other adults

Factor measured	Adults with Down syndrome	Other adults	F
Functional abilities	62.83	59.16	11.77 $p = .001$
Behavior problems	1.45	2.09	16.67 $p < .001$
Health status	2.31	2.32	0.01
Hearing impairment	0.34	0.14	10.38 $p = .001$
Vision impairment	0.16	0.28	1.00
Clarity of speech	2.05	2.31	3.40 $p = .066$

Data are expressed in terms of analysis of covariance (F) adjusted for the mothers' age and number of children in the family and for the age and gender of the adults with mental retardation.

with respect to activities of daily living (ADL) as compared with the other adults in the sample. Although not shown in Table 6, these adults had particular expertise in activities that are done around the house (e.g., bathing, making the bed, doing household chores). This is one example in which the reciprocal relationship between parental well-being and the well-being of the son or daughter with mental retardation is evident. Children learn daily living skills within the context of the family. Families that are less conflicted and feel less stressed and less burdened—as is the case with the families of adults with Down syndrome in the sample—might be more available to help their children acquire and refine daily living skills. Of course, there is a bidirectional relationship between families' well-being and their child's ADL skills, with children who have greater functional abilities being less stressful to their parents than those with lesser functional abilities (Seltzer & Krauss, 1984).

Also consistent with the hypothesis, the adults with Down syndrome had significantly fewer behavior problems than the other adults. Specifically, they were less likely to hurt themselves and others, to engage in offensive behavior, to be withdrawn, or to be uncooperative than were the adults with other types of mental retardation. This is another example of the possible influence of the family environment on the emotional development of a child. There are clearly bidirectional effects as well, with the behavior problems of a child influencing the level of conflict in the home and vice versa.

Counter to the hypothesis, the adults with Down syndrome were similar to the other adults in the study in terms of health status, with most of both groups (more than 85%) being in good or excellent health. This sample is apparently too young to have experienced the age-related health problems reported in older adults with Down syndrome. Consistent with expectations, however, the adults with Down syndrome were more likely to have a hearing impairment and had speech that was more difficult to understand (according to parental ratings) than were adults whose mental retardation was due to factors other than Down syndrome. There was no difference between the adults with Down syndrome and the other adults with respect to vision problems.

These patterns reflect characteristics observed in people with Down syndrome at earlier stages of the life course that have persisted over time. Taken as a set, these findings portray a favorable profile of the characteristics and abilities of adults with Down syndrome. With the exception of hearing problems and articulation impairments, adults with Down syndrome compared favorably (i.e., did not show impairments) with the adults with other types of mental retardation in important aspects of life such as ADL skills, behavior problems, and health. This pattern of skills and abilities in the adults with Down syndrome can account in part for the better psychological and social well-being of their mothers.

One adult with Down syndrome in the sample who fits this profile was age 38 at the time the research was conducted. He lives at home with his parents but has a separate apartment over the garage. He frequently visits his older brother, who lives in the same community. He does the housework in his apartment and often helps his mother with dinner preparation for the family. His mother said that it is easy to live with him because he is independent and cheerful. His father said, "Our son is so appreciative of what is done for him and tries so hard to be helpful. He strengthens the bonds between my wife and me. We have much to be thankful for."

The findings of this study underscore the importance of intergenerational research in accounting for the well-being of both generations because the well-being of the parents and that of their children varied in synchrony. Future research is needed to sort out the direction of effects and the mechanisms by which family characteristics foster development in their children across the life course and the mechanisms that account for how children's characteristics influence their families' functioning.

Future Plans for Adults with Down Syndrome

The final issue addressed in this chapter concerns the future plans that have been made by parents on behalf of their children with Down syndrome. In general, the families in the study have made a strong commitment to having their children live at home well beyond the time when adults ordinarily establish their own households. The families have chosen this lifestyle for several reasons. First, some families have a deep commitment to the idea of the family's taking care of its own. For others, placement is seen as highly problematic. Out-of-home placements may be judged as unavailable, unsatisfactory, too expensive, or having too long a waiting list. For these families, though the idea of placement is acceptable, they have judged that such an arrangement will not work out for them. Yet, other families prefer that their adult child with mental retardation remain at home because of an interdependence between the aging parents and the adult child, based on the physical assistance and emotional sustenance exchanged between them.

In all families in which the adult does not predecease the parents, however, a transfer of caregiving from the parents to some other family or nonfamily living arrangement can be expected. Some parents prefer that this transition occur during their lifetime so that they will be able to have some control over where their son or daughter will eventually live and to provide support to him or her during the transition period. As one parent explained, "We figured that anything could happen to either one of us [the mother or father]. Neither could take care of him alone. We'd like to have him settled so we know how he is. We don't know how he would manage if he lost either one of us and his home at the same time."

Other parents see the wisdom of making plans for the future living arrangements of their son or daughter but prefer not to implement these plans while they are still able to care for him or her. For example, one mother said, "She's on a waiting list because we won't live forever and I don't expect my other kids to care for her. But I'm in good health for an old lady, and I expect to take care of her until I die." Yet, other parents do not actively plan for or even think about the future, trusting that family members will come forward to take the primary caregiving responsibility. Still others express religious faith or a fatalistic sense that their son or daughter will be well cared for. The following quote illustrates this point: "She is my daughter. I think she should be at home. Where else would she be? The future will take care of itself."

During the first 5 years of the study, 18% of the parents of adults with Down syndrome arranged for the placement of their son or daughter into another living environment, primarily community residences. Of the families in which the adult with Down syndrome still lived at home, about one third (36%) were on a waiting list for a residential placement. The other parents had not made formal plans for having their son or daughter live away from the family.

Decisions regarding use of a waiting list for placement are not necessarily synonymous with parents' preferences regarding their children's future living arrangements, however. At times, professionals either actively encourage parents to, or discourage them from, placing their children's names on a waiting list. Also, preferences and plans change, but parents do not necessarily formalize these changes by removing their adult child's name from or adding it to a waiting list for a residential placement.

In order to directly assess the parents' preferences for future living arrangements of their adult children with Down syndrome who still live at home, they were asked two questions. First, parents were asked where they thought their sons or daughters would be living in 2 years. Next, parents were asked where they thought was the best place for their sons or daughters to be living in 2 years. Their answers are illustrative. Fully 86% of parents of adults with Down syndrome living at home expected that their sons or daughters with Down syndrome would be living at home 2 years hence. Fewer (60%) thought that living in the parental home would be the best living arrangement for their sons or daughters. Nearly one third (28%) thought that a community residence would be the best living arrangement for their sons or daughters, although far fewer (8%) expected that outcome to be achieved in the 2-year period.

Another option is having the adult with Down syndrome live with another family member, such as a sibling. It is interesting to note that though 83% of the parents said that there was a family member who would supervise the care received by the son or daughter with Down syndrome after the parents were no longer able to do so, only 6% either expected that the adult would live with another family member within 2 years or believed that living with other family members was the optimal arrangement.

To summarize, these data suggest that older parents of adults with Down syndrome do not expect much change in their sons' or daughters' living arrangements in the short run (i.e., within 2 years as defined in this study). A sizable difference exists, however, between what parents expect and what they prefer for the future living arrangements of their children with Down syndrome. These parents have elected to have their sons or daughters live at home until their children enter middle age. Yet, some recognize that this living arrangement is time limited, and about one third prefer a placement in a community residence even though few expected that transition to occur during the next few years.

CONCLUSIONS

This chapter focuses on the adulthood of people with Down syndrome and on the well-being of their aging parents. Parental care is a normative living arrangement for children and adults with mental retardation. However, little knowledge exists of the experiences of families as caregivers over the life course of adults with Down syndrome.

The research presented here exposes both the durability and the resilience of families of adults with Down syndrome. In comparison with mothers of adults with other types of mental retardation, the mothers of adults with Down syndrome reported higher satisfaction with their social support networks, lower levels of conflictive relationships within their immediate families, and less difficulty with their roles as parents or with their roles as caregivers to their adult children with Down syndrome. These salutary outcomes mirror those reported from research on families of younger children with Down syndrome.

The persistence of etiology-based differences in the context of caregiving is impressive and warrants further investigation.

For many adults with Down syndrome, adulthood is a vibrant stage of life. Consider the number of social roles that the adults with Down syndrome in the study occupied: Many (91%) were in a paid employment situation or participated in a regular day program, and most engaged in regular social activities with friends, co-workers, and family members. Furthermore, most (more than 85%) enjoyed good health and were independent in their personal grooming (70%), and some were able to participate independently in routine household activities such as meal preparation (41%). Most (68%) exhibited no behavior problems or just an occasional behavior problem, so their participation in social and recreation activities was not restricted by maladaptive behaviors. Although these findings do not ensure a high quality of life, they do represent important characteristics that would enable adults with Down syndrome to join in a variety of activities that would be expected and valued by any adult.

What does the future hold for these individuals and their families? This is, of course, a riveting question for adults with Down syndrome, their families, and society. The study found a range of projections. For some families, no change is foreseen in the near future with respect to where their son or daughter with Down syndrome will live, and no change is desired. For other families, the next 2 years were expected to mirror the present, but a shift in residential placement was preferred. The finding that most families did not anticipate a change does not imply that none was desired. There was clearly a deep ambivalence about the prospect of a transition to non–family-based care. This ambivalence stemmed from concerns about the quality of care available in nonfamily environments, the recognition that there are limited openings or long waiting lists for residential facilities, or a belief that continued family-based care is superior to any other arrangement. These beliefs may change with time, however, as new factors emerge that affect the choices and options that families confront.

Most families would wish for a crystal ball in which they could view what their future holds. The families participating in the research discussed here had no crystal ball when their children were born, and they had little access to other families in similar circumstances whose experiences could have served as a guide for them. Parents of young children with Down syndrome in the 1990s are the beneficiaries of more access to support groups and information about the experience of rearing children with Down syndrome, as well as more public acceptance and respect for the challenges they face. The older parents whose lives have been tracked bring a message of encouragement and pride to the younger families who will follow in their footsteps. As one parent stated,

> Having a retarded child is a terrible tragedy, but I wouldn't trade him for any normal child. If one can get beyond the grief and sorrow about what he has lost—and that takes some doing—experiencing life through his eyes and sharing a life with him so filled with joy and innocence has been an extraordinary path to take. I wouldn't have missed it for the world.

This parent's message is an important one and bears thoughtful reflection by the professionals and service providers who work with families that have a member with Down syndrome.

This chapter ends with a poem written by the father of a woman with Down syndrome. The poem was written after her first visit home following her move to a community residence.

Thoughts for Today

We had some joy come our way.
Darlene came home for a short stay.
She hadn't forgotten the dog and cat,
And gave them each an occasional pat.
Took her to Pizza Hut to eat,
Which to her was quite a treat.
Slept good all night, enjoyed her meals.
We couldn't ask for better deals.
Used the bathroom like a lady,
Just to show she's no baby.
Dressed herself and helped with chores,
The wife and I couldn't ask for more.
Listened to her tapes, threaded beads,
Looked at books, even though she can't read.
Wandered around, looking, all alone.
She knew for years it was her home.
We enjoyed having her back here.
It sure has brought us some cheer.

But time marches on much too fast.
We knew it just wouldn't last.
So, back to her new home tomorrow.
We still deal with heartbreak and sorrow.

Darlene's Dad

REFERENCES

Antonucci, T.C. (1986). Measuring social support networks: Hierarchical mapping technique. *Generations, 10,* 10–12.

Bruininks, R.H., Hill, B.K., Weatherman, R.F., & Woodcock, R.W. (1986). *Inventory for Client and Agency Planning* (ICAP). Allen, TX: DLM Teaching Resources.

Bumpass, L., & Sweet, J. (1987). *A national survey of families and households.* Madison: University of Wisconsin–Madison, Center for Demography and Ecology.

Carter, B., & McGoldrick, M. (Eds.). (1989). *The changing family life cycle: A framework for family therapy* (2nd ed.). Needham Heights, MA: Allyn & Bacon.

Clausen, J.A. (1986). *The life course: A sociological perspective.* Upper Saddle River, NJ: Prentice-Hall.

Erickson, M., & Upshur, C.C. (1989). Caretaking burden and social support: Comparison of mothers of infants with and without disabilities. *American Journal on Mental Retardation, 94,* 250–258.

Eyman, R.K., & Borthwick-Duffy, S.A. (1994). Trends in mortality rates and predictors of mortality. In M.M. Seltzer, M.W. Krauss, & M.P. Janicki (Eds.), *Life course perspectives on adulthood and old age* (pp. 93–105). Washington, DC: American Association on Mental Retardation.

Featherstone, H. (1980). *A difference in the family: Living with a disabled child.* New York: Penguin USA.

Friedrich, W.N., Greenberg, M.T., & Crnic, K. (1983). A short-form of the Questionnaire on Resources and Stress. *American Journal of Mental Deficiency, 88,* 41–48.

Fujiura, G.T., & Braddock, D. (1992). Fiscal and demographic trends in mental retardation services: The emergence of the family. In L. Rowitz (Ed.), *Mental retardation in the year 2000.* New York: Springer.

Gallagher, D., Rappaport, M., Benedict, A., Lovett, S., Silven, D., & Kramer, H. (1985). *Reliability of selected interview and self-report measures with family caregivers.* Paper presented at the 38th annual meeting of the Gerontological Society of America, New Orleans, LA.

Gallagher, J.J., Beckman, P., & Cross, A.H. (1983). Families of handicapped children: Sources of stress and its amelioration. *Exceptional Children, 50,* 10–19.

Gatz, M., & Hurwicz, M. (1990). Are old people more depressed? Cross-sectional data on Center for Epidemiological Studies Depression Scale factors. *Psychology and Aging, 5,* 284–290.

Goldberg, S., Marcovitch, S., MacGregor, D., & Lojkasek, M. (1986). Family responses to developmentally delayed preschoolers: Etiology and the father's role. *American Journal of Mental Deficiency, 90,* 610–617.

Greenspan, S., & Delaney, K. (1983). Personal competence of institutionalized adult males with or without Down syndrome. *American Journal of Mental Deficiency, 88,* 218–220.

Hetherington, E.M., Lerner, R.M., & Perlmutter, M. (Eds.). (1988). *Child development in life-span perspective.* Mahwah, NJ: Lawrence Erlbaum Associates.

Hodapp, R.M., & Dykens, E.M. (1994). Mental retardation's two cultures of behavioral research. *American Journal of Mental Retardation, 98,* 675–687.

Holroyd, J., & McArthur, D. (1976). Mental retardation and stress in the parents: A contrast between Down syndrome and childhood autism. *American Journal of Mental Deficiency, 80,* 431–436.

Johnson, R.C., & Abelson, R.B. (1969). The behavioral competence of Mongoloid and non-Mongoloid retardates. *American Journal of Mental Deficiency, 73,* 856–857.

Kazak, A.E. (1987). Families with disabled children: Stress and social networks in three samples. *Journal of Abnormal Child Psychology, 15,* 137–146.

Krauss, M.W., & Seltzer, M.M. (1993). Current well-being and future plans of older caregiving mothers. *Irish Journal of Psychology, 14,* 47–64.

Krauss, M.W., Seltzer, M.M., & Goodman, S.J. (1992). Social support networks of adults with retardation who live at home. *American Journal on Mental Retardation, 96*, 432–441.

Lakin, K.C., Hill, B.K., & Bruininks, R.H. (1988). Trends and issues in the growth of community residential services. In M.P. Janicki, M.W. Krauss, & M.M. Seltzer (Eds.), *Community residences for persons with developmental disabilities: Here to stay* (pp. 25–42). Baltimore: Paul H. Brookes Publishing Co.

Lawton, M.P. (1972). The dimensions of morale. In D. Kent, R. Kastenbaum, & S. Sherwood (Eds.), *Research planning and action for the elderly* (pp. 144–165). New York: Behavioral Publications.

Loveland, K.A., & Kelley, M.L. (1988). Development of adaptive behavior in adolescents and young adults with autism and Down syndrome. *American Journal on Mental Retardation, 93*, 84–92.

Mahoney, F.I., & Barthel, D.W. (1965). Functional evaluation: The Barthel Index. *Maryland State Medical Journal, 14*, 61–65.

Mink, I.T., Nihira, K., & Meyers, C.E. (1983). Taxonomy of family life styles: I. Homes with TMR children. *American Journal of Mental Deficiency, 87*, 484–497.

Minnes, P.M. (1988). Family resources and stress associated with having a mentally retarded child. *American Journal on Mental Retardation, 93*, 184–192.

Moos, R.H. (1974). *Family Environment Scale.* Palo Alto, CA: Consulting Psychologists Press.

Noh, S., Dumas, J.E., Wolf, L.C., & Fisman, S.N. (1989). Delineating sources of stress in parents of exceptional children. *Family Relations, 38*, 456–461.

Pruchno, R.A., Michaels, J.E., & Potashnik, S.L. (1990). Predictors of institutionalization among Alzheimer disease victims with caregiving spouses. *Journal of Gerontology, 45*, S259–S266.

Pruchno, R.A., & Resch, N.L. (1989). Mental health of caregiving spouses: Coping as mediator, moderator, or main effect. *Psychology and Aging, 4*, 454–463.

Radloff, L.S. (1977). The CES-D scale: A self-report depression scale for research in the general population. *Applied Psychological Measurement, 1*, 385–401.

Seltzer, G.B., Begun, A., Seltzer, M.M., & Krauss, M.W. (1991). The impacts of siblings on adults with mental retardation and their aging mothers. *Family Relations, 40*, 310–317.

Seltzer, M.M., Greenberg, J.S., & Krauss, M.W. (1995). A comparison of coping strategies of aging mothers of adults with mental illness or mental retardation. *Psychology and Aging, 10*, 64–75.

Seltzer, M.M., & Krauss, M.W. (1984). Placement alternatives for mentally retarded children and their families. In J. Blacher (Ed.), *Severely handicapped children and their families: Research in review* (pp. 143–175). San Diego: Academic Press.

Seltzer, M.M., & Krauss, M.W. (1989). Aging parents with mentally retarded children: Family risk factors and sources of support. *American Journal on Mental Retardation, 94*, 303–312.

Seltzer, M.M., & Krauss, M.W. (1994). Aging parents with co-resident adult children: The impact of lifelong caregiving. In M.M. Seltzer, M.W. Krauss, & M.P. Janicki (Eds.), *Life course perspectives on adulthood and old age* (pp. 3–18). Washington, DC: American Association on Mental Retardation.

Seltzer, M.M., Krauss, M.W., & Tsunematsu, N. (1993). Adults with Down syndrome and their aging mothers: Diagnostic group differences. *American Journal on Mental Retardation, 97*, 464–508.

Seltzer, M.M., & Ryff, C.D. (1994). Parenting across the lifespan: The normative and nonnormative cases. In D.L. Featherman, R. Lerner, & M. Perlmutter (Eds.), *Life-span development and behavior* (Vol. 12, pp. 2–40). Mahwah, NJ: Lawrence Erlbaum Associates.

Silverstein, A.B., Ageno, D., Alleman, A.C., Devecho, K., Gray, S.B., & White, J.F. (1985). Adaptive behavior of institutionalized individuals with Down syndrome. *American Journal of Mental Deficiency, 89,* 555–558.

Stone, R., Cafferata, G.L., & Sangl, J. (1987). Caregivers of frail elderly: A national profile. *Gerontologist, 27,* 616–626.

Zarit, S.H., Reever, K.E., & Bach-Peterson, J. (1980). Relatives of the impaired elderly: Correlates of feelings of burden. *Gerontologist, 20,* 649–655.

Zigman, W.B., Schupf, N., Lubin, R.A., & Silverman, W.P. (1987). Premature regression of adults with Down syndrome. *American Journal of Mental Deficiency, 92,* 161–168.

Zigman, W.B., Seltzer, G.B., & Silverman, W.P. (1994). Behavioral and mental health changes associated with aging in adults with mental retardation. In M.M. Seltzer, M.W. Krauss, & M.P. Janicki (Eds.), *Life course perspectives on adulthood and old age* (pp. 67–91). Washington, DC: American Association on Mental Retardation.

12

A View Toward the Future

Improving the Communication of People with Down Syndrome

Jon F. Miller, Mark Leddy, and Lewis A. Leavitt

Trying to predict the future is always tempting when concluding a discussion of the state of research on the communication development of individuals with Down syndrome. Having so thoroughly explored the present state of research, one's attention turns to the future. Everyone wants to believe that the future will be better for people with Down syndrome. Educational opportunities will be more open for them, communities will be more accepting of them, and employers will consider these individuals' strengths in conjunction with business needs.

There is reason to be optimistic about the future for people with Down syndrome in all of these areas. However, the future role of language and communication skills in society must also be evaluated. The demand for communication skills is of increasing importance in the workplace, particularly with regard to written and oral communication. Optimal communication skills development in children with Down syndrome requires that they receive early and continuing instruction. Research (Chapman, 1997; Fowler, 1995; Miller, 1995) has also demonstrated that changes in public policy are needed to deliver interventions from shortly after birth through the developmental period to optimize an individual's perceptual, motor, and cognitive development. Changes in public policy as well as targeted interventions are essential to prepare individuals with Down syndrome for the communication challenges of the future.

This book advocates changing public policy because research (Miller, 1996) on syndromes associated with mental retardation has shown differences in patterns of cognitive and language development and because categorizing children as having cognitive challenges or mental retardation often sets up misleading expectations of their uniformly low performance in communication. Research (Miller, 1996) on specific syndromes identified intervention needs that as of 1999 still are not generally being provided by U.S. schools or health care systems. When a child is born with Down syndrome, one can expect a number of specific challenges to the child's development of speech, language, and communication. Table 1 lists the major communication challenges that children with Down syndrome face.

If the challenges posed by Down syndrome are expected, children with Down syndrome should not have to wait until they are delayed at least 25% in one or more areas before they qualify for intervention services. Such waiting results in the loss of a crucial period of development, the first 3 years of life, for optimizing the child's brain and behavior functions. The more targeted stimulation that can be provided early in a child's life, the greater the chances of the child's overcoming or at least optimizing the neurophysiological differences associated with the syndrome. (See Chapter 4 for a detailed discussion of the neurophysiology of Down syndrome as it relates to speech and language skills.)

Table 1. Challenges that children with Down syndrome face

1. Children with Down syndrome will have persistent problems producing intelligible speech.
2. Children with Down syndrome will have better language comprehension skills than language production skills even at the earliest stages of development.
3. The majority of children with Down syndrome will demonstrate slower productive vocabulary development than their other cognitive skills would predict.
4. The productive syntax of children with Down syndrome will be significantly delayed.
5. Children with Down syndrome will have hearing difficulties. One third of them will have consistent mild to moderate hearing loss, one third will have mild to moderate losses of hearing intermittently, and one third will never exhibit hearing loss. The majority of these losses of hearing acuity can be linked to prolonged otitis media.
6. Variable hypotonia and other motor performance problems persist throughout childhood among children with Down syndrome.
7. Short-term memory will not develop as rapidly as the other cognitive skills of children with Down syndrome.

Public policy that reflects research findings would make available support for early intervention to enhance motor, perceptual, and cognitive development. A proper model of such support would have the goal of optimizing developmental progress, not correcting impairments identified later in childhood. This prevention and optimization model, rather than being a response-to-specific-disabilities model, incorporates specific individualized interventions to ensure that each child develops the language and communication skills necessary for independent living as an adult.

The details of research on Down syndrome document a number of persistent challenges affecting speech, language, and communication performance in individuals with Down syndrome. (See Chapter 2 for a more detailed discussion of unique communication profiles and Chapter 3 for a review of research on children and adolescents with Down syndrome.) These research data allow description of the skills and challenges that individuals with Down syndrome face in an increasingly technological society. The discussion in this chapter begins in the next section with a summary of expectations for communication development among people with Down syndrome drawn from the research literature to date. This summary focuses on what needs attention early in these individuals' development if their environments are to be optimized to establish a firm foundation for their future learning.

DEVELOPMENT OF OPTIMAL EARLY INTERVENTION PROGRAMS

Since the late 1970s, a number of advances in the development of early intervention programs have occurred. The success of these programs has been documented for both short-term and long-term gains (Guralnick, 1997; Guralnick & Bennett, 1987). This information, reflecting advances in research, has not prompted corresponding changes in service systems or in public policy. Policy in the late 1990s requires that each child must demonstrate significant developmental impairments before interventions can begin, a process that takes far too long and wastes precious early development time. Children with Down syndrome should be automatically placed in communication and motor intervention programs during the first year of life to optimize their future development. Such decisions are justified by expectations based on the biology of Down syndrome and should not be dependent on clinicians' first demonstrating the existence of developmental delays.

Service systems, particularly school systems, do not recognize the biological differences among children with specific syndromes associated with mental retardation and are not prepared to provide early intervention services to children without documented developmental delays. Although environments can optimize performance, the first years of life are crucial for optimizing the future communication development of children with Down syndrome. The criteria that many school systems use to qualify students for services require that a child be at least 3 years of age to evidence a significant delay in one or more of the following skill areas: perception, motor, cognition, or language. The level of impairment, combined with the lack of measurement sensitivity of most standardized tests measuring early development, has resulted in fewer younger students' than older students' meeting eligibility criteria. The result is the loss of valuable early intervention time.

The immediate solution in this situation is fourfold. First, public policy should be changed to recognize that children with syndromes including Down syndrome require intervention in several areas to ensure the same degree of access to educational opportunities extended to children who are developing typically. Access to early intervention should begin shortly after birth and should have automatic funding. Second, family intervention plans need to incorporate early intervention activities into daily routines. Part of this strategy is to work on prereading activities as early as the second year of life. Another focus should be to incorporate oral sensory stimulation in the first year of life with early speech motor control practice to optimize the child's development of intelligible speech. Third, the measurement of early speech, language, and cognitive skills needs to be improved. A number of advances have occurred since the late 1980s, such as the development of parent report measures (Fenson et al., 1993), that take advantage of the wealth of information that parents can provide about their children's development. Fourth, more research on language and communication interventions needs to be done. A great deal has been learned about the language and communication skills of children with Down syndrome that would allow the development of intervention plans that could be put in place immediately after birth.

These changes will not lead to changes in public policy without considerable effort being directed toward further research on biological and behavioral consequences of early intervention through the long-term investigation of developmental outcomes. As arguments are made in favor of early intervention to optimize development among children with Down syndrome, these individuals continue to show positive improvement in speech and language performance after interventions delivered in adolescence and adulthood. Unfortunately, the question seems to be more about who will pay the bill than whether intervention can help these individuals to gain the skills necessary for a productive, independent life.

Need for Communication Skills in the Future

Will there be more or less need for communication skills in the future? One can predict an increased demand for communication skills in some areas. Technology continues to invade people's daily activities, requiring that they have more interactions with electronic equipment to perform routine tasks. Consider electronic banking and the proliferation of automatic teller machines (ATMs), for example. They require reading instructions; remembering personal identification numbers and typing them accurately, in the proper order, and within a specified period of time; and indicating whether money is being withdrawn or deposited and from which account. ATMs are not all the same, and this requires adjustments in routine tasks. The use of ATMs thus requires that individuals read and respond to specific messages with the motor skills necessary to press and release keys quickly on a small keypad. Using a check card for shopping requires similar skills. The challenge of performing these tasks is that one has only a limited time in which to read and respond to each ATM command. ATM technology, though helpful for a great many people, presents significant obstacles for people with Down syndrome. Literacy skills are required to use computers and related technologies. Without the ability to read, people with Down syndrome would be denied access to essential services and learning opportunities, including the Internet with all of its increasing complexity.

Literacy skills will certainly play an increasingly larger role in gaining access to technology in the future. Alternatives to literacy are becoming available with advances in automatic speech recognition technology. Computer software allows computer speech recognition of words spoken at an almost typical speaking rate without extra pauses between words. The computer learns to recognize an individual's speech by practicing on several standard passages read into the computer. These passages are read into the computer several times to train the computer to recognize the speaker's speech patterns. Two problems may arise with regard to this procedure when undertaken by a person with Down syndrome. First, speech must be intelligible, though the limits of intelligibility for future software development are not known; second, the procedure requires that the individual read the standard passages. A great deal of research is being directed toward improving automatic speech recognition. Three problems are being addressed:

1. The need for greater security
2. Detection of individuals' voices even when their vocal quality is altered
3. Enhancement of speaking over writing for many applications

The promise of automation, however, requires more complex skills in another domain. Speech recognition software can provide access to computers without the motor skills required for typing, but reading is required to train the computer to recognize individuals' speech patterns. Internet access requires reading ability. There are "speaking" web browsers developed for people with visual impairments that may be of some value to individuals with limited literacy skills. A research project documenting the text difficulty of various web sites and their value for individuals with less-developed reading skills might be worthwhile.

LITERACY DEVELOPMENT IN CHILDREN WITH DOWN SYNDROME

Until the late 1960s, educational systems systematically excluded from academic curricula children with mental retardation requiring intermittent supports. Children were formerly labeled as "educable" if their IQ scores fell between 55 and 70 and as "trainable" if their IQ scores were between 35 and 55. These educational categories corresponded to the measured cognitive functioning categories of *mild mental retardation* and *moderate mental retardation* (since revised as *mental retardation requiring limited supports* and *mental retardation requiring intermittent supports* by the American Association on Mental Retardation [AAMR] [Luckasson et al., 1992]), respectively (Grossman, 1983). Most children with Down syndrome fall into the classification of mental retardation requiring intermittent supports. As of 1992, Connors revealed that only 35 studies had been published on reading skills among children with mental retardation requiring intermittent supports. Whereas none of these studies dealt with Down syndrome specifically, one can assume that many of the children participating in this research had Down syndrome. The studies were optimistic about the ability of these children to learn to read. They used three different approaches to instruction, and Connors concluded that sight-word instruction and word-level analysis are useful and appropriate approaches to instruction. She emphasized that no one method is best for all children and that individual differences require different approaches to instruction. This research contradicts those who claim that individuals with Down syndrome who can read are not representative of the skill levels possessed by most of the population with Down syndrome.

Most children with Down syndrome can learn to read at some level, though there is little research documenting their specific reading abilities. Oelwein (1995) published an excellent book for parents on teaching reading to children with Down syndrome based on her experience as a teacher in the Experimental Educational Unit at the Children's Center on Human Development and Disability at the University of Washington in the 1970s. The original reading program in the Experimental Education Unit was developed to foster the oral language skills of children with Down syndrome. This project demonstrated that most children with Down syndrome can benefit from reading instruction, regardless of how *reading* is defined. Oelwein provided a summary of individuals with Down syndrome who had learned to read despite the conventional wisdom of the 1960s and 1970s that children with mental retardation requiring intermittent supports could not learn to read.

Buckley (1995), a researcher at and Director of the Sarah Duffen Centre in Portsmouth, England, suggested that individuals with Down syndrome can master reading skills at an early age with an intensive, language-based early intervention program. Many of the children at 3 years of age who receive reading interventions at the center have sight vocabularies of up to 50 words. Buckley (1997) reported that the literacy accomplishments of children with Down syndrome participating in the British school system suggest that these children were maintaining their early reading skills and continued to make gains without special programming. These children participated in integrated general education classes; no special instruction was provided.

Buckley's work is important because it demonstrates that children with Down children can make significant educational progress without special programming. Although the rate of progress was slower for the children with Down syndrome than for the children who were developing typically, progress was evident. The curriculum for the Sarah Duffen Centre program was similar to that detailed by Oelwein (1995). It is interesting to note that both of these programs emphasized the relationship between oral language and written language. Buckley documented significant gains in oral language among those students participating in her reading instruction program.

STRENGTHS IN VISUAL SKILLS: SIGNING, READING, AND SYMBOL USE

The work of Oelwein and Buckley supports the observation that children with Down syndrome have strengths in processing visual information. Individuals with Down syndrome appear to have strengths in visual memory. Teachers and clinicians have reported anecdotally that the motivation and attention of children with Down syndrome improve if they are provided with visual support for the task at hand. This improvement is particularly true for verbal tasks. Computers provide the most striking example of this phenomenon. The use of word-processing programs to provide visual examples of words, word combinations, and specific features of grammar appear to provide a bridge to verbal expression for people with Down syndrome. The use of specific visual feedback on verbal intensity or clarity of speech sound production sustains these individuals' attention and promotes changes in their everyday verbal communication. These examples point out that the use of visual feedback should be explored with every child to determine how it can be used to promote the child's learning. Not all children learn at the same rate, and computer programs offer visual stimuli that provide a variety of opportunities to interest children in words to improve their speaking, listening, reading, and writing skills.

Another example of visual preference is the popular use of sign language systems as a communication tool. Sign systems have been used in the United States extensively with children with Down syndrome as a way of providing communication opportunities for these children who early in their development have extensive speech intelligibility problems. The idea behind using signs and gestures to enhance their language development appears to be straightforward, but the limitations of using it are rarely considered. First, if American Sign Language (ASL) is followed, school personnel must be mindful that it is a distinct, self-contained language with its own grammar, and the syntax used in ASL is different from spoken English. Most school systems use a version of Signed Exact English that provides grammatical markers and follows spoken English syntax. As a different language, there is no community of signers with whom children can communicate unless one is created, usually at home or at school or, ideally, in both places. Remember that one key ingredient necessary for learning a language is to participate in a community of speakers of that language. The purpose of language is communication. Speaking or signing without an interlocutor does not foster children's development of language skills. An ASL community is not usually created for children with Down syndrome. Personnel in schools frequently assume that teaching the signs is sufficient for the individual and that the rest of the child's classmates are not required to learn the signs as well. The benefit of sign instruction appears to be its use in the early stages of children's development, specifically during the first 5 or 6 years of life. Optimally, children find that signs allow communication with family and people at school, reducing their frustration and building their confidence that others are interested in their communications. As their speech becomes more intelligible, their sign use decreases in favor of speech that is much more efficient. This sequence has been reported repeatedly by parents participating in research since the late 1980s (Sedey, Rosin, & Miller, 1991).

In addition to signing, including reading in the early intervention curriculum provides another bridge for these children to verbally express their thoughts, feelings, and experiences. Buckley (1997) noted that reading is a "way in" to language for these children, meaning that language becomes more accessible when there is visual support. The spoken word is a transient event passing through the listener's ears quickly. A written word allows for stable processing over a longer period of time. Perhaps a better way to think about these two communication modes is that, after hearing a word or sentence, the visual representation can be accessed sequentially to aid in processing both the written and the spoken language. Finally, Buckley (1995) noted that gains in reading are linked to gains in language production skills, language comprehension, visual and auditory memory span, and speech intelligibility.

In addition to the advantages of signing and reading, the use of alternative symbol systems offers another opportunity to improve communication by taking advantage of visual processing strengths. In Chapter 9, Murray-Branch and Gamradt describe the use of augmentative and alternative communication (AAC) strategies to improve communication skills. AAC uses alternative symbol systems, graphic symbols, pictures, photographs, gestures, sign systems, and written language to augment children's speech. The easier these alternative symbols can be learned, the broader the language community available to the user. Every communication requires a speaker and a listener, and the listener must know the language used by the speaker in order for communication to be successful. Graphic symbol systems usually include the written words that they represent. This allows the literate listener to interpret the message intended by the speaker as they point to individual symbols on their communication board. The symbols provide all of the advantages of written words (i.e., stability of the image), with the added benefit of ease of learning because most of these symbols share features of the objects represented. People and objects are easily represented by drawings, whereas adjectives modifying nouns are more difficult; and relationships coded by verbs and adverbs are more difficult still. Abstract ideas are almost impossible to communicate graphically with picture systems. Written language and the language of mathematics are best suited for these complex communication tasks. The use of alternative symbol systems can be productive as a transition to help children grasp the idea that words represent objects, people, and relationships and that these words can be used to communicate experiences to others. Communication—the exchange of messages—must be the primary focus when interacting with children with Down syndrome. Message form (e.g., clear speech, proper syntax) follows as these children's skills improve. Make sure that communication is a fun and successful activity for children with Down syndrome.

MAJOR BARRIER TO
IMPROVING COMMUNICATION SKILLS

The relationship between speaking and listening and the impact of the speaker on a listener suggest that speech clarity is central to the communication process. A great deal can be communicated even when one is speaking only one word at a time. Speech intelligibility determines how much of the message the listener can receive. When speakers become aware of their limited intelligibility, they begin to alter their speech patterns by searching for words that can be spoken clearly, selecting words that have fewer syllables, and reducing sentence length and complexity. When this process begins early in a child's development, the child experiences fewer language-learning opportunities because practice in expressing ideas, thoughts, feelings, needs, and wants is greatly curtailed. Reduced practice results in the child's reduced facility with the language and reduced oral language development. Children who experience significant lack of success in communicating reduce the number of their attempts to communicate. This reduction in communicative exchange not only severely limits their practice with the language but also significantly reduces their opportunities to learn the social conventions of language use. The intricacies of learning to wait one's turn and to identify the cues that signal the opportunity to take one's turn to speak must be learned by practice rather than by direct instruction. How else would one come to understand that, in everyday speech, a pause of only 2 seconds or less signals to a speaking partner that he or she can begin speaking? Practice is essential for the development of good oral communication skills. One of the advantages of early literacy training is the focus on the shared content of words or stories, providing practice for the speaker with limited demand on the listener to understand the speaker's message. The benefits of early literacy activities in advancing oral language skills and oral language development are crucial for the development of literacy.

DO LANGUAGE AND COMMUNICATION
SKILLS CONTINUE TO DEVELOP INTO ADOLESCENCE?

Two papers (Buckley, 1993; Chapman, Ross, & Seung, 1993) documented continued growth in language and communication through age 20. Chapman and colleagues reported a longitudinal study of people ages 5.5–20.5 years with Down syndrome. The greatest gains were reported for comprehension of vocabulary that exceeded nonverbal cognitive skills, comprehension of syntax, and expressive syntax. (See Chapter 3 for further discussion.) Only two of nine individuals showed gains in expressive language beyond 16 years of age. Buckley reported on a study that used reading to improve the morphosyntax of teenagers with Down syndrome. She found that all but one of the individuals in the study made significant gains, using longer and more complex utterances in their conversations at the end of the yearlong study. Leddy and Gill (see Chapter 10) also report improvements in vocabulary, syntax, and conversational skills in adults with Down syndrome who participated in weekly individual and group therapies. These data provide support for continued research to document intervention paradigms for optimizing specific skills acquisition in later childhood and adolescence.

RESPONSIBILITY FOR THE DEVELOPMENT OF COMMUNICATION SKILLS

Everyone—parents, teachers, and speech-language pathologists—is responsible for the development of communication skills of people with Down syndrome, but parents have the most pervasive role in the process. Hart and Risley (1995) documented the contribution that parents make to their children's language development in the first 3 years of children's lives. Hart and Risley studied 42 families for more than 2 years, visiting them once per month for an hour to record all conversations and verbal interactions between parents and their children. The 42 families represented the broad spectrums of race and socioeconomic status in the United States. What Hart and Risley discovered from their study places new emphasis on both the first 3 years of life and the significant role that parents play in their children's language development process. Their results support what has been known for some time about language development:

1. Parents are their children's first teachers of speech, language, and communication skills.
2. Children follow their parents' model of communication action and style.
3. Social relationships are central for the development of children's communication skills.

The striking findings of Hart and Risley's research document that the amount of talk that parents address to their children between the ages of 1 and 3 had a significant and lasting impact on their children's development of communication skills. Parents who talked to their children the most, as measured by the amount of talk per hour, helped their children to develop vocabulary at a faster rate than parents who talked to their children less frequently. Furthermore, these parents' children's rates of vocabulary growth predicted the children's cognitive and language performance at age 3. These data suggest that the more parents talk to their children and engage them in communicative activities, the more they promote their children's development of language and cognitive skills.

Clearly, children do not optimally learn language passively by, for example, listening to the television or radio. Language facility requires a social context with speakers and listeners exchanging messages in an active way to achieve specific communication goals such as informing, commenting, questioning, responding, and persuading. The Hart and Risley (1995) study documented the types of parental communications that are most helpful. Children whose parents had styles that were responsive and encouraging progressed faster than children whose parents were directive and discouraging.

In Chapter 6, Roach and her colleagues provide a detailed discussion of parental style in families of children with Down syndrome. The role of directiveness is not as simple as one might first assume. A directive style is not always associated with children's slower development; and, among mothers of children with Down syndrome, directiveness may serve an essential function of task focus and completion. The importance of the Hart and Risley (1995) study cannot be overemphasized. It confirms that what parents say to their children and how often they talk in the first 3 years of life have an enormous impact on how much language children learn and use. Furthermore, parents' speech input styles predicted their children's test performance at age 3 and ages 9 and 10. The quality of early language input had a significant and lasting effect on the children's development of language and cognitive skills.

The importance of how parents' communication with their children affects their children's development is supported by another longitudinal study of early language development (Huttenlocher, Haight, Bryk, Seltzer, & Lyons, 1991). Huttenlocher and colleagues found that the size of children's vocabulary at age 3 years was predicted by the number of different words addressed to children during the second year of life. Parents who used a richer, more diverse vocabulary had children who at age 3 years had larger vocabularies. These studies confirm the pervasive impact that parents have in their everyday interactions with their children.

The advances in research on the brain as well as in longitudinal research on the development of communication point to the importance of the early years of life for sustaining central nervous system development. The impact of stimulation and the quality of language input affect children's rates of language and cognitive development. Child-appropriate environments promote positive early development, which forms the scaffolding for learning through childhood and beyond. Parents are at the center of this process, and many early childhood curricula are aimed at making parents better teachers of their children as well as better members of the intervention team. The extent to which parents need direct intervention so that they can improve their communication with their children is best addressed at the individual family level. The behavioral research documents that children adopt their family's communication style, whether it facilitates or suppresses their developmental progress. Individual family styles should become the focus of study so that researchers can improve their understanding of the causes and consequences of family interactions, communication effectiveness, and the rates of positive stimulation to promote change. Can family styles be changed if they are found to be unfavorable to children's developmental progress? Can these styles be identified early enough to make a difference? Only continued research can answer these questions.

EFFECTIVE PARENTAL COMMUNICATION WITH THEIR CHILDREN WITH DOWN SYNDROME

Research on typical children documenting the frequency of input as a major force in promoting language and communication development for families of children with Down syndrome has found that children's language and cognitive development can be improved by parents' simply talking more and producing more and longer utterances as well as utterances using more complex vocabulary. This research ignores the status of children's ability to comprehend language addressed to them and how parents adjust their language to optimize their children's chances of understanding their message. Parents adjust their language to children on almost every linguistic dimension—phonological, syntactic, and semantic—including slowing their rate of speech. The advice to talk more to children must be understood to mean "Talk more while adjusting your language to meet the child's level of language comprehension to facilitate the processing of the message."

Communication is the product of this game. More talk in the absence of the rest of the features necessary for successful communication cannot improve children's language development. If this were not true, children's language would improve as a function of the amount of time they spent listening to the radio or watching television. Families that are successful communicators perhaps talk more to their children, but their increased talking is in the context of exchanging messages. These families' communication styles are generally encouraging, urging their children to try new experiences, discussing their activities, and providing new challenges. In the context of increasing the frequency of communication with children with Down syndrome, families' communication styles are similar to those of typical children whose parents adjust their language and encourage performance through attention and support for task completion. Increasing the frequency of talk addressed to these children should be encouraged in the context of family communication about the child's daily activities.

Guidelines for developing optimal environments for talking with children include the rules of thumb listed in Table 2, which were derived from research conducted since the 1930s on language development (Miller, 1981). These can be thought of as "Grandma's rules" for talking with children because grandmothers have had long experience in talking with many children of various ages. This experience helps in developing a template of language expectations for children of various ages as well as effective strategies for encouraging communication. By articulating these rules, 40–50 years of direct experience in developing effective strategies for talking with children can be saved. "Grandma's

Table 2.   Grandma's rules to guide communicative interactions with children

1. *Be enthusiastic:* No one wants to talk with someone who does not appear to be interested in what he or she is saying.

2. *Be patient:* Allow children time and space to perform.
    Don't be afraid of pauses.
    Don't overpower the child with requests or directions.

3. *Listen and follow the child's lead:* Help maintain the child's focus (topic and meaning) with your responses, comments, and questions.
    Use open-ended prompts and questions when possible (e.g., "Tell me more," "And then what happened?")
    Add new information where appropriate.
    Maintain the child's pace; do not rush to the next topic.

4. *Value the child:* Recognize the child's comments as important and worth your individual attention. Do not patronize the child. Demonstrate unconditional positive regard.

5. *Do not play the fool:* A valued conversational partner has something to say that is worth listening to, so pay attention. Refrain from asking questions for which the child knows that you know the answer. Refrain from making the usual remarks children hear from adults.

6. *Learn to think like a child:* Consider that the child's perspective of the world is different at different levels of cognitive development. The child's awareness of varying perspectives of action, time, space, and cause evolve over time as a product of development. Adapt your language to the level of the child's development of language comprehension. Shorten utterances, simplify vocabulary, and reduce complexity.

rules" have one thing in common: They put the child, not the adult, first. If parents can increase the amount of time that they talk with their children in the context of these six rules, then improved communication, not to mention more family fun, should result.

STRATEGIES THAT FAMILIES CAN USE TO ENHANCE COMMUNICATION WITH THEIR CHILDREN

Research on language learning in children with Down syndrome has documented that language learning occurs in childhood and continues throughout adolescence (Chapman, 1997). Research on family communication style and frequency of communication may indicate why some children with Down syndrome learn language more rapidly than other children (see Chapter 6). Families whose children are making good progress with their language and communication skills development share the following features:

1. Language levels are selected relative to the child's ability to understand the message and not with regard to the child's ability to produce messages.
2. The families have realistic communication goals for children.
3. The families expect all children to learn to read.
4. The families focus on understanding the content of children's messages and should not be as concerned with the forms that children's messages take.
5. Hearing testing is scheduled every 6 months until the child is 8–10 years of age.
6. The families provide children with frequent and varied experiences outside the home.

These features or strategies are described in detail in the rest of this section.

   1. *Language levels are selected relative to the child's ability to understand the message and not with regard to the child's ability to produce messages.* Language comprehension will be significantly more advanced than language production skills in children with Down syndrome than in typical children. Language that is too simple does not motivate the child's learning of new vocabulary or expose the child to new grammatical structures. Language that is too complex will not be understood at all. The ideal utterance is composed of 90% words and grammatical structures that the child knows and 10% new words or grammatical features. This composition of already-learned and new words and syntax allows the child to use the context of the utterance to figure out what is meant by the new features. Slobin (1973) wrote

out a series of rules that children who are developing typically use in learning their language. One of the most prominent rules was for adults to use new forms (words) with old structures (grammar) or old forms (words) with new structures (grammatical features). Another rule suggested that children are best at learning one new thing at a time rather than acquiring several features simultaneously. These rules seem to be particularly appropriate for use with children with Down syndrome.

2. *The families have realistic communication goals for children.* The communication goals of children who are learning to speak tend to be forgotten with regard to children with Down syndrome. Instead, the focus is fixed on children's acquiring new words, speaking more clearly, or using longer utterances. The question is, Why are these changes the focus rather than the message? A great deal can be communicated by using single-word utterances. A single word, spoken clearly, communicates more than a long, unintelligible utterance. Longer utterances or new vocabulary should serve the communication needs of the child rather than the needs of the adults with whom the child is communicating every day. Remember that typical children learn what the environment presents relative to their individual communication needs within their families and schoolrooms.

3. *The families expect all children to learn to read.* Families rarely set out to teach new words, but they do provide a great deal of experience with language through everyday verbal exchanges and through bedtime reading. Reading experts have suggested that typical children in middle-class families are exposed to several thousand hours of reading before they enter school at age 5. Children with developmental disabilities are not usually expected to benefit from being read to, nor are they expected to learn to read. Oelwein (1995) documented that these children are not read to at home, which denies them vital exposure to print, the relationship between the printed word and the spoken word, and experience with the ways in which books work. This neglected early exposure to storytelling and print might not be overcome with later education programs. Here expectations are vital to providing early experience. If one expects children to learn to read, one reads to them. If one does not expect children to learn to read, the fulfillment of that expectation is ensured by not having provided the necessary early exposure to print materials. Programs that are designed to teach reading to children with Down syndrome are language based. Children who are making progress in reading are also making progress in their oral language skills development.

4. *The families focus on understanding the content of children's messages and should not be as concerned with the forms that children's messages*

take. Children who are not understood become frustrated and reduce their attempts to communicate. If communication partners always correct the form of a child's message, the child learns that the form of the message is more important than its content. Correct only at specified times; otherwise, take all forms equally—gestures, facial expressions, body postures, signs, graphic symbols, and spoken words. When trying to improve a child's pronunciation of individual words, focus on a small set of words that are important for the child's communication goals and work on those, supplementing oral practice with visual feedback, printed words, or pictures.

5.   *Hearing testing is scheduled every 6 months until the child is 8–10 years of age.* Research (Sedey, Miolo, Murray-Branch, & Miller, 1992) showed that only about 33% of children with Down syndrome never have a mild hearing loss, meaning that 67% have some type of hearing loss. Half of the children with hearing loss experienced the loss every time they were evaluated. The other half had mild to moderate hearing loss at some testing sessions but not at others. These mild to moderate hearing losses may contribute to their speech intelligibility problems. Fluctuating hearing loss through the developmental period may contribute to the inconsistent speech patterns of these children and their delayed language production.

6.   *The families provide children with frequent and varied experiences outside the home.* Nelson (1985) documented that children who were taken on more outings had faster language acquisition rates than children who were taken on fewer outings. Outings may be any experience outside the daily routine, such as going to the zoo, to the park to play, or to visit friends. Making new friends to play with or visits to extended family are rich experiences for children, as is travel by any means. Exposing a child to different languages and cultures within the city in which or near which his or her family lives can also expand the child's world. Riding on public transportation can expose children to new people and places. All of these experiences provide wonderful topics for conversations and event narratives to be shared with other family members and friends at home or at school. New and repeated experiences are necessary for children's growth in knowledge through active participation. These experiences provide the substance as well as the motivation to share them through language.

CONCLUSIONS

This chapter attempts to predict the future of children with Down syndrome relative to the increasing demand for language, communication, and literacy skills in American society. As American society relies more on electronic means for accomplishing activities of daily living, individuals with communication challenges will become less integrated into the dominant culture. There are several actions that will help children with Down syndrome to overcome these increasing demands as well as the limitations of their biological status. These actions include the need for early intervention, which can take many forms delivered both in the home and by professionals in other contexts. Next, all education and therapeutic activities should emphasize the use of visual stimuli to support and improve learning and communication. Finally, more family involvement in and focus on improving their children's communicative effectiveness is needed (i.e., "Grandma's rules").

Need for Early Intervention

Interventions to foster child development should be considered in the broadest possible terms. The actors can be family members, preschool teachers, physical therapists, occupational therapists, speech-language pathologists, physicians, or nurses. A supportive environment for promoting communication through everyday participation is important. A family focus in providing interventions delivers early and continuous intervention in a natural context. Some families may need training to accomplish this type of supportive environment, and others may not. It is necessary to evaluate the family context and do as much as possible to improve communicative effectiveness because children spend the most time in this environment. Families should employ general rules to promote communication (see Table 2) and should not worry about conducting specific therapy with their children.

Preschool- and school-based interventions should focus on children's cognitive and linguistic skill development within the curriculum. School environments that foster communication through group activities, storytelling, dramatic play, and small-group projects are best suited to meet the needs of children with Down syndrome. Excellent examples of this type of preschool curriculum can be found in Bricker, Pretti-Frontczak, and McComas (1998) and Rice and Wilcox (1995).

Both family- and school-based programs emphasize the power of modeling appropriate language and communication skills and work to provide the best possible models within the context of their intervention programs. Dodd, McCormack, and Woodyatt (1994) documented a direct relationship between the parental modeling of speech skills and the speech intelligibility of their children's speech. Using parents in intervention programs requires that parents first become the objects of change and then become the agents of change.

Parents as therapists or therapists as parents—how should parents juggle time, intensity, and having fun with their children? Intervention programs focusing on parents' behavior run the risk of turning parents into therapists and abandoning their role as loving, supportive, and accepting adults. The goal of providing children with perfect models can take two forms: environments that reinforce all therapeutic moments or models focusing on the more general features of the communication model, exchanging messages effectively.

The question for intervention research is, How should parents' interventions be structured at the message level or at the sound, word, and utterance levels? Research (Hart & Risley, 1995) on typical children suggests that a more global focus on parental style is a powerful influence on children's communication ability by providing models focusing on frequent communication exchanges about daily experiences. Addressing the sound, word, and utterance levels focuses on the form of the message and therefore can confuse the child about the goal of verbal exchanges. Therapies that focus on message form should be delivered by professionals in contexts that cannot be confused with everyday communication contexts.

A rich source of family activities promoting speech, language, and communication in their children with Down syndrome can be found in Kumin's (1994) excellent book for parents entitled *Communication Skills in Children with Down Syndrome: A Guide for Parents,* which discusses Down syndrome and expectations through the early periods of children's development. Kumin provides activities to stimulate children's speech and language skills at each period of their development. Her book also includes useful discussions of assessment techniques and how to work with professional teams. Two other books aimed at families of typical children may be of value in finding activities to promote language learning. Crystal (1986) wrote an account of the child's acquisition of language that provides a detailed discussion of the factors that promote language growth with sample activities to enhance language learning at each stage of a child's development. Fowler (1990a, 1990b) addressed children's joint development of language and cognitive skills through the early developmental period.

Use of Visual Stimuli

All education and therapeutic activities should emphasize the use of visual stimuli to support and improve learning and communication. The use of visual stimuli to support auditory information is discussed in some detail in this chapter. The use of written language, computer software, and paper and pencil cannot be overemphasized. The success of many AAC systems, including ASL, can probably be traced to their reliance on visual information. Take every opportunity to reinforce children's verbal messages to improve the comprehensibility of their messages.

Importance of Family Involvement

More family involvement in and focus on improving children's communicative effectiveness (i.e., "Grandma's rules") is greatly needed. Have fun, and enjoy children's attempts to communicate. Be patient, and remember that children with Down syndrome acquire their language skills at less than half the rate of children at the same chronological age who are developing typically. Their slower rate of language development gives the illusion that they are making little progress. Therefore, it is useful for their parents to audiotape- or videotape-record their communication attempts at least every 3 months. Parents should record their children performing similar tasks for comparison so that they can see their children's progress. They should relax and enjoy their children as they are. There are no magic bullets to cure language and communication difficulties. Children's communication skills can be optimized by parents' focusing on their abilities.

Parents versus Professionals

Crutcher (1993) powerfully presented the key issues underlying the tensions between parents and professionals with regard to the speech and language development of children with Down syndrome. She articulated several issues that parents perceive as limitations of speech-language interventions. The first encompasses professionals' lack of time, lack of awareness, or unwillingness to explore therapeutic techniques specifically for the individual child. Second is the failure to modify formal therapeutic techniques to create strategies that fit a family's natural lifestyle. The time constraints under which most clinicians work promote a "one size fits all" mentality. A lack of sensitivity to individual family styles and needs renders many family intervention programs ineffective. Families may be perceived to be uninterested when in fact it is the therapists who have failed. The third limitation is the failure of speech-language pathologists to realize that families have other aspects of their lives that need attention (i.e., activities of daily living, financial challenges, health concerns, other educational issues, other family members). Crutcher also pointed out that most therapeutic environments allow limited time for evaluating family interactions, perhaps annual visits. Although most of these limitations can be attributed to employment environments, the family context must not be overlooked when designing effective intervention sequences for children with Down syndrome.

Crutcher also listed the 16 most frequent concerns expressed by parents about speech and language interventions. At the top of the list is an overemphasis on perfect articulation followed by lack of carry-over to promote generalization and the underemphasis of rate and volume of speaking, eye contact, and maintaining appropriate spatial distance in therapy. These concerns of parents emphasize the lack of dialogue with speech and language professionals. Speech and language professionals must pursue improved communication between professionals and parents in the service of children with Down syndrome. There is simply too much to be gained.

REFERENCES

Bricker, D., Pretti-Frontczak, K., & McComas, N. (1998). *An activity-based approach to early intervention* (2nd ed.). Baltimore: Paul H. Brookes Publishing Co.

Buckley, S. (1993). Developing speech and language skills of teenagers with Down syndrome. *Down Syndrome Research and Practice, 1,* 63–71.

Buckley, S. (1995). Improving the expressive language skills of teenagers with Down syndrome. *Down Syndrome Research and Practice, 3,* 110–115.

Buckley, S. (1997, April). *Links between literacy, language and memory development in children with Down syndrome.* Paper presented at the 2nd International Conference on Language and Cognitive Development in Down Syndrome, Portsmouth, England.

Chapman, R.S. (1997). Language development in children and adolescents with Down syndrome. *Mental Retardation and Developmental Disabilities Research Reviews, 3,* 307–312.

Chapman, R.S., Ross, D., & Seung, H. (1993). *Longitudinal change in language production of children and adolescents with Down syndrome.* Paper presented at the 6th International Congress of the Study of Child Language, Trieste, Italy.

Connors, F. (1992). Reading instruction for students with moderate mental retardation: Review and analysis of research. *American Journal of Mental Deficiency, 69,* 577–597.

Crutcher, D. (1993). Parent perspectives: Best practice and recommendations for research. In A.P. Kaiser & D.B. Gray (Eds.), *Communication and language intervention series: Vol. 2. Enhancing children's communication: Research foundations for intervention* (pp. 365–373). Baltimore: Paul H. Brookes Publishing Co.

Crystal, D. (1986). *Listen to your child.* New York: Penguin USA.

Dodd, B., McCormack, P., & Woodyatt, G. (1994). Evaluation of an intervention program: Relation between children's phonology and parents' communicative behavior. *American Journal on Mental Retardation, 98,* 623–645.

Fenson, L., Dale, P.S., Reznick, J.S., Thal, D.J., Bates, E., Hartung, J., Pethick, S., & Reilly, J. (1993). *MacArthur Communicative Development Inventories (CDI).* San Diego: Singular Publishing Group.

Fowler, A. (1995). Linguistic variability in persons with Down syndrome: Research and implications. In L. Nadel & D. Rosenthal (Eds.), *Down syndrome: Living and learning in the community* (pp. 121–131). New York: Wiley-Liss.

Fowler, W. (1990a). *Talking from infancy: How to nurture and cultivate early language development.* Cambridge, MA: Brookline Books.

Fowler, W. (1990b). *Talking from infancy: How to nurture and cultivate early language development* [Videotape]. Cambridge, MA: Brookline Books.

Grossman, H. (Ed.). (1983). *Classification in mental retardation.* Washington, DC: American Association on Mental Deficiency.

Guralnick, M.J. (Ed.). (1997). *The effectiveness of early intervention.* Baltimore: Paul H. Brookes Publishing Co.

Guralnick, M.J., & Bennett, F. (Eds.). (1987). *The effectiveness of early intervention for at-risk and handicapped children.* San Diego: Academic Press.

Hart, B., & Risley, T. (1995). *Meaningful differences in the everyday experiences of young American children.* Baltimore: Paul H. Brookes Publishing Co.

Huttenlocher, J., Haight, W., Bryk, A., Seltzer, M., & Lyons, T. (1991). Early vocabulary growth: Relation to language input and gender. *Developmental Psychology, 27*(2), 236–248.

Kumin, L. (1994). *Communication skills in children with Down syndrome: A guide for parents.* Bethesda, MD: Woodbine House.

Luckasson, R., Coulter, D.L., Polloway, E.A., Reiss, S., Schalock, R.L., Snell, M.E., Spitalnik, D.M., & Stark, J.A. (1992). *Mental retardation: Definition, classification and systems of supports* (Special 9th ed.). Washington, DC: American Association on Mental Retardation.

Miller, J.F. (1981). *Assessing language production in children: Experimental procedures.* Baltimore: University Park Press.

Miller, J.F. (1995). Individual differences in vocabulary acquisition in children with Down syndrome. In C. Epstein, T. Hassold, I. Lott, L. Nadel, & D. Patterson (Eds.), *Etiology and pathogenesis of Down syndrome: Proceedings of the International Down Syndrome Research Conference* (pp. 93–103). New York: Wiley-Liss.

Miller, J.F. (1996). The search for a phenotype of disordered language performance. In M.L. Rice (Ed.), *Toward a genetics of language* (pp. 297–314). Mahwah, NJ: Lawrence Erlbaum Associates.

Nelson, K. (1985). *Making sense: Development of meaning in early childhood.* San Diego: Academic Press.

Oelwein, P. (1995). *Teaching reading to children with Down syndrome: A guide for parents and teachers.* Bethesda, MD: Woodbine House.

Rice, M.L., & Wilcox, K.A. (1995). *Building a language-focused curriculum for the preschool classroom: Volume I. A foundation for lifelong communication.* Baltimore: Paul H. Brookes Publishing Co.

Sedey, A., Miolo, G., Murray-Branch, J., & Miller, J.F. (1992, November). *Hearing status and language development in children with Down syndrome.* Poster presented at the annual meeting of the American Speech-Language-Hearing Association, San Antonio, TX.

Sedey, A., Rosin, M., & Miller, J.F. (1991, November). *A survey of sign use among children with Down syndrome.* Poster presented at the annual convention of the American Speech-Language-Hearing Association, Atlanta, GA.

Slobin, D. (1973). Cognitive prerequisites for the development of grammar. In C. Ferguson & D. Slobin (Eds.), *Studies in child language development* (pp. 175–276). Austin, TX: Holt, Rinehart & Winston.

Appendixes

A

Resource List

The following resource list includes books of interest to parents and professionals and discusses activities for improving communication skills in general as well as in individuals with Down syndrome or mental retardation and for enhancing children's development in general.

ACTIVITIES FOR IMPROVING LANGUAGE, COMMUNICATION, AND LITERACY SKILLS

The books listed in this section are written for parents of children who may or may not have any developmental challenges. Readers should focus on their families' interaction styles and select activities that complement their families' natural interaction patterns. These activities are most helpful as supplements to typical communication exchanges and not intended as a recipe for changing the family's structure. Also, readers should make sure that the activities selected are ones that fit their children's interests so that their children will be motivated to participate. After all, participation is the objective of these activities. Readers may want to develop a set of activities for their children and then discuss the activities with their children's teachers and speech-language pathologists. Because these books are organized developmentally, they also give readers an idea of what to expect next as their children progress through the developmental periods. Begin with activities with which children can be successful to encourage the notion that communication is a fun activity.

Crystal, D. (1986). *Listen to your child: A parent's guide to children's language.* New York: Penguin USA.

Fowler, W. (1990). *Talking from infancy: How to nurture and cultivate early language development.* Cambridge, MA: Brookline Books.

Hart, B., & Risley, T.R. (1995). *Meaningful differences in the everyday experiences of young American children.* Baltimore: Paul H. Brookes Publishing Co.

Kumin, L. (1994). *Communication skills in children with Down syndrome: A guide for parents.* Bethesda, MD: Woodbine House.

Kumin, L. (Ed.). *Communicating Together: A News Letter Dedicated to the Children, Devoted to Parents and Caring Professionals.* Post Office Box 6395, Columbia, Maryland 21045-6395.

McCabe, A. (1987). *Language games to play with your child.* New York: Fawcett Columbine.

Moore, C. (1990). *A reader's guide for parents of children with mental, physical, or emotional disabilities.* Bethesda, MD: Woodbine House.

Oelwein, P. (1995). *Teaching reading to your children with Down Syndrome: A guide for parents and teachers.* Bethesda, MD: Woodbine House.

Schwartz, S., & Heller Miller, J.E. (1988). *The language of toys: Teaching communication skills to special-needs children.* Bethesda, MD: Woodbine House.

Weiner, H.S. (1988). *Talk with your child: Using conversation to enhance language development.* New York: Penguin USA.

MENTAL RETARDATION

Mental retardation has been used as a general classification for children who do not perform as well as their age-matched peers on standardized tests of intelligence and do not develop as rapidly or perform as well as their peers with regard to activities of daily living such as speech, language, and communication. The technical definition of *mental retardation* used by professionals has changed since the late 1940s, specifically with the American Association on Mental Retardation (AAMR) 1992 definition, which moves the definition from its earlier reliance on intelligence testing to incorporating environment, etiology, psychological and social considerations, and adaptive skills. It is important to understand that the term *mental retardation* represents a classification based on performance and is not a determination of an individual's potential, even though that is how the term is understood by the general public. Every parent and professional should read *Mental Retardation: Definition, Classification, and Systems of Supports* (Luckasson et al., 1992), the AAMR's definition and classification manual. It provides a historical perspective on mental retardation as well as an appreciation of the complexities of defining intellectual performance. Also listed in this section is *How the Mind Works,* by Pinker (1997), who discusses research on the brain from the viewpoint of several disciplines and incorporates it into a readable book on the complexities of brain function, with a particular focus on the acquisition and use of language. Essentially, one needs to be humble about one's knowledge of human intellectual performance, particularly with regard to how to improve it. The volumes listed in this section should emphasize that there are no magic cures, only the careful emphasis of language, communication, and literacy in as many of children's daily activities as possible.

Anderson, W., Chitwood, S., & Hayden, D. (1990). *Negotiating the special education maze: A guide for parents and teachers* (2nd ed.). Bethesda, MD: Woodbine House.

Luckasson, R., Coulter, D.L., Polloway, E.A., Reiss, S., Schalock, R.L., Snell, M.E., Spitalnik, D.M., & Stark, J.A. (1992). *Mental retardation: Definition, classification, and systems of support* (Special 9th ed.). Washington, DC: American Association on Mental Retardation.

Pinker, S. (1997). *How the mind works.* New York: W.W. Norton.

Trainer, M. (1991). *Differences in common: Straight talk on mental retardation, Down syndrome, and life.* Bethesda, MD: Woodbine House.

DOWN SYNDROME

Keeping up with the advances in research on Down syndrome is important. New findings must be integrated into instruction programs and therapies focused on improving the developmental progress of people with Down syndrome. Professionals who keep up with research advances in this area gain a better appreciation of the complexities of parenting a child with Down syndrome. Parents who increase their understanding of Down syndrome are better able to manage their children's medical and education programs because unfortunately most of the burden for promoting health and educational opportunities falls to families. One should not miss the opportunity, for example, to read about some exceptional people with Down syndrome described so well by Rondal of the University of Liege, Belgium. These individuals provide a challenge to understand how the extra copy of chromosome 21 alters human performance.

Burke, C., & McDaniel, J. (1991). *A special kind of hero: Chris Burke's own story.* New York: Doubleday.

Cicchetti, D., & Beeghly, M. (1990). *Children with Down syndrome: A developmental perspective.* New York: Cambridge University Press.

Cunningham, C. (1987). *Down's syndrome: An introduction for parents* (2nd ed.). Cambridge, MA: Brookline Books.

Kingsley, J., & Levitz, M. (1994). *Count us in: Growing up with Down syndrome.* Orlando, FL: Harcourt Brace & Co.

Lott, I., & McCoy, E. (1992). *Down syndrome: Advances in medical care.* New York: Wiley-Liss.

Nadel, L. (1988). *The psychobiology of Down syndrome.* Cambridge, MA: MIT Press.

Nadel, L., & Rosenthal, D. (1995). *Down syndrome: Living and learning in the community.* New York: Wiley-Liss.

Pueschel, S.M. (1990). *A parent's guide to Down syndrome: Toward a brighter future.* Baltimore: Paul H. Brookes Publishing Co.

Pueschel, S.M., & Pueschel, J.K. (Eds.). (1992). *Biomedical concerns in persons with Down syndrome.* Baltimore: Paul H. Brookes Publishing Co.

Pueschel, S.M., & Šustrová, M. (Eds.). (1997). *Adolescents with Down syndrome: Toward a more fulfilling life.* Baltimore: Paul H. Brookes Publishing Co.

Reilly, A.P. (Ed.). (1980). *The communication game: Perspectives on the development of speech, language and non-verbal communication skills* (Vol. 4) (Johnson & Johnson pediatric roundtable series). New Brunswick, NJ: Johnson & Johnson Baby Products Co.

Rondal, J. (1995). *Exceptional language development in Down syndrome.* New York: Cambridge University Press.

Stray-Gundersen, K. (1986). *Babies with Down syndrome: A new parents guide.* Bethesda, MD: Woodbine House.

EARLY INTERVENTION

The books listed in this section are aimed at a professional audience, but most are written in a clear and lucid style that can be understood by parents. These books provide insight into how preschool education classrooms can be organized to provide children with both the experiences and the language models necessary to promote advances in their language skills.

Bagnato, S.J., Neisworth, J.T., & Munson, S.M. (1997). *LINKing assessment and early intervention: An authentic curriculum-based approach.* Baltimore: Paul H. Brookes Publishing Co.

Bird, G., & Buckley, S. (1994). *Meeting the educational needs of children with Down's syndrome: A handbook for teachers.* Portsmouth, England: University of Portsmouth.

Donahue-Kilburg, G. (1992). *Family-centered early intervention for communication disorders: Prevention and treatment.* Rockville, MD: Aspen Publishers.

Meisels, S.J., & Fenichel, E. (Eds.). (1996). *New visions for the developmental assessment of infants and young children.* Washington, DC: ZERO TO THREE: National Center for Infants, Toddlers and Families.

Neel, R.S., & Billingsley, F.F. (1989). *IMPACT: A functional curriculum handbook for students with moderate to severe disabilities.* Baltimore: Paul H. Brookes Publishing Co.

GENERAL DEVELOPMENT

Most of the books listed in this section are not necessarily new, but they provide a comprehensive description of child development and describe all aspects of the developing child. There are newer books published, but few are as user-friendly as the ones listed below. After the 1997 White House Conference on Child Development, *Newsweek* magazine published a special issue on the most recent research on brain development, speech, language, and motor development of children by leading U.S. scholars. The *Newsweek* special issue is a readable treatment of this fast-developing and complex area of scientific research. Readers are also encouraged to browse through the child development section of their local book stores to expand their horizons. Keep in mind that each system—motor, cognition, speech, and language— can be described separately; but children must master them all simultaneously. The synchrony of development across all aspects of human performance should not be overlooked.

Caplan, F. (1971). *The first twelve months of life: Your baby's growth month by month.* New York: Bantam Books.

Caplan, F., & Caplan, T. (1977). *The second twelve months of life: Your baby's growth month by month.* New York: Bantam Books.

Caplan, T., & Caplan, F. (1983). *The early childhood years: The 2 to 6 year old.* New York: Bantam Books.

Smith, R. (Ed.). (1997, Spring/Summer). *Your Child: A Special Edition of Newsweek* [Entire issue].

Steele, D.A. (Ed.). (1987). *Your growing child.* Alexandria, VA: Time-Life Books.

B

World Wide Web Sites on Down Syndrome and Related Topics

Helen Hartman

Helen Hartman is an administrative assistant at The Waisman Center, University of Wisconsin–Madison, and she is the mother of Hannah, a child with Down syndrome. Hannah was born on December 25, 1988, and is an elementary school student in an inclusive classroom in the Madison Metropolitan School District. Helen has spent a great deal of time learning about Down syndrome and its associated health and educational challenges. Helen has become an Internet guru, constantly surfing the World Wide Web for new web sites offering information that will help promote Hannah's education program. She has compiled in this appendix the list of web sites that have been particularly helpful to her and her daughter. Keep in mind that because the World Wide Web is everchanging, new web sites related to Down syndrome and related issues are constantly being created. For a fast update, check the National Down Syndrome Society web site (http://www.ndss.org/) or The Sarah Duffen Centre web site (http://www.downsnet.org/). The web site addresses listed in this appendix provide readers with an excellent beginning of a search for relevant Down syndrome information.

Evaluating the accuracy of web site material is a major problem. Consider that professional journal articles go through a rigorous peer review process to establish that each article presents new and accurate information. Most book publishers seek outside reviews in addition to subjecting manuscripts to a thorough editorial process. Anyone can publish a web site, however, without consultation or professional review. Adhering to the following procedure may help establish the value of web site information: Find out who wrote the material on the web site in which you are interested, establish the person's professional reputation and institutional affiliation, find out what other trustworthy sources (e.g., the National Down Syndrome Society, the Sarah Duffen Centre) have to say about the material published at that web site, and be skeptical and demand confirmation before acting on any web-based information.

COMMUNICATION AND DOWN SYNDROME

Downs ED
http://www.downsnet.org/

The Downs ED (DownsNet) web site is affiliated with The Sarah Duffen Centre, established in 1981 by the University of Portsmouth, England, and The Down's Syndrome Trust. The Centre is involved in research, consulting, training, and publishing. The caliber of articles available at this web site is outstanding, with information for parents and practitioners from the *Down Syndrome Educational Trust Newsletter* and research from the *Journal of Down Syndrome: Research and Practice.* A wide range of topics, from early reading to adult issues, is covered.

GENERAL DOWN SYNDROME

Down Syndrome Quarterly
http://www.denison.edu/dsq/

To use the *Down Syndrome Quarterly* web site fully, one must subscribe to the journal. The web site does post position papers as well as good health guidelines that can be accessed without subscribing to the journal. This excellent, high-quality web site is linked with the Family Village web site listed later in this appendix.

MEDICAL CONCERNS RELATED TO DOWN SYNDROME

Disability Solutions
http://www.teleport.com/~dsolns/news.htm

Disability Solutions is available both on-line and through the mail. It presents research about Down syndrome, is sensitive to parents' needs, and is presented in an easily understandable format. Each issue focuses on a theme. Funded by The Enoch-Gelbard Foundation, the publication is free of charge, although it does accept tax-deductible contributions.

Len Leshin, M.D., F.A.A.P.
http://www.davlin.net/users/lleshin/

Dr. Leshin, a pediatrician and father of two children, one of whom has Down syndrome, has posted his essays concerning medical issues affecting children with Down syndrome. His web site includes helpful information lists, links to related web sites, and abstracts of recently published information.

National Association for Down Syndrome
http://www.nads.org/

The National Association for Down Syndrome (NADS) was founded in 1961 by parents of children with Down syndrome to provide support and up-to-date information to new parents and to educate the general public about Down syndrome. Its web site includes an excellent bibliography, a media guide, and a section on speech and language; and it advertises products such as posters to promote awareness about Down syndrome.

National Down Syndrome Congress
http://members.carol.net/~ndsc/

The mission of the National Down Syndrome Congress (NDSC) is to be the national advocacy organization for Down syndrome and to provide leadership in all areas of concern related to people with Down syndrome.

National Down Syndrome Society
http://www.ndss.org/

The National Down Syndrome Society (NDSS) supports young researchers seeking the causes of and answers to many of the medical, genetic, behavioral, and learning problems associated with Down syndrome; sponsors internationally renowned scientific symposia; advocates on behalf of families and individuals affected by Down syndrome; provides information and referral services through its toll-free telephone number; and develops educational materials, many of which are distributed free of charge.

Trisomy 21 Foundation
http://www.geocities.com/HotSprings/9438/t21hmpg.htm

The Trisomy 21 Foundation was created by a small group of parents of young children with Down syndrome. The foundation is organized to fund results-oriented research that has a practical and applicable benefit for infants, children, and adults with Down syndrome. This web site can be accessed through Family Village; the links to it are the same as the Family Village links.

GENERAL DISABILITY

Family Village
http://www.familyvillage.wisc.edu/

As its name implies, the Family Village web site is an all-encompassing site designed for use by people with mental retardation and other disabilities, their families, and those who provide them with services and supports. It integrates information, resources, and communication opportunities for these individuals. This web site provides a user-friendly doorway into a vast array of information. For web sites specific to Down syndrome, click on Library, Specific Diagnosis; then scroll down to Down syndrome and click.

COMMUNICATION/LANGUAGE DELAYS

Hanen Centre
http://www.hanen.org/

The Hanen Centre provides early speech-language interventions for young children with special needs and speech-language delays. Their programs are based on research that is translated into practical terms for parents, community-based intervention programs, and professionals who work with all age groups, ranging from families of infants to adults with developmental delays.

ASSISTIVE TECHNOLOGY

Trace Center
http://www.trace.wisc.edu/

This web site focuses on assistive technology for people with cognitive, perceptual (i.e., hearing and vision), and motor disabilities. One can access information about technologies for environmental control, computer access for people who are blind or have physical impairments, and augmentative or alternative communication. This web site is of value for exploring assistive technology options or when comparing assistive technology systems.

C

Medical Care of
Children with Down Syndrome

Children with Down syndrome have a greatly increased risk for a variety of physical disorders. These include heart disease, gastrointestinal disease, eye disease, musculoskeletal disease, and endocrine disease, as well as the auditory system problems discussed in this book. Not all of these problems are evident at the time of initial diagnosis of Down syndrome. Some, such as thyroid disease, may not develop until late in childhood. It is therefore important for parents and those involved in supervising health care (e.g., nurses, pediatricians, general practice physicians) to modify their usual approaches to health care visits. It is necessary to perform screening tests for conditions associated with Down syndrome according to the child's age and developmental status. Table 1 lists the recommended evaluations proposed by the American Academy of Pediatrics in May 1994. Parents and nonmedical professionals who are committed to improving the quality of life of children with Down syndrome will find it useful to familiarize themselves with health supervision needs as well as growth charts developed specifically for children with Down syndrome (Cronk et al., 1988).

REFERENCES

Cronk, C., Crocker, A.C., Pueschel, S.M., Shea, A., Zackai, E., Pickens, G., & Reed, R. (1988). Growth charts for children with Down syndrome: 1 month to 18 years of age. *Pediatrics, 81,* 102–110.

Committee on Genetics. (1994). Health supervision for children with Down syndrome. *Pediatrics, 93,* 855–859.

Table 1.   Health supervision for children with Down syndrome

	Pre-natal	Infancy						Early childhood, 1–5 years					Late childhood, 5–13 years, annual	Adolescence, 13–21 years, annual
		Neo-natal	2 months	4 months	6 months	9 months	12 months	15 months	18 months	24 months	3 years	4 years		
Diagnosis														
Karyotype review†	•	•												
Phenotype review	•	•												
Recurrence risks	•	•												
Anticipatory guidance														
Early intervention services	‡	‡	•	•	•	•	•	•	•	•	•	•		
Reproductive options														
Family support	•	•	•			•	•							
Support groups	•	•	•				•							
Long-term planning							•					•	•	•
Sexuality													•§	•§
Medical evaluation														
Growth		○	○	○	○	○	○	○	○	○	○	○	○	○
Thyroid screening		○¶					○			○	○	○	○	○
Hearing screening		S/○	S/○	S/○	S/○	S/○	S/○‡	S/○	S/○	S/○‡	S/○‡	S/○	S/○§	S/○
Vision screening		S/○	S/○	S/○	S/○	S/○‡	S/○	S/○	S/○	S/○	S/○	S/○	S/○∥	S/○
Cervical spine roentgenogram											○			
Echocardiogram	•	○												
Psychosocial														
Development and behavioral	S/○	S/○	S/○	S/○	S/○	S/○	S/○	S/○	S/○	S/○	S/○	S/○	S/○	S/○
School performance											○	○	S/○	S/○
Socialization							S						S/○	S/○

From Committee on Genetics. (1994). Health supervision for children with Down syndrome. *Pediatrics*, 93, 856. Used with permission of the American Academy of Pediatrics. Copyright © 1994 by American Academy of Pediatrics.

Note: This table is designed to ensure compliance with the American Academy of Pediatrics Recommendations for Preventive Pediatric Health Care.

•, to be performed; S, subjective by history; and ○, objective, by a standard testing method.

† Or at time of diagnosis   ‡ Discuss referral to specialist   § Give once in this age group   ¶ According to state law   ∥ As needed

Index

Page references followed by "t" or "f" indicate tables or figures, respectively.

AAC, *see* Augmentative and
    alternative communication
AAMR, *see* American Association on
    Mental Retardation
Activities, 265–266
Adaptive inputs, 172
Adolescents with Down syndrome
    cognition, 46–47
    communication skill development
        in, 250–251
    language development in, 41–60,
        250–251
        historical background, 41–43
        research description, 43–45
        research findings, 45–47
        omitted words from, 54, 54t
Adults with Down syndrome
    clinical methods for working with,
        207–208
    comparisons with other adults,
        230–233, 231t
    contemporary life circumstances
        of, 223–226
    enhancing speech and language
        skills of, 205–213
    families of, 217–240
    future plans for, 233–235
    intervention case studies, 208–212
    measures of well-being for, 223,
        224t
Adults with mental retardation,
    families of
    background characteristics,
        222–223, 223t
    sample characteristics, 221t,
        221–222
Advocacy groups, 201–203
AEPS, *see* Assessment, Evaluation,
    and Programming System for
    Infants and Children
Aided language stimulation, 174
    modeling with, 178, 179f

ALB, *see* Assessing Prelinguistic and
    Early Linguistic Behavior in
    Developmentally Young
    Children
Alexander (case study), 210–212
    learning to improve speech
        intelligibility, 210–212
Alternate methods to express ideas,
    175–176
American Association on Mental
    Retardation (AAMR), 17, 246,
    266
American Sign Language (ASL), 166,
    248
Apraxia, developmental, 143–144
Articulation, speech sound, 66–67
ASL, *see* American Sign Language
Assessing Prelinguistic and Early
    Linguistic Behavior in
    Developmentally Young
    Children (ALB), 125
Assessment(s), 117–118
    approaches to, 126–129
    authentic, 123
    current views of, 122–125
    developing protocols for, 126
    functional, 123
    of language comprehension, 125
    of language production, 124
    parents' contribution to, 126
    play-based, 123
    principles of, 121–129
Assessment, Evaluation, and
    Programming System (AEPS)
    for Infants and Children, 125
Assistive technology, 161–204
    case studies, 182–192
    key terms, 164t
    support with, 171–182
    web sites, 274
Auditory short-term memory
    impairment, 48

Augmentative and alternative communication (AAC), 249
Authentic assessments, 123
Automatic speech recognition, 245

Bayley Scales of Infant Development–Mental Scale, 23, 100
Bead Memory subtest (Stanford-Binet Intelligence Scale), 44, 47
Behavior
  frequencies of, 103, 103t
  maternal directive, 95, 95t
  play, 102–103
Behavior coding, 100–101
  definitions, 101, 102t
Behavioral measures, 101–104
Behavioral phenotype, 52–53
Bill (case study), 62–63, 189–192
  enhancement of social relationships in general education classrooms, 189–190
  high-technology communication aid, 190, 190f
  history/intervention program, 190–191
  outcomes and future considerations, 191–192
BoardMaker software, 170–171
Books, 200–201
  wallet-size, 166, 168f
Brain, in individuals who are developing typically versus individuals with Down syndrome, 74, 75f
Build a Scene software, 172
Bulletin boards, 203–204

Caregiving, lifelong, 226–228
CDI, see MacArthur Child Development Inventory
Child development
  MacArthur Child Development Inventory (CDI), 34, 124
  White House Conference on Child Development, 268–269
Child Talk model, 55–56, 57

Children
  behavior code definitions, 102t
  behavior frequencies, 103, 103t
  communication goals for, 256
  communicative interactions with Grandma's rules to guide, 254t, 254–255
    maternal, 105t, 105–106
    strategies to enhance, 255–257
  messages from, 256–257
  play behavior, 102t, 102–103
  vocal behavior, 102t
Children with developmental disabilities, limitations of standardized tests for, 123
Children with Down syndrome
  assessment principles for, 121–129
  assistive technology for, 171–182
    case studies, 182–192
  challenges facing, 242, 242t
  computers and communication aids for, 162–171
  conversational samples, 44
  current views of assessment and, 122–125
  early vocabulary development in, 31–33
  health supervision for, 275, 276t
  hearing abilities of, 120–121
  intelligibility production measures in, 49, 49t
  language abilities of, 120–121
  language development in, 41–60
    communication aid and symbol features that support, 168–171
    course of, 41–42
    historical background, 41–43
    research description, 43–45
    research findings, 45–47
    research participants, 43–45, 44t
  language development profiles, 11–39, 19f, 20f
    studies, 18–20
  lexical production measures in, 49, 49t
  medical care of, 275
  mothers' communication with, 93–115
  parental communication with, 253–255

pragmatic production measures in, 49, 49*t*

speech, language, and hearing abilities of, 120–121

speech intelligibility of, 133–159

strategies and tools for enhancing communication skills of, 161–204

syntactic comprehension measures for, 45, 45*t*

syntax production measures in, 49, 49*t*

teaching
  features of communication aids helpful for, 166–171
  features of computers helpful for, 163–166

vocabulary acquisition in, 30–35
  individual differences in, 34–35

vocabulary comprehension measures for, 45, 45*t*

see also Young children with Down syndrome

Children's Center on Human Development and Disability, University of Washington, 246–247

Choices, line drawings for constructing short phrases to make, 178, 179*f*

Classrooms, general education, 189–190

Clinical methods for working with adults, 207–208

Cluttering, 68, 84–85

Cognition, 46–47

Cognitive skills in language learning, 14–18

Columbia Test, 47

Communication, 1–7
  characteristics of people with Down syndrome, 9–10
  complete model for, 4
  development of
    findings, 122
    Sequenced Inventory of Communication Development (SICD), 23
  evaluation of, 119–132
  family, 255–257
  goals for children, 256

Grandma's rules to guide, 254*t*, 254–255

maternal
  group differences in, 94–97
  individual differences in, 93–115
  sample characteristics, 99–104
  study procedures, 99–104
  model for, 3
  observation form for documenting, 176, 177*f*
  parental, 253–255
  picture symbols, 167*f*
  vocal, mothers', 101–102, 102*t*
  web sites, 272

Communication aids
  for children, 162–171
  construction of, 170–171
  for early reading skills, 171
  for Erica (case study), 183, 183*f*
  features helpful for teaching, 166–171
  features that support language learning and use, 168–171
  high-technology
    for Bill (case study), 190, 190*f*
    handheld, 175, 175*f*
    for Jenny (case study), 187, 188*f*
  motor skill requirements, 170
  for Neil (case study), 185, 185*f*
  portable digitized electronic, 169, 169*f*
  voice output, 163, 165*f*
  wallet-size books, 166, 168*f*

Communication and Symbolic Behavior Scale (CSBS), 125

Communication intervention(s), 133–159, 171–182

Communication inventory, 176, 177*f*

Communication/language delays, web sites, 274

Communication profiles
  Alexander (case study), 210–212
  Jay (case study), 142–143
  Maria (case study), 136
  Molly (case study), 147–148
  Nicholas (case study), 208–210

Communication skills
  activities for improving, 265–266
  barriers to improving, 250

Communication skills—*continued*
  development of, 241–262
    into adolescence, 250–251
    responsibility for, 251–253
  future need for, 245–246
  strategies and tools for enhancing,
    161–204
Communicative effectiveness, 81–91
  speech production impairments'
    influence on, 87–89
Complex object play, 103
  correlation with maternal
    communication, 105*t*,
    105–106
  definition of, 102*t*
  frequencies of, 103, 103*t*
Complex sentences, 51–52, 52*t*
Comprehension problems,
    accommodating, 187
Computers, 162–171
  features helpful for teaching,
    163–166
  significant features, 163
  supporting thinking skills with,
    171–173
Conferences, 199
Criterion reference procedures, 123
Critical period hypothesis, 49–50
CSBS, *see* Communication and
    Symbolic Behavior Scale

Databases, 203–204
Development
  child
    MacArthur Child Development
      Inventory (CDI), 34, 124
    White House Conference on
      Child Development, 268–269
  communication, 241–262
    findings, 122
    Sequenced Inventory of
      Communication Development
      (SICD), 23
  early sentence, for Neil (case
    study), 185
  early vocabulary, research on,
    31–33
  expressive vocabulary, for Erica
    (case study), 182
  general, resources, 268–269

language
  into adolescence, 250–251
  assessing, 22–24
  with Down syndrome, 41–60
  responsibility for, 251
language development profiles,
    11–39
literacy
  in children with Down
    syndrome, 246–247
  in people with Down syndrome,
    121
  Mental Development Index
    (MDI), 100
  of writing skills, with Down
    syndrome, 121
Developmental apraxia, case study,
    143–144
Developmental disabilities
  limitations of standardized tests for
    children with, 123
  see also Children with
    developmental disabilities
Digitized electronic communication
    aids, portable, 169, 169*f*
Directive behavior
  definition of, 102*t*
  frequencies of, 103*t*, 104
  maternal, 95, 95*t*
Directiveness, maternal, 95, 96*f*,
    96–97, 104–106
Disability
  developmental
    limitations of standardized tests
      for children with, 123
  web sites, 274
Documenting communication, 176,
    177*f*
Down syndrome
  assessment principles for,
    121–129
  assistive technology case studies,
    182–192
  challenges facing children with,
    242, 242*t*
  clinical methods for working with,
    207–208
  communication aids for children
    with, 162–171
  communication characteristics
    with, 9–10

communication skills with
developing, 241–262
strategies and tools for
enhancing, 161–204
computers for children with,
162–171
contemporary life circumstances
with, 223–226
early vocabulary development
with, 31–33
families with, 217–240
health supervision for children
with, 275, 276t
hearing abilities with, 120–121
intervention case studies, 208–212
language abilities with, 120–121
language development profiles,
11–39
language development with,
41–60, 241–262
literacy development with, 121,
246–247
medical care for children with,
275
mothers of young children with,
93–115
parents of children with, 253–255
resources, 267–268
speech intelligibility characteristics
with, 120
speech intelligibility with, 133–159
speech with, 120–121
biological bases of, 61–80
enhancing, 205–213
verbal language characteristics
with, 120
vocabulary acquisition with,
30–35
World Wide Web sites, 204,
271–274
writing development with, 121
see also Adults with Down
syndrome; Children with
Down syndrome; Families
with Down syndrome; Young
children with Down
syndrome

Early intervention
need for, 258–259

program development, 243–246
resources, 268
Early reading skills, communication
aids for, 171
Early sentence development, for Neil
(case study), 185
Electronic communication aids,
portable digitized, 169, 169f
Elicitation tasks
for Maria (case study), 139, 140t
for oral motor system, 155–159
respiration, 158–159
Environmental engineering, 174
Erica (case study), 182–184, 183f
case history/intervention program,
183–184
communication aids, 183, 183f
development of expressive
vocabulary, 182
outcomes/future considerations,
184
Experimental Educational Unit,
Children's Center on Human
Development and Disability,
University of Washington,
246–247
Expressive language development,
for Erica (case study), 182
Expressive language impairments,
49
Expressive Vocabulary subtest
(Stanford-Binet Intelligence
Scale), 44

Facial expression, muscle variations,
72–73, 73f
Facilitative techniques to increase
vocabulary and phonetic
inventory, for Maria (case
study), 138–139
Families
communication goals for children,
256
communication with children
features of, 255
strategies to enhance, 255–257
expectation for reading, 256
importance of, 260
well-being, comparison of, 229,
229t

Families with Down syndrome,
217–240
communication characteristics of,
9–10
comparisons with other families,
228–230
diagnostic differences in
background characteristics,
222–223, 223t
study description, 220–223
study findings, 226–235
Families with mental retardation
diagnostic differences in
background characteristics of,
222–223, 223t
sample characteristics, 221t,
221–222
Fast mapping, 56
Fluency, 67–68
description, 65t
verbal, 81–91
impairments, 88–89
Fragile X syndrome, language development profile with, 18, 19f
Functional assessments, 123
Future directions, 215–216, 241–262

General development resources,
268–269
General education classrooms,
enhancement of social
relationships in, 189–190
Go Fish software, 181
Grammatical morpheme
impairment, 53–54
Grandma's rules for communication
with children, 254t, 254–255
Group differences in mothers'
communication, 94–97

Handheld high-technology communication aids, 175, 175f
Hard palate, observation and
elicitation tasks for, 157
Health supervision, 275, 276t
Hearing, 128–129
of children with Down syndrome,
120–121
Hearing status, 48

Hearing testing, 257
Historical background, of language
development with Down
syndrome, 41–43
Hoarse voice production, factors that
contribute to, 68

I Can Play Too software, 181
Iconicity, 170
Ideas, alternate methods to express,
175–176
IFSPs, see Individualized family
service plans
Impairments
auditory short-term memory, 48
expressive language, 49
grammatical morpheme, 53–54
intellectual, adaptive inputs for
individuals with, 172
pervasive sequencing, 47–48
speech production, 87–89
verbal fluency, 88–89
Individual differences
in maternal communication,
97–99, 104–110
in vocabulary acquisition rates,
34–35
Individualized family service plans
(IFSPs), for Maria (case
study), 141
Informal tests, 123
Intellectual impairments, adaptive
inputs for individuals with,
172
Intelligibility, 134
etiological and interactive factors,
134t, 134–135
production measures, 49, 49t
speech, 64–66, 86–89
characteristics with Down
syndrome, 120
improving, 133–159
influence on communicative
effectiveness, 87–88
learning to improve, 210–212
International Phonetic Alphabet, 24
Internet sites, 204
Intervention(s), 117–118
for adults with Down syndrome,
208–212

for Bill (case study), 190–191
communication, 133–159,
    171–182
early
    need for, 258–259
    program development, 243–246
    resources, 268
for Erica (case study), 183–184
Jay's story (case study), 141–147
for Jenny (case study), 187–189
Maria's story (case study),
    135–141
medical, 137
Molly's story (case study),
    147–151
for Neil (case study), 185–186
overall goals
    for Jay (case study), 142–143
    for Maria (case study), 136–137
    for Molly (case study), 148–149
principles of, 135
speech-language
    for Jay (case study), 143–146
    for Maria (case study), 137–139
    for Molly (case study), 149–150
target selection, 144

Jaw, observation and elicitation tasks
    for, 157
Jay (case study), 141–147
    communication profile, 142–143
    language, 146
    multidisciplinary team meeting
        for, 146–147
    overall intervention goals,
        142–143
    phonology, 145–146
    speech-language intervention,
        143–146
        input modification, 144–145
        target selection, 144
Jenny (case study), 187–189
    communication system, 187, 188f
    history/intervention program,
        187–189
    language comprehension
        problems, 187
    outcomes and future
        considerations, 189
Journals, 199–200

Keyboards, alternate, 166f

Language
    aided language stimulation, 174
    expressive, impairments, 49
    for Jay (case study), 146
    for Maria (case study), 140–141
    unique features with Down
        syndrome, 120–121
    verbal, characteristics with Down
        syndrome, 120
Language-based hypothesis for
    stuttering, 84–85
Language comprehension, 46
    accommodating problems of, 187
    assessment of, 125
    research implications, 46
Language delays, 28, 28t
    web sites for, 274
Language development
    assessing, 22–24
    with Down syndrome
        conversational samples, 44
        historical background, 41–43
        narrative language samples, 44
        reliability, 45
        research, 41–60
        research description, 43–45
        research findings, 45–47
        research participants, 43–45,
            44t
        research procedures, 43–44
        scoring, 45
        transcriptions, 44
    factors associated with, 14
    responsibility for, 251
Language development profiles,
    14–30
    of children with Down syndrome,
        11–39, 19f, 20f
    change over time, 27–30
    defining, 24–26
    individuals studied by, 26, 26t,
        28, 28t
    lessons learned, 29–30
    longitudinal change in, 21–22,
        22t
    studies, 18–20
    of children with fragile X
        syndrome, 18, 19f

Language development profiles—
    continued
  of children with Williams
      syndrome, 18, 19*f*
  definition of, 15–16, 16*f*
  importance of, 16–18
  Profile Discovery Process (PDP),
      25
    results, 26–27
Language intervention services,
    36–37
Language learning
  acquisition processes, 55–57
  cognitive skills in, 14–18
  communication aid and symbol
      features that support, 168–171
Language levels, selecting, 255–256
Language performance
  criteria for determining, 24, 25*t*
  investigating, 16–18
Language production, 48
  assessment of, 124
  implications for defining
      behavioral phenotype, 52–53
  individuals delayed in, 28, 28*t*
Language production age, criteria for
    establishing, 24, 25*t*
Language skills
  activities for improving, 265–266
  developing, 241–262
  enhancing, 205–213
  evaluating communication to
      improve, 119–132
Language use, communication aid
    and symbol features that
    support, 168–171
Larynx, observation and elicitation
    tasks for, 157–158
Learning
  to improve speech intelligibility,
      210–212
  to increase sentence meaning and
      length, 208–210
  language
    cognitive skills in, 14–18
    communication aids and symbol
        features that support,
        168–171
  to use symbols, 173–175
  vocabulary, progress rates, 33–34
Lexical production measures, 49, 49*t*

Lifelong caregiving, 226–228
Line drawings, for constructing short
    phrases to make choices, 178,
    179*f*
Lips, observation and elicitation
    tasks for, 155
Literacy development
  activities for improving, 265–266
  with Down syndrome, 121,
      246–247
Living Books software, 163

MacArthur Child Development
    Inventory (CDI), 34, 124
Madison Metropolitan School
    District (Wisconsin), 271
Mapping, fast, 56
Maria (case study), 135–141
  communication profile, 136
  individualized family service plan
      (IFSP), 141
  language, 140–141
  medical intervention, 137
  motor awareness and control,
      increasing, 139
  observation and elicitation tasks,
      139, 140*t*
  overall intervention goals for,
      136–137
  speech-language intervention
      goals and methods, 137–139
  speech production, 137–139
  vocabulary and phonetic
      inventory, 138–139
Maternal communication
  correlation with children's
      characteristics, 105*t*, 105–106
  individual differences in, 104–110
Maternal directive behavior,
    categorization of, 95, 95*t*
Maternal directiveness, 95, 96*f*,
    96–97, 104–106
Maternal praise, 106–107
Maternal responsive structuring,
    103–104
Maternal restriction, 107–108
Maternal well-being
  comparison with normative
      samples, 226, 227*t*
  measures of, 223, 224*t*

Mazes, 85
MDI, *see* Mental Development Index
Mean length of utterance (MLU), 52
Medical concerns, web sites, 272–273
Medical intervention
  for children with Down syndrome,
    275
  for Maria (case study), 137
Melodic intonation therapy (MIT),
  150
Memory, 127–128
  short-term, auditory impairment,
    48
Mental Development Index (MDI),
  100
Mental retardation
  American Association on Mental
    Retardation (AAMR), 17
  definition of, 266
  families of adults with
    background characteristics,
      222–223, 223t
    sample characteristics, 221t,
      221–222
  language development profile of
    child with, 15, 16f
  mild, 246
  moderate, 246
  requiring intermittent supports,
    246
  requiring limited supports, 246
  resources, 266–267
  see also Adults with mental
    retardation; Families with
    mental retardation
Messages
  content of, 256–257
  frequently needed for Neil (case
    study), 186
Miller–Chapman procedures, 23
Miniboards, 176
MIT, *see* Melodic intonation therapy
MLU, *see* Mean length of utterance
Modeling, with aided language
  stimulation, 178, 179f
Molly (case study), 147–151
  communication profile, 147–148
  improving speech intelligibility,
    149–150
  overall intervention goals,
    148–149

reevaluation of progress, 150–151
  speech-language intervention,
    149–150
Morphemes, grammatical,
  impairment, 53–54
Mothers
  communication with young
    children, 93–115
    behavior coding, 100–101
    behavioral measures, 101–104
    group differences in, 94–97
    individual differences in, 97–99
    sample characteristics, 99–104,
      100t
    sample population, 99–100
    study procedures, 99–104
  differences in, 228–229
  vocal communication with young
    children, 101–102
    behavior code definitions, 102t
    measures of, 101–102
Motor awareness and control,
  increasing, 139
Motor limitations, 128
Motor skills, communication aid
  requirements, 170
Multidisciplinary team meeting, for
  Jay (case study), 146–147
Multisensory approach to
  phonology, 145–146
Muscular system, 72–74
  facial expression muscles, 72–73,
    73f

National Down Syndrome Society,
  (NDSS), 271
NDSS, *see* National Down Syndrome
  Society
Negative vocalizations
  correlation with maternal
    communication, 105t,
    105–106
  definition of, 102t
  frequencies of, 103, 103t
Neil (case study), 184–187
  communication wallet, 185, 185f
  development of early sentences,
    185
  history/intervention program,
    185–186

Neil (case study)—*continued*
  messages frequently needed, 186
  outcomes and future considera-
    tions for, 187
Nervous system, 74–76
Networks, 203–204
Newsletters, 199–200
Newsweek, 268–269
Nicholas (case study), 208–210
Nonspeech tasks
  for jaw, 157
  for tongue, 156
Nonvocal play behavior, 102–103

Object play
  complex, 103
    correlation with maternal com-
      munication, 105t, 105–106
    definition of, 102t
    frequencies of, 103, 103t
  simple, 102–103
    correlation with maternal com-
      munication, 105t, 105–106
    definition of, 102t
    frequencies of, 103, 103t
Observation and elicitation tasks
  for jaw, 157
  for larynx, 157–158
  for lips, 155
  for Maria (case study), 139, 140t
  for oral motor system, 155–159
  for respiration, 158–159
  for tongue, 155–157
  for velopharynx and hard palate,
    157
Observation forms, 176, 177f
Omitted words, 54, 54t
Oppositional play, 103
  correlation with maternal com-
    munication, 105t, 105–106
  definition of, 102t
  frequencies of, 103, 103t
Oral motor system, observation and
  elicitation tasks for, 155–159
Outings, 257

Palate
  hard, observation and elicitation
    tasks for, 157

normal versus steeple, 71–72,
    72f
Parents
  contribution to assessment, 126
  effective communication with
    children, 253–255
  versus professionals, 260–261
Pattern Analysis subtest (Stanford-
    Binet Intelligence Scale), 44,
    47
PDP, *see* Profile Discovery Process
Peabody Picture Vocabulary
    Test–Revised, 24
Peers, establishing social
    relationships with, 180–182
PepTalk software, 163
Pervasive sequencing impairment,
    47–48
PFCI, *see* Preschool Functional
    Communication Inventory
Phonetic inventory, facilitative tech-
    niques to increase, 138–139
Phonology, 145–146
  multisensory approach to, 145–146
Picture Communication Symbols,
    167f
Play
  children's behavior, 102–103
    behavior code definitions, 102t
  complex object, 103
    correlation with maternal
      communication, 105t,
      105–106
    definition of, 102t
    frequencies of, 103, 103t
  oppositional, 103
    correlation with maternal
      communication, 105t,
      105–106
    definition of, 102t
    frequencies of, 103, 103t
  simple object, 102–103
    correlation with maternal
      communication, 105t,
      105–106
    definition of, 102t
    frequencies of, 103, 103t
Play-based assessments, 123
Portable digitized electronic
    communication aids, 169,
    169f

Pragmatic production measures, 49, 49t
Praise
    definition of, 102t
    frequencies of, 103t, 104
    maternal, 106–107
Preschool Functional Communication Inventory (PFCI), 125
Primary motor cortex, 74, 75f
Professionals, 260–261
Profile Discovery Process (PDP), 25
    results, 26–27
Progress reevaluation, 150–151

Reading, 247–250
    communication aid support for, 171
    family expectation for, 256
Relationships, social, 180–182
Remediation techniques, 149–150
Research
    on early vocabulary development, 31–33
    on language development, 43–45
Resources, 265–269
    list, 198–204
Respiration, observation and elicitation tasks for, 158–159
Responding, consistency of, 127
Responsive vocal structuring, 108–110
Restriction
    definition of, 102t
    frequencies of, 103t, 104
    maternal, 107–108

SALT: Systematic Analysis of Language Transcripts, 24, 44, 124
Sarah Duffen Centre, 247, 271
Self-help and advocacy groups, 201–203
Sensory input, continua of, 139, 140t
Sentences
    complex, 51–52, 52t
    early development of, 185
    longer
        understanding, 178–180

using words in combination to create, 176–177
    meaning and length of, learning to increase, 208–210
    simple, syntactic ceiling at, 50–52
Sequenced Inventory of Communication Development (SICD), 23
Sequencing impairment, pervasive, 47–48
Short phrases to make choices, line drawings for constructing, 178, 179f
Short-term memory impairment, auditory, 48
SICD, see Sequenced Inventory of Communication Development
Signed Exact English, 248
Signing, 247–250
Simple object play, 102–103
    correlation with maternal communication, 105t, 105–106
    definition of, 102t
    frequencies of, 103, 103t
Skeletal system, 71–72, 72f
Social relationships
    establishing, 180–182
    in general education classrooms, 189–190
Software programs
    important features of, 165
    resources, 198
    see also specific programs by name
Speech
    biological systems affecting, 70–76
    case study, 62–63
    with Down syndrome
        biological bases of, 61–80
        enhancing, 205–213
        unique features of, 120–121
Speech characteristics, 64–70
    terminology, 64, 65t
Speech intelligibility, 64–66, 86–89
    description, 65t
    with Down syndrome
        characteristics of, 120
        improving, 133–159
            for Alexander (case study), 210–212
            for Molly (case study), 149–150

Speech intelligibility—*cotninued*
  influence on communicative
    effectiveness, 87–88
  poor, 66
    alternate methods to express
      ideas for, 175–176
    remediation techniques for,
      149–150
Speech-language intervention
  inputs
    modification of, 144–145
    suggestions for, 144–145
  for Jay (case study), 143–146
  for Maria (case study), 137–139
  for Molly (case study), 149–150
Speech motor basis for stuttering,
  83–85
Speech production
  disfluent, 83
  evaluating communication to
    improve, 119–132
  impairments, 87–89
  increasing frequency and variety
    of, 137–139
  mechanisms of, 82–83
Speech recognition, automatic, 245
Speech sound articulation, 65*t*, 66–67
Speech tasks
  for larynx, 157–158
  for tongue, 156
  for velopharynx and hard palate,
    157
SpeechViewer software, 163
Standardized tests, 122–123
  limitations for children with
    developmental disabilities, 123
Stanford-Binet Intelligence Scale
  (Fourth Edition), 23
  Bead Memory subtest, 44, 47
  Expressive Vocabulary subtest, 44
  Pattern Analysis subtest, 44, 47
Steeple palate, 71–72, 72*f*
Structuring, responsive vocal, 108–110
Stuttering, 68
  cluttering or language-based
    hypothesis for, 84–85
  definition of, 84
  speech motor basis for, 83–85
Syllable structure complexity,
  modifying, 144
Symbolic Play Test, 23

Symbols
  features that support language
    learning and use, 168–171
  learning to use, 173–175
  permanent, 169–170
  picture communication, 167*f*
  recognition of, 170
  use of, 247–250
  visual, 168–169
Syntactic ceiling at simple sentences,
  50–52
  examples, 51
Syntax comprehension, 46
Syntax comprehension measures,
  45, 45*t*
Syntax production measures, 49, 49*t*

TACL–R, *see* Test for Auditory
  Comprehension of
  Language–Revised
Target phrases, suggestions for
  crafting, 144
Teaching
  features of communication aids
    helpful for, 166–171
  features of computers helpful for,
    163–166
Teams
  characteristics of, 192
  multidisciplinary, meeting, 146–147
Technology
  assistive, 161–204
    web sites, 274
  computer, 171–173
Terminology
  assistive technology, 164*t*
  speech characteristics, 64, 65*t*
Test for Auditory Comprehension of
  Language–Revised (TACL–R),
  23, 44
Tests
  informal, 123
  new and improved methods,
    125–126
  standardized, 122–123
Thinking skills, supporting through
  computer technology, 171–173
Tongue, observation and elicitation
  tasks for, 155–157
Topic boards, 176

University of Washington, Children's Center on Human Development and Disability, 246–247
University of Wisconsin–Madison, The Waisman Center, 124, 128, 271

Velopharynx and hard palate, observation and elicitation tasks for, 157
Verbal fluency, 81–91
  characteristics with Down syndrome, 120
Verbal fluency impairments, influence on communicative effectiveness, 88–89
Vision, 128
Visual skills, strengths in, 247–250
Visual stimuli, use of, 259
Vocabulary, expressive, development of, 182
Vocabulary acquisition
  with Down syndrome, 30–35
  facilitative techniques to increase, 138–139
  individual differences in rates of, 34–35
  progress rates, 33–34
Vocabulary comprehension, 46
Vocabulary comprehension measures, 45, 45t
Vocabulary development, early, 31–33
Vocal behavior, children's, 102–103
  code definitions, 102t
Vocal communication, mothers', 101–102
  behavior code definitions, 102t
Vocal structuring, responsive, 108–110
Vocalizations
  correlation with maternal communication, 105t, 105–106
  definition of, 102t
  frequencies of, 103, 103t
  negative, 102
    correlation with maternal communication, 105t, 105–106

definition of, 102t
  frequencies of, 103, 103t
  simple, 102
Voice output communication aids, 163, 165f
Voice production, 68–70
  description, 65t
  hoarse, factors that contribute to, 68

The Waisman Center, University of Wisconsin–Madison, 124, 128, 271
Wallets, communication, 166, 168f
  for Neil (case study), 185, 185f
Well-being
  comparison with normative samples, 226, 227t
  components of, 229
  family, 229, 229t
  maternal
    comparison with normative samples, 226, 227t
    measures of, 223, 224t
  measures of, 223, 224t
White House Conference on Child Development, 268–269
Williams syndrome, language development profile with, 18, 19f
Words
  in combination, 176–177
  fast-mapping phase, 56
  omitted, 54, 54t
World Wide Web sites, 271–274
Writing skills, development of, 121

Young children with Down syndrome
  mothers' communication with behavior coding, 100–101
  behavioral measures, 101–104
  individual differences in, 93–115
  sample characteristics, 99–104, 100t
  sample population, 99–100
  study procedures, 99–104
  see also Children with Down syndrome